111 Days to Zion

By Hal Knight and Dr. Stanley B. Kimball

Illustrations by Robert R. Noyce

Maps by Richard F. Carter

 *111 Days to Zion*

BIG MOON
Traders

Published by Big Moon Traders
676 Desoto Street
Salt Lake City, Utah 84103
(801)359-0306 Fax (801)533-9379

First Big Moon Traders edition, 1997
          9 8 7 6 5 4 3 2 1
Cover Photograph: Charles Savage, *Mormon Pioneers*, 1866.
Courtesy of Utah State Historical Society, Salt Lake City, Utah

 **"The Spirit of Pioneering, 1847-1997"**

Preface

The exodus of the Mormon pioneers in the decades between 1847 and 1869 has been described as a great and exciting epic in American history.

The migration crossed America's broad, Indian-occupied plains and moved into the towering, untamed Rocky Mountains. It ended in the sagebrush blanketed valley of the Great Salt Lake. More than 68,000 Mormon pioneers made the journey, mostly with ox-drawn, canvas-bonneted wagons, but some with only handcarts. The covered wagon era ended with the completion of the transcontinental railroad on May 10, 1869.

The exodus actually began Feb 4, 1846, at Nauvoo, Ill., on the banks of the Mississippi River. Here, members of The Church of Jesus Christ of Latter-day Saints, known as Mormons, in seven years had built Nauvoo to a size comparable to Chicago, boasting a population of more than 11,000.

But enemies rose up against the Mormons in Nauvoo, causing them to look to the Rocky Mountains for an isolated haven where they could worship unmolested. Under their able prophet-leader, Brigham Young, they crossed Iowa in 1846. They endured the winter of 1846-47 in tents, dugouts and crude log huts in what they called Winter Quarters on the west bank of the Missouri River.

The trek from Winter Quarters began April 5, 1847, with the departure of the first wagons in Brigham Young's advance pioneer company. There were 144 men, three women and two boys in the group. Brigham Young arrived in Salt Lake Valley on July 24, 1847. Under his leadership and with Salt Lake City as a base, the Mormons founded more than 350 communities in the Rocky Mountains and as far away as California, Canada and Mexico.

The Congress of the United States in 1978 officially designated the Mormon Pioneer Trail as a national historic trail. While the legislation was under consideration, the Deseret News published a day-by-day account of the trek of that first company of Mormon pioneers from Winter Quarters to Salt Lake Valley. The daily series matched the dates of the 111-day journey by the pioneers.

The installments were written by Hal Knight, veteran Deseret News reporter, in consultation with Dr. Stanley B. Kimball of Southern Illinois University, a historian who has studied the Mormon Trail in detail and traveled it many times. Dr. Kimball prepared the maps on which Secretary of the Interior Cecil D. Andrus generally based his recommendations to Congress that the trail be designated a national historic trail.

Weekly, the Deseret News published with the trail stories its own detailed map, showing campsites of the first Mormon pioneer company, historic markers, and neighboring highways in the area covered that week by the 1847 pioneers. The maps were executed by Deseret News artist Richard F. Carter.

Each of the stories was accompanied by a line drawing — 111 of them — created by Robert R. Noyce, another Deseret News artist, to illustrate events of that particular day's journey.

The back cover was taken from a water color painting and map of the Mormon Trail by Utah artist Ferrell Collett. The painting was commissioned by the Deseret News and copies were made available to readers.

Dee Chipman, Deseret News associate news editor, did the editing, wrote the page titles, and supervised preparation of the text.

In these installments, Mr. Knight and Dr. Kimball have brought to readers not only an informative, interesting narrative. They have also captured the spirit and feelings of those intrepid Mormon travelers who braved the unknown for a thousand wilderness miles. Drawing on a number of first-hand diaries, the authors have described the pioneers' vivid impressions of the scenery, their concerns about Indians and about the supply of game for food. The authors have faithfully recorded the adventure and geography of the journey and also the little human incidents that caused surprises, humor, and at times, irritation.

Many of our approving readers, while the series was appearing in the Deseret News, inquired if the articles, illustrations and maps would be published in a book.

This volume is the answer.

This book has been sized to fit in the glove compartment of a car. It has been designed by Charles Nickerson, Deseret News graphics director, so that a highway traveler can easily locate the Mormon Pioneer Trail and also trace the campsites and story spots. Hopefully, it will encourage families, as well as history lovers, to seek out the trail, pause at significant places, and relive some of the stirring experiences of the pioneers.

If, through this little book, 111 Days to Zion, we have provided a useful guide to this great national trail . . . if we have helped build a greater appreciation of America and of the Mormon pioneers who have done so much to strengthen and expand this nation, then we shall be pleased.

Wendell J. Ashton
Publisher, Deseret News

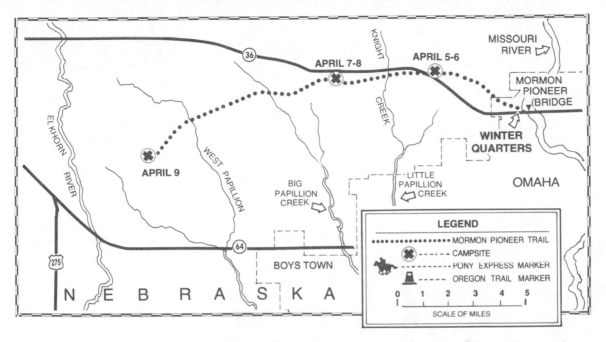

The great exodus had a modest beginning

April 5 - 9

The beginning of the great exodus west by the Mormon pioneers was modest — hardly an indication of the flood of emigrants to follow in the next 22 years.

Only a handful of wagons left Winter Quarters in the first few days of the trek. And those wagons departed at different times and took slightly different routes, traveling very few miles before halting on the prairie.

The pioneer company soon would be well organized, but at the start, small parties headed out as they were ready, their first objective being the Elkhorn River some 20 miles to the west. The river had been adopted as the staging ground and jumping off place.

1

April 5

Six wagons slowly began epic journey

Despite rainy weather, Heber C. Kimball led six loaded wagons from the Mormon refugee town of Winter Quarters on the west bank of the Missouri River and moved toward the open prairie to the west.

With the river at their backs, the teams slowly made their way just three miles before halting and setting up camp on the plains of what is now Nebraska. In 1847 it was strictly Indian country.

This brief march by a handful of wagons hardly was an impressive event, but it was the beginning of an exodus destined to become an epic in American history — the trek of the Mormon pioneers across a thousand-mile wilderness to what is now Utah.

In the next 22 years, before the transcontinental railroad was linked in 1869, more than 68,000 pioneers, 9,600 wagons and 650 handcarts would make the long trip in search of religious freedom.

Unlike the Hollywood version, the first Mormon wagon train to embark on the journey did not neatly line up, say goodbye, and set forth with a "westward ho" cry.

Instead, Kimball's wagons were slowly followed by a half dozen similar small groups in subsequent days, leaving at different times, taking slightly different routes and camping at scattered places on the prairie.

Even after departing Winter Quarters, many men in these groups rode back repeatedly to take care of last-minute business, hold conferences and meet with missionaries returning from abroad.

Not until about 10 days later did all the wagons assemble on the banks of the Platte River some 35 miles northwest of Winter Quarters and get fully organized under the leadership of Brigham Young.

That the 46-year-old Kimball was the first on the trail was not surprising. Since encountering Mormon missionaries in Mendon, N.Y., he had been a dedicated and driving force in the fledgling Church of Jesus Christ of Latter-day Saints.

A 6-foot, 200-pound barrel-chested blacksmith, he said of his meeting with the missionaries in late 1831: "As soon as I heard them, I was convinced they taught the truth." He never looked back.

He joined the church in April, 1832, and within four years was a member of its original quorum of 12 apostles. He served eight proselyting missions, including the founding of the enormously successful British mission.

By the time of the Mormon exodus he was second to Brigham Young in seniority among the apostles and was Brigham's trusted friend and right-hand man.

As his tiny group camped in the darkness on the prairie that first night, they were once more without a roof over their heads — a situation they had shared often with other members of the church since its founding.

The church was organized in Fayette, N.Y., in April, 1830, with six members. It grew rapidly, but persecution drove the followers to Ohio, to Missouri and finally to Illinois where they built Nauvoo, at the time the largest city in the state.

The Mormons prospered in Nauvoo for a few years, but their growing numbers and influence brought more persecution. Finally, their leader Joseph Smith and his brother, Hyrum, were killed by mob action in 1844.

A year and a half later the Mormons began to abandon their thriving city under the threat of massive mob violence. They struggled across Iowa in the winter and spring. They froze and starved and the living left behind hundreds of loved ones in unmarked graves. The physical and emotional suffering was intense.

Their history of one exodus after another, the persecutions, beatings and even murders, had convinced the Mormons that their only safety lay in leaving settled portions of the United States and moving to the distant Rocky Mountains, at that time in the hands of Mexico.

Now, on April 5, that journey had begun. Ahead lay the unknown. But Kimball and his associates were in high spirits. They worried about family and friends left behind, but ahead was not just a trail of tears. There was also freedom — freedom from persecution, freedom to be themselves, to hunt, fish and explore new lands.

Typically, Kimball never complained about any of the trek's hardships. Instead, his journals indicate he seems to have had a great time. Most of those early pioneers probably did.

The site of Kimball's first camp is near a little-used section of old State Highway 36 in Nebraska. Where his oxen hauled the wagons at a slow two miles an hour, aircraft now hurtle overhead to and from the nearby North Omaha Airport.

The surrounding area is one of small farms and pleasant homes just outside the metropolis of Omaha, which was laid out in 1854, shortly after the Nebraska Territory was organized by Congress.

April 6

TUESDAY

The trek west paused for annual conference

No move west was made by the Mormon pioneers this day. Most of Heber C. Kimball's small band, which was camped on the prairie four miles away, hurried back to Winter Quarters for an important event — the 17th annual conference of The Church of Jesus Christ of Latter-day Saints.

Nearly all the church members were destitute, having lived through two terrible winters on the open prairie or in refugee settlements like Winter Quarters. Now they were getting ready to move again.

"I did not think there had ever been a body of people . . . who had done so little grumbling under such unpleasant circumstances," Brigham Young once said.

Despite the suffering of the past three years since the murder of their Prophet Joseph Smith, the faithful crowded into a log meeting house to listen to Brigham and to follow where he would lead them.

Brigham, by this time 45 years old, had earlier rallied the stricken church members after the death of their prophet in 1844. In his role as president of the twelve apostles, he had taken charge of events and most of the church accepted his leadership.

A remarkable organizer, Brigham was a man of many gifts and a commanding personality. His blunt, straightforward language left no doubt about his feelings or views.

A copy of the Book of Mormon fell into his hands at Mendon, N.Y., in 1830 and he was deeply impressed by it. He studied the book thoroughly, visited branches of the church, and traveled to Canada to share the new religion with his brother, Joseph Young, a Methodist minister. The two of them returned to Mendon and were baptized in 1832.

Just three years later, Brigham was called as an apostle. He filled missions in New York, Ohio, among the Indians and in Great Britain, frequently at great physical hardship and sacrifice.

Now, in 1847, he stood before a congregation in Winter Quarters, prepared to lead the people to the largely unknown West. A larger group would follow in two months.

Brigham spoke very briefly. Most of the detailed instructions had been given earlier. He voiced his love for the people, "but to say I love those who do wickedly — I do not," referring to persecutors of the church.

He said he was willing to be charitable "to those that deserve it." He said if the mobs who had driven them from their homes would give back a 100th part of what was taken, "it would carry us over the mountains."

Brigham prayed for God to soften the hearts of their enemies "until we are out of their grasp." The last part of his sermon was a short discourse on the evils of dancing, which he called "a snare." If people want to be merry, they should sing hymns, he said.

After his talk, he was unanimously sustained once more as president of the twelve apostles. The First Presidency of the church had not been reorganized after the death of Joseph Smith. But about eight months later, in that same log building in Winter Quarters, Brigham would be approved as president of the church — a post he would hold for 29 years, longer than any other man.

When the 1847 conference broke up at noon, people hurried to their homes to continue preparations for the great journey into the wilderness. No afternoon meeting was held. It was a time for action.

The advance guard under Brigham's leadership originally was to be 144 men, representing 12 men for each of the 12 tribes of Israel. But this nicely balanced plan didn't last long. One woman insisted on being taken along.

Harriet Young, the wife of Brigham's younger brother, Lorenzo Dow Young, suffered from asthma and declared she would die if left in Winter Quarters. She said she would rather take her chances on the trail.

Brigham at first objected, but finally agreed when Lorenzo said he wouldn't go if he couldn't take Harriet.

But Harriet couldn't travel as a lone woman in a party of men, so Brigham took one of his wives, Clara, a daughter of Harriet by a previous marriage, and Heber C. Kimball took his Norwegian wife, Ellen. Both men left other wives and children at Winter Quarters.

Brigham's troubles with Harriet weren't over. She also insisted on taking two children. As a result, the makeup of the starting party was 144 men, three women and two children. It didn't stay that way for the entire journey. Some men were left behind along the trail for special assignments and other pioneers joined the group while it was traveling. A number of teen-age youths were in the party, but they were counted as men.

April 7

One by one, four small groups of wagons headed for the prairie

One by one, four small groups of Mormon pioneer wagons pulled away from Winter Quarters toward the prairie land.

First to leave this day was a small band headed by Wilford Woodruff, 40, an apostle destined one day to become the fourth president of the church. It was said of him he was the most energetic man in the entire pioneer company.

The eight wagons in his command departed before noon, but camped for the night after covering only seven miles across the prairie.

Shortly afterwards, a company led by Orson Pratt, 36, another apostle, also moved away from Winter Quarters. Pratt was the scientist among the Mormons, a self-taught man who became an expert in higher mathematics.

On the heels of this group came another party with Brigham Young. The three companies, totalling about 25 wagons, met at the same campsite that night and shared a meal in weather described as "cold and windy."

Brigham's brother, Lorenzo, (whose wife had already altered the makeup of the advance pioneer party by insisting on going along) had another idea which drew an objection from Brigham.

Lorenzo had a fine milk cow he wanted to include on the trip. Brigham said such an animal would hinder their progress, but Lorenzo said if she slowed them by one hour, he would abandon her on the prairie. The cow made the entire trip and provided milk and butter along the way.

In the late afternoon of April 7, a fourth group, including the wagons of Willard Richards, 43, to be a counselor in the First Presidency within a year, and Thomas Bullock, 31, a former clerk to Joseph Smith, also left Winter Quarters.

This last party didn't get far before dark and camped uncomfortably on the open prairie without wood or water and exposed to the chilling wind.

As the pioneers left Winter Quarters, many of them did so with extreme sadness because they were leaving behind families who were almost destitute and, in some cases, very sick.

Sylvester Henry Earl, 31, was perhaps typical of many when he wrote: "It is hard to leave my family here, sick and among the howling wolves and roaming savages . . . but the servants of the Lord say go."

His wife and three daughters survived until he was able to return to Winter Quarters that fall. But the youngest girl died after his return and before the family could be moved across the plains.

Andrew Purley Shumway was only 14, but was allowed to accompany his father, Charles Shumway, on the journey. His mother was one of those who had died in Winter Quarters. Two sisters were left behind in the care of others, but one of the girls was dying. The Shumways, father and son, were both sick when they left, but recovered their health on the trail.

Those chosen for the advance party were picked for their abilities and skills. They weren't just going for themselves, but to pave the way for all the others who would follow in the coming months and years.

Among the first party were Indian experts, road and bridge builders, farmers, hunters, teamsters, blacksmiths, horsemen, scouts, masons and stonecutters, carpenters, stockmen and barrel makers. Like many men of their day, they were usually adept in a variety of skills.

For those left behind at Winter Quarters, Council Bluffs and other camps, preparations continued for their own move west. In June another group, called the Big Company, divided into nine parties totalling 1,489 persons, would depart Winter Quarters under the general command of John Taylor, 38, another apostle destined to become church president after the death of Brigham Young.

Winter Quarters was quickly emptied of residents after the summer of 1848. Those who had not gone west moved back across the Missouri River to Council Bluffs. By 1853 all that remained of Winter Quarters was a cemetery.

In 1856 other settlers moved to the area and named it Florence, hoping to build a great commercial center. But it eventually succumbed to the growth of nearby Omaha and became a suburb of that city.

Memories of the Mormon pioneers are still to be found in Florence. There is a Mormon Bridge Road and the steel spans of the Mormon Pioneer Memorial Bridge. There is a Mormon Street, a Young Street and the pioneer cemetery with the graves of 600. Impressive historical markers are found at the cemetery and in a little park on 30th Street.

Several small parties joined on prairie to form large group

Although chosen well in advance, the Mormon pioneers departed Winter Quarters in small groups as they were ready. Few followed exactly the same route. They camped in scattered locations on the prairie.

Several small parties met April 7 about seven miles from town and formed a larger body. They remained camped this day as other wagons joined them, some carrying news.

Brigham Young was with this main gathering on the prairie and the latest wagons from Winter Quarters brought a report to him that Parley P. Pratt, a member of the Twelve, had arrived from England where he had been serving a mission.

John Taylor had also sent word that he was on his way home from the same mission and would reach Winters Quarters in a few days.

Brigham wanted to talk to Pratt, 40, a prolific writer who served one mission after another and traveled thousands of miles for the church. The president also wanted to collect $500 worth of scientific and surveying instruments from Taylor who was bringing the equipment from England.

Taylor and Pratt were to be named heads of the next expedition to follow in the footsteps of the advance party of pioneers in about two months. In the meantime, they would be in charge of things at Winter Quarters and Brigham desired to give them final instructions.

Pratt had little formal education, but like his brother, Orson, was widely read and self-taught to a remarkable degree. He authored books on history and theology and wrote one of the most famous tracts in Mormon missionary work, the "Voice of Warning."

After the arrival of the pioneers in the Salt Lake Valley, he helped draft the first provisional government constitution and later served in the Territorial Legislature.

Pratt sacrificed much for the church and once spent eight months in prison in Missouri without trial as mobs rampaged against Mormons in that state.

In May, 1857, while on one of his many missions for the church, he was shot and killed near the Arkansas border by a man whose wife had joined the Mormon faith.

As Brigham made preparations for a return to Winter Quarters to confer with Pratt and Taylor, other groups of pioneers still were leaving the community.

Despite the different departure times and different routes, all were headed for a known crossing at the Elkhorn River which had been chosen as a staging area and jumping off place for the trek across the open prairie.

A party of seven wagons, headed by John Brown and William Crosby, passed the larger pioneer encampment during the day and continued toward the river.

Howard Egan and some people with him also left town and traveled three miles before making camp. Just after they stopped, O. Porter Rockwell rode up to tell of Pratt's arrival from England.

"We went back home in the carriage to pass the night," Egan said. A number of others not far from Winter Quarters did the same.

Meanwhile, those camped with the main party spent much of the day hunting, but with limited success. Wilford Woodruff said they saw deer, geese and ducks, but weren't able to bag them.

Finally, four squirrels were killed, the first wild game collected on the trip. It was agreed to give the small animals to Brigham as a present.

However, Brigham and others already had left camp for Winter Quarters and a visit with Pratt — a meeting that would last only a few hours. By the next day the president would be back in the pioneer camp.

Largest group waited for Brigham

Small parties of Mormon pioneers continued their scattered and leap-frog approach to the Elkhorn River, but the largest group — about 30 wagons — remained camped awaiting the return of Brigham Young.

The weather was cool and some of the men in camp engaged in a little dancing to pass the time. They probably felt it was safe in Brigham's absence.

Finally Wilford Woodruff saddled a horse and rode toward Winter Quarters to meet Parley P. Pratt as Brigham and others had done the day before. He made most of the seven-mile trip and was within a half-mile of home when he saw the others headed back to camp.

Woodruff turned around and went back to the camp with them. However, some other men in the camp took the opportunity to slip back to Winter Quarters for a few hours.

Howard Egan, Heber C. Kimball and others who had returned to spend the previous night at their homes, set forth once more onto the prairie.

Kimball joined Brigham for the trip to the main camp. Egan's company passed the larger pioneer group in the early afternoon and continued another three miles before halting on the open prairie.

Egan, 31, was to be one of the captains for the trek. Born in Ireland, he emigrated to America with his family while still a young child. Left an orphan by the death of his father, he became a youthful sailor. He later gave up the sea and became a rope maker in Salem, Mass., where he heard Mormon missionaries and joined the church in 1842.

A rugged outdoorsman and a former major in the Nauvoo Legion, he crossed the plains three times, made innumerable trips to California, and led an adventurous life as a Pony Express rider, a policeman and a bodyguard to Brigham Young.

After Brigham rejoined the main body of pioneers this day, they broke camp about 3 p.m. The men burst into cheers when it was announced they finally would get moving again.

Brigham already had decided that the pioneers should not stop on the east bank of the Elkhorn River to get organized.

Rather than use the Elkhorn as a staging area, he felt it would be better to put that barrier behind them and travel another 20 miles to the Platte River.

Brigham said he would stay with the group until they were across the Elkhorn. Then he would turn back with the apostles one more time for a meeting in Winter Quarters with John Taylor and collect the scientific equipment Taylor was bringing from England.

Pulling away from Little Papillon Creek where they had camped for three days, the pioneers climbed a nearby hill and found themselves in rough and broken country.

The wagons soon entered a swampy area and began to bog down. About 30 men pulled on ropes to help the oxen drag the wagons through the mire.

The group camped on the open prairie that night after traveling about eight miles. There was a sprinkling of grass for the cattle, but no wood for fires.

Brigham and others went to work with knives, cutting and gathering grass for the cattle. The well-being of the animals was more important than the comfort of the people.

All of the teams were carefully inspected to make sure they hadn't suffered any harm in the day's march, especially the pull through the mire.

Because of additional parties who joined the company during the day, a total of 64 wagons were in camp that night — the majority of those taking part in the trek.

Among those in camp was William Kimball, who was accompanying the pioneers to help them cross the Elkhorn River. After that he would return to Winter Quarters.

Ferrying Elkhorn River a difficult project

One of the first obstacles facing the Mormon pioneers was the Elkhorn River and it proved a difficult crossing, all the wagons being ferried over on a raft.

From the Elkhorn they made their way to the north bank of the Platte River, which would be their guide and companion for the next 600 miles. Water had to be close at all times for the animals. This forced the pioneers to follow the river — but that was the best route anyway.

The company remained camped on the banks of the Platte for several days, awaiting the return of Brigham Young and other leaders who had made a final visit to Winter Quarters on some last-minute business.

After his return, Brigham laid down rules for the conduct of the march, divided the pioneers into a quasi-military organization of divisions and companies of 10, and set their faces to the west.

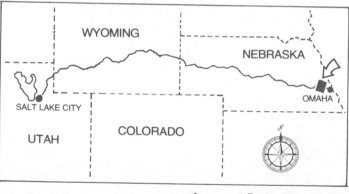

April 10-16

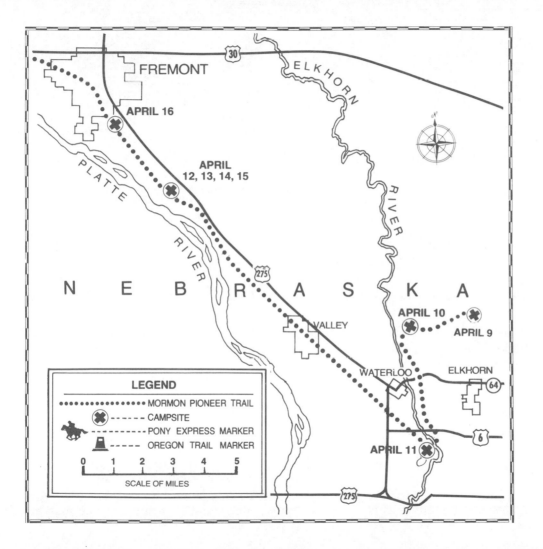

13

Wood was scarce, and any creek an obstacle

Camping on the open prairie was no picnic for the Mormon pioneers. One of the biggest problems was the lack of wood for fires to cook food.

The scarcity of trees across the Nebraska prairie made wood a valuable commodity. Trees and brush occasionally could be found along the rivers, but not every day.

As the pioneers broke camp April 10, many did not have wood to make fires so they skipped breakfast. However, the men cut considerable grass to feed the cattle.

Jolting along in their wagons, the party crossed Big Papillion Creek during the morning. Any body of water, from a small creek to a large river, was a barrier for the company. The creeks usually were narrow, but with high, steep banks. Getting across was accomplished by everybody grabbing shovels and digging the banks down. Wagons were then driven through the gap. The water normally was quite shallow.

At the Big Papillion the pioneers found a few cottonwood trees. Some they promptly chopped down and most of the party cooked and ate the breakfast they had missed earlier on the prairie.

A few had managed a meal before breaking camp that morning and these continued their journey after

14

crossing the creek. They reached the Elkhorn River about noon and then followed the river eight miles to a known crossing point where there was plenty of timber.

The advance wagons found a raft built and waiting for them — the work of a few men sent ahead several days earlier for just that purpose.

Working quickly because of coming darkness, a number of the leaders floated their wagons across the Elkhorn. The river at this point was about 160 feet wide and the water was four feet deep in places. The Elkhorn was the first major milestone on the trip.

Getting across was wet work. The horses were ridden through the water to the other side and the cattle driven along with them. The raft was controlled by cattle pulling guide ropes on both sides of the river.

Seen in modern times, the Elkhorn doesn't look too formidible — a fairly shallow body of water and not too wide. But for the pioneers it was a time-consuming obstacle. In 1978 the crossing site is surrounded by cornfields. A Union Pacific railroad line spans the river nearby and Highway 6 is about a mile to the south.

During the evening many of the pioneers who had stopped to eat at Big Papillion Creek arrived on the scene and lent a hand with the rafting. This group had run into a marshy creek along the way and the men had to help pull the wagons through. Writing in his journal that night, Lorenzo Young called it "a hard day's work."

Nightfall found members of the party camped on both sides of the river. Eight men were posted for guard duty throughout the night because several pioneers reported seeing Indians prowling around the area.

Not everybody bringing up the rear reached the river by dark. Some of the main party, including the wagons with Brigham Young, camped near the banks of the Elkhorn, but about four miles upstream from the rest of the group.

Howard Egan, whose wagons were still traveling separately from the others, covered about 15 miles, which was pretty good marching time. He camped for the night on the open prairie "near a ravine which provided us water."

The pioneers' traveling speed was dictated by the oxen, who could make only about two miles an hour — slower than a man could walk. Thus the pace had to be rather leisurely. No one had any trouble keeping up.

To properly appreciate the pioneer route, it is necessary to understand that the trail was not a narrow pathway in the same sense as a road. Rather, it was a corridor which might be a few dozen yards wide to several miles in width, depending on the terrain. Wagons moving along the trail traveled anywhere in that corridor, the exact path depending on available grass for cattle, campsites, and other factors.

The main group of pioneers who camped April 10 on both sides of the Elkhorn was not far from the site of the future town of Waterloo, a Union Pacific Railroad community laid out in 1871 and named after the famous European battlefield.

By late afternoon, 72 wagons had ferried 'The Horn'

Darkness had halted the rafting of wagons across the Elkhorn River the night before, but the task resumed shortly after dawn on this Sunday.

The work continued most of the day as more companies of Mormon pioneers reached the river. The wagons were pulled across on a raft made of "dry cottonwood logs."

Willard Richards, who was with the last group to reach the river, reportedly had some bad luck. The lead mare for his wagon was "either strayed or stolen by Indians" the previous night.

By late afternoon a total of 72 wagons had been ferried to the west bank of the Elkhorn, or "the Horn" as the pioneers called it.

After collecting their cattle, the pioneers moved parallel to the river for about two miles to a place where a grove of trees provided shade, shelter and wood for fires.

The day had been a warm one, thanks to a "smart breeze from the south," according to Thomas Bullock, who was serving as record keeper for the party. The warm weather would help the prairie grass to grow, noted Norton Jacob, who turned out the horses to graze near camp.

Jacob, 42, one of the captains for the journey, was like many of the pioneers who sacrificed much for their religious beliefs.

He left a pregnant wife and six small children in Winter Quarters. One of those children was fated to die on the plains the next year while he was taking his family to their new home in the Salt Lake Valley.

Before leaving Nauvoo in 1846, Jacob worked full time making wagons for the trek westward. He was a skilled carpenter and cabinet maker. For his year's work he was paid with one of the wagons he had constructed.

When he finally settled in the Valley with his family, Jacob devoted 10 years to working on the construction of the Salt Lake Temple.

Brigham Young called a meeting of the pioneers after they were settled under the trees near the Elkhorn River. He explained that he and seven other apostles in the company would return to Winter Quarters the next day to meet with apostles coming back from missions in England.

He asked the company if they wanted to stay at the present campsite until he and the others returned or if they would rather push on another 14 miles to the Platte River, designated earlier as a staging point and jumping off place. "The feeling was to go ahead," Bullock wrote.

Heber C. Kimball then spoke to the assembled pioneers and reminded them that despite the hard work they had done in getting the wagons across the Elkhorn, it was still the Sabbath.

He said he hoped the men would not go hunting or fishing, but if they did, they would not prosper because "this was a day set apart for the service of the Lord and not for trivial amusement." The pioneers usually would remain camped each Sunday on their trek across the plains.

The rest of the day was spent in private activities. Some of the men wrote letters to their families because mail would be carried by the apostles as they returned to Winter Quarters the next day.

Wilford Woodruff said the Platte River could be seen from the pioneer campsite. The river would be their constant companion for the next 600 miles, always at their left hands as they kept to the north bank. That route had been used by others in earlier years, but never on such a large scale as the Mormons. For that reason it became known as the Mormon trail.

Both sides of the Platte River were considered part of the famed Oregon trail. It eventually would be used by thousands of emigrants and gold seekers, but most followed the south side of the river after coming up from the usual jumping off place at Independence, Mo.

The Mormons, with their bitter experiences of persecution and mob violence, preferred to keep the river between themselves and any other travelers going west. And there were many others on the Oregon trail.

Brigham and seven apostles left the company

At daybreak the men who had been standing guard roused the rest of the people in the Mormon pioneer company "and the bustle of camp life commenced."

After breakfast, Brigham Young and the other apostles with the pioneers, Heber C. Kimball, Willard Richards, Wilford Woodruff, Orson Pratt, George A. Smith, Amasa M. Lyman and Ezra T. Benson, went back over the Elkhorn River and headed for Winter Quarters.

With them went a number of other men, including Norton Jacob, who said he returned to "pick up my cow and rifle." But this trip was so brief that "I didn't get to see my family," he sadly noted.

Woodruff said the apostles found an Indian trail on the way back and it proved to be a shortcut, requiring only 20 miles of travel instead of the 35 they had covered in an indirect route to the Elkhorn River. The party reached home about 6 p.m., moving more rapidly because they were on horseback or in horse-drawn carriages instead of the slow ox-drawn wagons.

Meanwhile, the rest of the pioneer company packed up and moved 14 miles to the banks of the Platte River. They had decided to travel ahead without their leaders in order to cross a dozen miles of river bottom land "before the water should rise and the road get muddy," Howard Egan explained.

He said the width of the Platte "much surprised me." The river is more than a mile wide in places, but so shallow that it can't be navigated by even small boats. The water is studded by so many sandbars of varying size that the river seems to be divided into several parallel streams.

Early-day travelers didn't think too highly of the Platte, describing it on occasion as a mile wide and six inches deep, too thick to drink, too thin to plow, hard to cross because of quicksand, impossible to navigate, too yellow to wash in and too pale to paint with.

Springs floods frequently changed the course of the river in pioneer times and very little timber was to be found along its banks. One solitary giant cottonwood tree was a major landmark on the flat prairie until a storm blew it down in 1865. Many cottonwood trees line the river today, but they are mostly relatively recent.

After reaching the Platte, the pioneers set up camp to await the return of their leaders. That evening the company was called together by Stephen Markham, 47, who had been left in charge. He earlier had led a company of 200 in the flight from Nauvoo and across Iowa to the Missouri River.

Markham was still mending from an injury he suffered in Winter Quarters. While training some oxen to pull wagons for the trip west, he caught his hand in a chain and lost a finger.

Despite the injury, he was taken along for his skill as a road and bridge builder. He later would lead more pioneers across the plains and help settle Spanish Fork, serving as one of the first bishops in the Utah Territory.

At the meeting on the banks of the Platte, Markham said the apostles wanted men who knew something about the prairie to be sent ahead of the main party as scouts.

James Case, 53, one of the captains in the company, and Return Jackson Redden, 29, an adventuresome frontiersman, were chosen along with two others to move out the next day and see what lay ahead.

The campsite on the river was near the present-day town of Fremont, Neb., which was founded in 1856 and named after John C. Fremont, then a candidate for president. Legend has it that the town was established by some Republicans in answer to another community 25 miles away which Democratic settlers had named Buchanan.

The town of Fremont prospered because it was on the military road between Omaha and Fort Kearney. Merchants made a good living from people going west in the gold rush days. When the Union Pacific railroad was laid through in 1866, residents had high hopes Fremont would become a major industrial center. But those dreams never materialized. The town today is a pleasant agricultural center with a small college.

Blacksmiths kept busy fixing wagon wheels, shoeing some horses

The Mormon pioneers hadn't come far since leaving Winter Quarters, but they used a three-day delay while camped near the Platte River to repair and clean their wagons.

Three blacksmiths in the company set up forges and began fixing the iron-rimmed wagon wheels and shoeing some of the horses among the livestock.

The blacksmiths were James Davenport, 44, a Vermonter who was to cross the plains another half-dozen times; Thomas Tanner, 43, an Englishman who was killed in an accident in Salt Lake City eight years later, and Burr Frost, 31, who helped produce the first nails from ore mined in Iron County.

Others in the camp were busy cleaning their wagons after the muddy crossing of the Elkhorn River. The women in the party did washing.

Howard Egan reported that he propped up his wagon, removed the running gear and "Brother Harper went to work and put in two new axletrees."

"Brother Harper" was Charles Alfred Harper, 30, a wheelwright and carriage maker by trade, who had worked night and day building wagons in Nauvoo before the Mormons left that city for the trek to the west.

Meanwhile, the men who had been sent ahead to scout trail returned to camp. R. Jackson Redden, called "Redding" by his fellow pioneers; James Case, and the others, said the bottom land ahead was low and flat and probably couldn't be crossed in wet weather.

"And it has the appearance of rain this evening," Egan wrote in his journal.

As darkness began to fall, Stephen Markham, who had been left in charge of the camp, called the people together, issued some general instructions and posted guards for the night.

Back in Winter Quarters, the apostles, under the direction of Brigham Young, worked hard to raise additional money and prepare extra wagons they planned to take to the advance pioneer group.

"I was very busy," reported Wilford Woodruff. "Painted a wagon to sell and met with the Council of Twelve Apostles until midnight." The council had gathered to hear John Taylor, who returned that very evening from a mission in the British Isles.

Taylor brought valuable equipment he had purchased in England. Among the articles were two barometers, two sextants, two artificial horizons, one circle of reflection and one telescope. He exhibited these to the council members and they voiced pleasure the instruments had arrived in time for the trip across the plains.

The pioneers wanted the equipment to help them lay out roads and bridges for the 70,000 who were to follow. Unlike most emigrants, they weren't going for themselves, but were the advance party for many others.

After the items were inspected, they were carefully boxed for the rough trip. Taylor also brought money donated by church members in England. This was most welcome because the pioneers were desperately short of hard cash.

When the lengthy council meeting ended, the leaders went to their homes, doubtless feeling much like Woodruff, who noted it was "the last night I shall spend at Winter Quarters for a long time."

Earlier, Thomas Bullock and others had taken some of the extra wagons prepared during the day and set out once more to join the pioneers on the Platte River.

This small group traveled only a short distance before darkness overtook them and they camped on the open prairie.

Four yelling Indians were cause for delay

A small party of men with Thomas Bullock had camped on the prairie after leaving Winter Quarters the previous day and arose at dawn to continue the journey.

But the Indians were up even earlier.

"While I was in the act of hitching my cattle," Bullock wrote, "four Omaha Indians came rushing down upon us, waving their standards covered with turkey feathers and hallooing and yelling like savages."

The noise frightened his cattle and they broke away from the wagon tongue "as if they were mad," and ran back in the direction of Winter Quarters "and I after them at full tilt," Bullock recorded.

He finally caught up with the animals two or three miles away, but one of the Indians also had given chase and drew his bow and arrow, "threatening to shoot one of my oxen."

The pioneers tried to calm the Indians by giving them bread. "They were not satisfied with that and demanded more to take with them," Bullock said. "One had the boldness to come to my wagon and attempt to take the front of my wagon cover for a headress, but I repelled him and he went away in anger."

Norton Jacob, who was with the party of wagons,

said he heard a gun fired and some whooping. "Soon four of them came to us and were very saucy because we would not give them our provisions."

The confusion caused by the Indian raid created considerable delay and the wagons were late getting on the trail that day.

Brigham Young and the rest of the apostles left Winter Quarters around noon the same day. Wilford Woodruff wrote in his journal that he called his family together, "blessed them and left them in the hands of the Lord." The group took the Indian shortcut they had followed earlier to Winter Quarters.

With Brigham was William Clayton, who would serve as scribe and historian for the trip. He hadn't expected to be with the group. He was sick in bed with "rheumatism of the face" (which turned out to be an infected tooth) when Brigham and Willard Richards walked in and told him to be ready to leave in half an hour.

With the help of his family, he quickly gathered his clothing and a few supplies, said his farewells and became a passenger in Heber C. Kimball's carriage.

Taking Clayton was a fortunate move. Without his excellent journal and his "Emigrant's Guide," published in 1848, knowledge of the Mormon trail experience wouldn't be as complete as it is today.

Brigham's party traveled 19 miles, according to Clayton, and then pitched camp. Those with the group had what Woodruff called "a splendid supper." It consisted of fried catfish, pork beans, shortcake and honeycomb. "I ate hearty," Woodruff noted.

Because darkness had fallen and the slower-moving, ox-drawn Bullock wagons hadn't appeared, Brigham ordered signal fires to be kept burning. Bullock saw the lights and finally joined the group for the rest of the night.

Meanwhile, the main body of pioneers at the Platte continued to rest in camp. A rain soaked them during that morning, but the weather cleared as a sharp wind began blowing.

Howard Egan said two of his horses had strayed the night before. He borrowed a horse from R. Jackson Redden and rode back toward the Elkhorn River. He found the animals, but could only catch one of them and finally left the other.

John S. Higbee, 43, Redden, and four or five other men went up the Platte River looking for a good place to fish and returned that evening with a catch of about a dozen, which were eaten for supper.

Higbee actually should have been in California. He had volunteered the year before to join the Mormon Battalion in the war with Mexico, but by the time he reached Council Bluffs to march with the troops, they had already left.

He was called to be a captain in the advance pioneer company, even though he had no wagon of his own. His supplies were carried in a friend's wagon.

Higbee didn't reach the Salt Lake Valley that summer. He was assigned to stay behind at a crossing of the Platte River and help operate a ferry. His family eventually joined him there and they entered the valley in September, 1847.

Now it was time to face west with a single objective

All the running back and forth between Winter Quarters and the pioneer staging area 35 miles away on the Platte River was about ended.

From now on, the faces of the Mormon pioneers would be turned to the west and the settlement on the banks of the Missouri River would not be seen again for many months.

Once the break was made, there would be little chance for communication. An occasional traveler met on the trail might agree to carry some letters, but for the most part, the pioneers and those they left behind could only worry and wonder about each other during the long months of separation.

Brigham Young and those with him had left Winter Quarters the previous day and spent the night on the prairie after traveling an estimated 19 miles.

Now they were on the march again and reached the Elkhorn, using the raft left behind there to ferry their wagons across the water. By late afternoon they rejoined the remainder of the pioneers at the Platte River.

In the evening, Jesse C. Little, 31, who had been serving as president of the church's Eastern States

Mission, rode into camp. He had reached Winter Quarters and found the pioneers gone, so he pushed ahead to catch them.

He brought greetings from Col. Thomas Kane, a gentile friend of the Mormons, along with some small gifts for the apostles from the colonel. Little stayed with the company for the journey west, but next fall returned to his mission and served nearly four more years.

Brigham called the camp together that night for instructions on the thousand-mile march that lay ahead. He told them to take good care of their teams and "cease all music, dancing and light-mindedness."

He exhorted them to prayer and faithfulness and warned that persecutions weren't ended. He said traders and preachers were stirring up Indians to attack the Mormons and steal their horses and goods. But he promised all would come through safely if they were faithful and obeyed counsel.

Nine rules were laid down for the trip and everyone was expected to be obedient. The rules were:

1. A bugle will blow each day at 5 a.m. and every man is expected to arise and pray, then attend to his team, get breakfast and be prepared to travel at 7 a.m.

2. Each man is to walk at the side of his team with his gun loaded and within reach.

3. The camp will halt about noon to rest the animals. People must have their dinner pre-cooked so as not to delay camp by fixing meals.

4. At night the wagons are to be drawn into a circle and the animals placed inside the circle when possible.

5. The bugle will blow at 8:30 p.m. when every man must return to his wagon and pray, except the night guard. Fires must be out and people in bed by 9 p.m.

6. The camp will travel in close order and no man is to get farther than 20 rods away (about 330 feet) without permission from his captain of 10.

7. Every man is to help take care of his brother's cattle. No man will be indulged in idleness.

8. Every man is to have his rifle and pistol in perfect working order. A piece of leather should be kept over the firing mechanism to protect it from moisture.

9. All persons will start together and keep together. A company guard will attend the cannon in the rear and see that nothing is left behind at each stopping place.

Stephen Markham was named chief of the guard and told to pick 50 men in whom he had confidence. These were to be divided into groups of 12 to stand watch — one group to be on duty the first half of a night and a second 12 to take the last half of the night.

On those occasions when the horses and cattle are staked out some distance from camp instead of being inside the wagon circle, extra guards will be posted with the animals. These extra guards will be chosen from men not already among the 50 picked for sentry duty.

25

April 16
FRIDAY

Company organized, and rules reviewed

After breakfast, Brigham Young called the Mormon pioneer company together once again to organize for the trek and to remind them of the rules adopted for safety and discipline.

Norton Jacob said the president issued a stern admonition to the assembled group, saying that if any do not like to obey the necessary rules, without murmuring, they should "turn back now."

Bishop Newell K. Whitney, who had accompanied the pioneers thus far, but was scheduled to return to Winter Quarters, also spoke and promised he would do all he could "to help the families of those who are going."

After some remarks by several other speakers, Brigham had the company count off and nominate their officers. The pioneers were formed into two divisions, with Stephen Markham and Albert P. Rockwood as leaders. Rockwood, 41, was a former general in the Nauvoo Legion. He later became the first warden of the territorial prison.

The pioneers were further organized into groups of 10, each with a captain. The groups, although they would change in some respects before the trip was over, were recorded as follows this day:

— First 10: Wilford Woodruff, captain; Jacob D. Burnham, Joseph Egbert, Marcus B. Thorpe, George Wardle, John S. Fowler, Orson Pratt, John M. Freeman, George A. Smith.

— Second 10: Ezra T. Benson, captain; Thomas Grover, Barnabas L. Adams, Roswell Stevens, Amasa M. Lyman, Sterling Driggs, Albert Carrington, Thomas Bullock, George Brown, Willard Richards, Jesse C. Little.

— Third 10: Phineas H. Young, captain; John Y. Green, Thomas Tanner, Brigham Young, Addison Everett, Truman O. Angell, Lorenzo D. Young, Briant

Stringham, Albert P. Rockwood, Joseph S. Schofield.

— Fourth 10: Luke S. Johnson, captain; John Holman, Edmund Ellsworth, Sidney Alvarus Hanks, George R. Grant, Millen Atwood, Samuel Fox, Tunis Rappleye, Harvey Pierce, William Dykes, Jacob Weiler.

— Fifth 10: Stephen H. Goddard, captain; Tarlton Lewis, Henry G. Sherwood, Zebeedee Coltrin, Sylvester H. Earl, John Dixon, Samuel H. Marble, George Scholes, William Henrie, William A. Empey.

— Sixth 10: Charles Shumway, captain; Andrew Shumway, Thomas Woolsey, Chauncey Loveland, Erastus Snow, James Craig, William Wardsworth, William Vance, Simeon Howd, Seeley Owen.

— Seventh 10: James Case, captain; Artemas Johnson, William C.A. Smoot, Franklin B. Dewey, William Carter, Franklin G. Losee, Burr Frost, Horace Datus Ensign, B. Franklin Stewart, Monroe Frink, Eric Glines, Ozro Eastman.

—Eighth 10: Seth Taft, captain; Horace Thornton, Stephen Kelsey, John Eldgredge, Charles Barnum, Almon Williams, Rufus Allen, Robert T. Thomas, James W. Stewart, Elijah Newman, Levi Kendall, Francis Boggs, David Grant.

— Ninth 10: Howard Egan, captain; Heber C. Kimball, William A. King, Thomas Cloward, Hosea Cushing, Robert Baird, George Billings, Edson Whipple, Philo Johnson, William Clayton.

— Tenth 10: Appleton M. Harmon, captain; Carlos Murray, Horace K. Whitney, Orson K. Whitney, Orrin P. Rockwell, Nathaniel T. Brown, R. Jackson Redden, John Pack, Francis Pomeroy, Aaron Farr, Nathaniel Fairbanks.

— Eleventh 10: John S. Higbee, captain; John Wheeler, Solomon Chamberlain, Conrad Kleinman, Joseph Rooker, Perry Fitzgerald, John H. Tippets, James Davenport, Henson Walker, Benjamin Rolfe.

— Twelfth 10: Norton Jacob, captain; Charles A. Harper, George Woodward, Stephen Markham, Lewis Barney, George Mills, Joseph Hancock, John W. Norton, Andrew Gibbons.

— Thirteenth 10: John Brown, captain; Shadrach Roundy, Hans C. Hansen, Levi Jackman, Lyman Curtis, Matthew Ivory, David Powell, Hark Lay, Oscar Crosby.

— Fourteenth 10: Joseph Mathews, captain; Gilbroid Summe, John Gleason, Charles Burke, Alexander Chesley, Rodney Badger, Norman Taylor, Green Flake, Ellis Eames.

In addition, there were three women, the wives of Brigham Young, Heber C. Kimball and Lorenzo Young, and Lorenzo's two children, a grand total of 149 persons.

As can be seen, a company of 10 wasn't always made up of 10 persons. Sometimes there were nine in a group and sometimes as many as 12. No explanation was offered by the pioneers for these differences.

After getting organized and bidding goodbye to those returning to Winter Quarters, the company moved out at 3 p.m., traveling just three miles before halting for the night.

"The wind blew from the north, very cold," Egan wrote. William Clayton shared a single blanket with Philo Johnson that night, saying he "suffered much and took a very bad cold."

Good progress over the flat Nebraska plain

The fairly level Nebraska prairie allowed the Mormon pioneers to make good time as they followed the north bank of the Platte River.

Each day the company paused for an hour or two in the middle of the march to allow the animals to rest, drink and graze. Otherwise the teams would exhaust themselves before it was time to make camp in the evening.

The pioneers passed a large Indian village on April 21 near what is now Columbus, Neb., and more than 200 Pawnee turned out to greet them and ask for gifts.

Late in the week, the Loup River took the company away from the Platte and forced the pioneers to cross the wide stream to get back to the banks of the Platte. Attempts to ford the Loup were frustrated on April 23 because of quicksand under the shallow water.

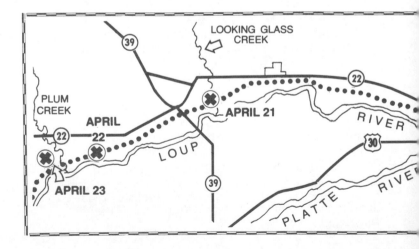

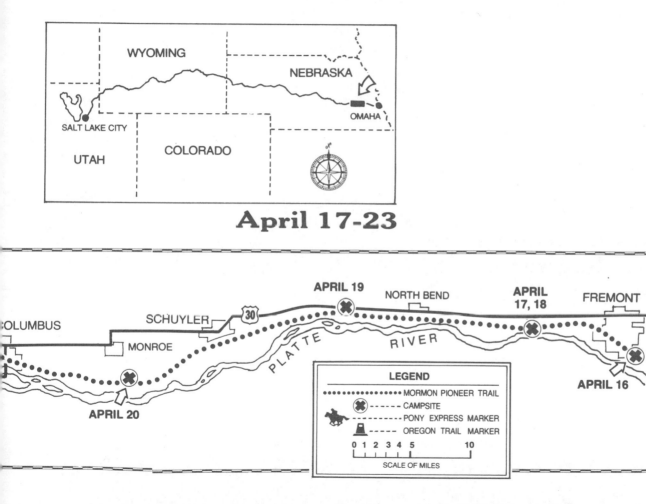

April 17-23

WYOMING

NEBRASKA

OMAHA

SALT LAKE CITY

UTAH

COLORADO

APRIL 19

NORTH BEND

APRIL 17, 18

FREMONT

COLUMBUS

SCHUYLER

30

MONROE

PLATTE RIVER

APRIL 16

APRIL 20

LEGEND

●●●●●●●●●● MORMON PIONEER TRAIL

⊗ - - - - - CAMPSITE

🏇 - - - - - PONY EXPRESS MARKER

⛫ - - - - - OREGON TRAIL MARKER

0 1 2 3 4 5   10

SCALE OF MILES

Pioneers awoke to ice on water buckets, traveled only 7 miles

The night was bitter cold and when the Mormon pioneers awoke at 5 a.m. they found ice an inch thick in the camp's water buckets. Men who had been on guard duty "complained much of the severity of the weather."

Keeping as usual between the river on their left and the sand bluffs on the right, the company moved slowly along a sandy track, bothered by a "disagreeable" wind.

The group stopped about noon after moving only seven miles and established camp where they would spend the time until Monday morning.

A grove of small cottonwood trees was nearby and the men chopped down "hundreds" of them to feed their teams and save their precious corn for treeless parts of the prairie still to come. A small lake was nearby, but scouts said the water was no good. The pioneers filled their buckets in the Platte River, about a half-mile from the campsite.

At 5 p.m. Brigham Young called the camp together and warned once again that this was Indian country. He reminded them of camp rules about keeping loaded guns at hand at all times and staying close to the wagons.

A military organization was formed with Brigham as lieutenant general and commander-in-chief; Stephen Markham as a colonel and John Pack and Shadrach Roundy as majors.

Pack, 37, had been an officer in the Nauvoo Legion. He was to later help settle Carson Valley, Nev., and in his Salt Lake home were held the first classes of what was to eventually become the University of Utah.

Roundy, 58, was one of the oldest in the pioneer company. He was to cross the plains another five times helping later emigrant parties. He was involved in forming the cooperative which later became ZCMI.

Concern of the pioneers about Indians became more intense because they knew a large Pawnee village was nearby. An estimated 4,000 warriors were rumored to be there. The Pawnee generally were considered friendly to whites, but the Mormons were taking no chances.

Shortly before dark, a wagon driven by traders entered the Mormon camp and pitched their tents about a quarter mile away. They had been trading at the Indian village and the wagon was loaded with furs and pelts.

The traders "had plenty of buffalo meat and gave us what we wished," Wilford Woodruff reported.

That night after dinner, two of the men, Ellis Eames and Hans C. Hansen, got out their violins and entertained the camp until the bugle sounded at 9 p.m.

Eames was to give up the trek and leave the camp in less than 24 hours, but made it later to the Rocky Mountains and served as mayor of Provo.

Hansen, 40, a native of Denmark, was the only Scandinavian in the group. A former seaman, he was on shore leave in Boston when he learned of the new religion and joined the church. An accomplished violinist, he settled in Salina where he lived out his life as a bachelor, performing at local dances and social events.

After the music the pioneers retired to their tents and wagons under the watchful eyes of the night guard, but "all was peace and quietness," wrote William Clayton.

The campsite was near what is now the Ames Post Office. The tiny community was founded by the Union Pacific Railroad Co. and was named after one of the company officials.

During the day the pioneers had traveled through the area now occupied by Fremont, Neb. A historical marker in a small park west of town notes the community is on what was the Oregon-Mormon trail.

Because the Mormon pioneers used the best route they could find, with the fewest hills and obstacles, their path was later chosen for the Omaha-Fort Kearny Road and finally became the right-of-way for the Union Pacific railroad.

Eventually, Highway 30, the famous Lincoln Highway, was built along the same corridor. Motorists on Highway 30 between Fremont and Columbus, Neb., are right on the trail.

31

A welcome rest day, and an opportunity to send mail back

"Today, being the day set apart by Almighty God for His people to rest, we do not intend to travel."

This feeling, recorded by Howard Egan, was shared by all of the Mormon pioneer company. The practice was kept for most of the journey across the plains.

Ellis Eames decided this day to pull out of the trek and go back to Winter Quarters "on account of poor health, spitting blood, etc.," William Clayton reported.

Egan was less charitable, writing that Eames was leaving in consequence of sickness, "so he said." But added, "I think he is weak in the faith."

Some of the pioneer company took the opportunity to write letters to loved ones at Winter Quarters. Eames would carry the mail with him.

Heber C. Kimball penned a few lines to his wife, Vilate, explaining that he was well and in good spirits. Although he had taken several wives in the practice of polygamy, he wrote to Vilate, his first wife, that she had "the love of my youth, which is first, last, now and forever," and urged her to be of good cheer.

He called his tender letter "a private epistle," not to be shared with others of the extended family.

Although he obviously missed his wife, Kimball was enjoying the trek across the plains. After it was all over, he wrote: "It was pretty hard and laborious, I admit, but it was one of the pleasantest journeys I ever performed."

The weather was cold and a light snow fell on this Sunday morning as Eames turned his wagon eastward in company with the traders who had camped near the Mormons the previous night. He arrived safely in Winter Quarters a few days later.

More traders' wagons, seven in all, drove up and camped near the pioneers later this day. All were loaded with buffalo robes and various furs. Clayton ate some of the buffalo meat provided by the traders, "which I thought tasted very good."

Life in camp was relaxed this Sunday. The pioneers took care of their livestock and did some reading, although Wilford Woodruff complained as he read some newspapers brought several days earlier,

that he "did not find much news."

Some excitement was caused during the afternoon when James Case was cutting down a tree and a sudden gust of wind "blew it in a contrary direction." A branch of the falling tree struck an ox owned by John Taylor. At first the pioneers feared the animal would be blinded, but the injured eye recovered in a few hours.

The sun broke through overcast skies and the weather moderated later in the day. Some of the men walked the half mile to the banks of the Platte River.

Woodruff said that strolling along the bank of the Platte was "like walking on the edge of a smooth sea beach where a man or horse can drink. But here and there he can suddenly sink into quicksand. The more he struggles to get out, the more he will sink and soon perish if assistance is not near."

The bugle announcing the end of the day blew at 8:30 p.m., giving the pioneers a half hour to get ready for bed and extinguish their campfires. The wagons were pulled in a circle when the company halted the night before. Now the cattle were placed inside the circle for the night.

Some of the pioneers bedded down in their wagons among all the supplies. Others had brought tents along. These were pitched near the wagons, outside the circle.

The groups of 10 kept their individual campsites close together under the command of the particular captain who was responsible for their safety and conduct.

Wagons on the move down an easy corridor

It had been a restful weekend. Now the Mormon pioneer wagons were on the move again, traveling in double file. The route was "very level" as the Platte River flood plain provided an easy corridor about 15 miles wide.

William Clayton, still bothered by a pounding toothache, left camp a few minutes early, going on foot ahead of the wagons "with my rifle on my shoulder."

As the company slowly moved along, the pioneers saw a series of small lakes or ponds with many ducks. Some of the men unlimbered their guns and started shooting. They managed to bag several ducks before the rest flew away.

In the early afternoon the pioneers stopped for about two hours near a bend in the river and let the cattle graze. They had covered an estimated dozen miles since morning, but their mileage at this point was just a guess.

While the company was stopped here, four men rode into camp. They were Jesse C. Little, R. Jackson Redden, N. Thomas Brown and O. Porter Rockwell. They came from Winter Quarters where they had gone to help Little collect his baggage.

Little had reached the pioneers several days earlier after returning from a mission to the Eastern States, but had not stopped for his belongings in Winter Quarters, so had to ride back for them.

Not much is known about Brown, who accompanied him, except that he was highly regarded by Brigham Young and that he was killed in 1848 in an accidental shooting at Council Bluffs, Iowa. He had returned to the area to help other pioneers after reaching the Salt Lake Valley.

Rockwell, 31, a rugged frontiersman, had been a faithful bodyguard to Joseph Smith and once was imprisoned in Missouri for his allegiance to the Mormon cause.

A slight, wiry man, he wore his hair braided and pinned at the back of his head. Although loyal to church leaders, he attended religious meetings infrequently, feeling out of place with his rough, gun-toting manner. He rode thousands of miles in the service of the church and was effective in dealing with Indians.

He was later a Pony Express rider and a lawman. He had a fearsome reputation, and lawbreakers generally went far out of their way to avoid him.

When Brown, Rockwell, and the others reached camp they brought a most welcome gift — mail from home. Many of the men in the pioneer party received letters from family and friends and were deeply relieved that all was well at Winter Quarters.

The riders also brought some small but useful items to share among the pioneers. Clayton said Rockwell gave him some fishhooks, a ball of fish line and three pencils.

Along with the mail and gifts, the four men also brought a horse belonging to Willard Richards. Some days earlier Richards had reported the animal was strayed or stolen near the west bank of the Elkhorn River.

During the day's march the pioneer company passed a mass Indian grave about a quarter mile wide and bordered by a ridge of dirt. "We thought this was some ancient battlefield," Thomas Bullock wrote in his journal.

After making camp that evening, some of the men took a leather boat, which they called the Revenue Cutter, to a nearby lake in an effort to catch some fish. The boat, being lightweight, was carried in one of the wagons and used for fishing and ferrying supplies in river crossings.

This fishing expedition didn't have much luck, returning with two small catfish, some turtles and a duck.

Clayton, who had walked to the fishing site and back, was exhausted and footsore and went straight to bed, "but had no rest on account of the severe pain in my head and face."

Chase for deer failed, but fishermen succeeded

Some men in the Mormon pioneer company were up very early — about 4:30 a.m. — to take their cattle out to graze in the dew-soaked prairie grass, a two-hour chore.

Howard Egan said he prepared a "first-rate breakfast" from wild ducks bagged the day before. Despite the good food, William Clayton "ate but little" because his aching tooth was keeping him in misery.

The company began the day's march in two lines, about a quarter mile apart. A stiff early wind blew considerable sand but finally died down. The day turned out to be warm and dusty as the iron-rimmed wagon wheels cut into the prairie turf.

As the party moved along they could see large numbers of waterfowl near the Platte River. Some of the birds were geese, "but mostly sandhill cranes which fly in large flocks on every side of us," Wilford Woodruff said.

The wagons came to a large prairie dog village covering about six acres. The pioneers also saw many gopher holes, some with dirt heaped up two or three feet high and others "resembling a potato patch, which makes it rough waggoning over them," Woodroff wrote in his journal.

While stopped near some ponds of water about midday to let the animals feed, the company saw three deer and O. Porter Rockwell and Thomas Brown went after them. "They had a fine chase of four or five miles, but did not get them," Norton Jacob reported.

Stephen Markham, John S. Higbee and Luke Johnson took the camp's leather boat and went ahead to some small lakes to try their hands at catching fish for dinner that evening.

Johnson, 39, was an early apostle and effective missionary, but was disfellowshipped from the church for a time. He returned and was rebaptised in 1846 and later became a bishop at a settlement in Nevada. He was in charge of the boat for the pioneers.

The rest of the pioneer company pushed on during the afternoon and camped near a grove of cottonwood trees on the banks of the river. Blacksmiths got out their forges and repaired some wagon wheels before darkness fell.

A number of men cut down cottonwood trees to feed the livestock, but took care to leave plenty for the many companies who would be following. The cattle gnawed off the bark "as readily as they would eat corn," Woodruff said.

The fishermen returned to camp that evening after a highly successful expedition. They had thrown

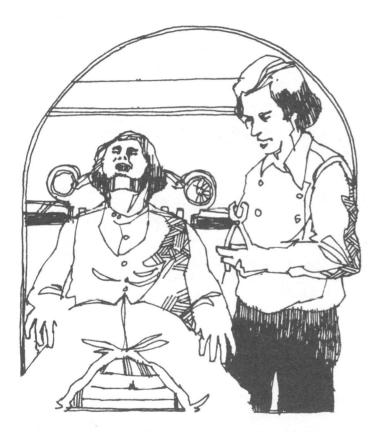

nets into a lake and pulled in more than 200 fish, mostly carp. The fish were divided among the camp, one large fish to each person.

Clayton went down to the river and bathed his feet which were dusty and sore. "I also washed my socks as well as I could in cold water without soap."

After taking care of his weary feet, he decided to do something about his aching face. He approached Luke Johnson and asked if he would pull the offending tooth.

"He willingly agreed," Clayton said and got out his instruments. Johnson served as doctor for the group. He sat Clayton in a chair and bent to his work. He lanced the swollen gum and yanked the tooth out with a pair of nippers, the "the whole operation taking less than a minute."

Unfortunately, "he only got half the tooth, the balance being left in the jaw," Clayton said. "After this, my head and face pained me more than before. I ate but little supper and then lay down, but could not sleep for pain until near morning."

As they traveled that day, the pioneers veered slightly south of, but parallel to present-day Highway 30 and the Union Pacific railroad line.

They passed the place where Schuyler, Neb., would one day be built. The town was laid out 42 years after this first party of Mormon pioneers came through. It was named after Schuyler Colfax, vice president of the U.S. at the time (1869) and it became the first shipping point on the U.P. railroad for cattle driven north from Texas after the Civil War.

Pawnees paid visit to collect tribute, handshakes for all

Having half a tooth pulled seemed to have helped William Clayton. He awoke with his face feeling less painful, although still swollen and sore.

He ate some fish for breakfast, but couldn't take the bread, "it being very dry and hard. I could not bear to put it in my mouth."

During the morning's travel an Indian appeared and rode full speed toward the wagons and then pulled to a stop. He dismounted and seemed very sociable, shaking hands all around. Eight others also put in a brief appearance.

Despite the friendliness, the Mormon pioneers were very cautious, "knowing the Pawnee will show every sign of friendship and at the same time be watching and laying plans to steal our horses, etc.," said Heber C. Kimball.

Later in the day, the pioneer company passed a large Pawnee village. There were more than 100 lodges, set close together and in good order. The lodges were all made of skins, Kimball said, the usual houses or cabins at the old village having been burned by the Sioux.

As the pioneers continued on their way, a large number of Indians trailed after them until the Mormons pitched camp for a midday rest across the Platte River and out of sight of the Indian village.

About 200 Pawnees gathered on the far side of the river and finally some 75 rode through the shallow water to the wagons. Among them was an old chief.

The Indians presented Brigham Young with certificates from other travelers declaring that the grand chief of the Pawnee was friendly and that those previous visitors had given him presents of powder, lead, salt and other items.

Some of the pioneers gave gifts of tobacco, fishhooks, flour and salt, but the old chief wasn't satisfied with the quantity. He said he "didn't like us to go west through their country. He was afraid we should kill their buffalo and drive them off," Clayton said.

"But there was no appearance of hostility," he added. In fact, all the Indians who came to the camp wanted to shake hands and would "run from one side to the other so as not to miss one."

However, two horse bridles and a copper wash pan were discovered missing after the Pawnee visit.

When the pioneers passed the Indian village, they noticed squaws at work digging for roots, while the men walked about with the air of great overlords, being "perfectly listless and idle," Norton Jacob reported.

After this encounter, the pioneers moved on. The skies clouded over and a heavy rain began to soak the company. The rain was punctuated by "heavy peals of thunder and vivid flashes of lightning."

The pioneers camped for the night at the mouth of Looking Glass Creek on the bank of the Loup Fork of the Platte River. This fork had parted them from the Platte itself and would have to be crossed soon. The company covered an estimated 25 miles that day, the best day's travel since leaving Winter Quarters.

Because of the nearness of Indians, Brigham called for extra volunteers to stand guard and 100 men responded. They were divided into two groups of 50, each group taking half of the night watch.

Wilford Woodruff, who rode a mule on picket duty outside the camp, said the weather was foul. He wrapped himself in a buffalo hide "and let the wind and rain beat on me."

Earlier that day the pioneers passed the place where Columbus, Neb., would be founded in 1856 by a group of settlers from Columbus, Ohio. Germans, Swiss and Poles were among the early inhabitants. The community has grown into a modest, but thriving industrial center.

April 22
THURSDAY

Sleeping guards were taught lesson by a joke

Many extra guards were on duty during the night — 50 per shift — because of the nearness of the large Pawnee Indian village which the Mormon pioneers passed the previous day.

Several of the guards fell asleep and when they awoke in the morning, two of them discovered their rifles were missing and a hat was gone from a third man.

The embarrassed guards were the objects of considerable jokes about having fallen victim to prowling Indians during the night. But other sentries finally confessed they took the hat and guns from the sleeping men "as a warning."

However, William Clayton sympathized with the guards, noting that it was "difficult for men to keep awake night after night, while traveling 20 miles in a day, taking care of teams, cooking, etc."

The few sentries who fell asleep did not cause security problems. Plenty of other men were alert, but there was no sign of any Indian activity around the camp during the night.

The pioneers resumed their march at 7:30 a.m. and soon crossed Looking Glass Creek, which was named by Heber C. Kimball. The name was appropriate, according to Norton Jacob, because the water was "clear as crystal."

Later the company forded Beaver Creek. Here the crossing was less pleasant. The stream was 20 feet wide and two feet deep, but the west bank was very steep. A rope was hooked to the tongue of each wagon and 12 men hauled the wagons one at a time up the nearly vertical creek bank.

In the afternoon the pioneers reached a deserted Pawnee missionary station near Plum Creek, a stream the pioneers found especially attractive.

The missionary outpost and some nearby government buildings were established eight years earlier, but were abandoned in the fall of 1846 when Sioux raiders drove off the Pawnee. The attackers burned the government buildings but left the missionary structures intact.

The Mormons took possession of the farmyard at the station, observing that there were a number of good log houses and considerable improved land enclosed by rail fences, plus plenty of hay and fodder lying about.

This feed for cattle was especially welcome because of the limited supplies carried by the pioneers and the frequent lack of good grass on the prairie. Brigham Young said the company could use all the hay desired but gave strict orders not to touch anything else at the abandoned station.

Scattered around the buildings were "large lots of iron, several plows, a drag and two stoves, all apparently left to rot," Clayton said. Such iron products were scarce and extremely valuable to the pioneers.

The burned-out government buildings were about a quarter mile from the missionary station. The area was familiar to James Case, one of the members of the pioneer company. He had been employed at the station as a government farmer the year before.

Jacob said the area around the abandoned station was "excellent country with rich land." He said the surrounding slopes were covered with the "richest kind of grass which serves to feed those immense herds of buffalo. Although, by the by, we haven't seen any yet," he added.

One of the pioneer company had a close call that day. George A. Smith, destined one day to become a counselor to Brigham Young, was watering his horse when it became mired in the mud and lunged forward, knocking him flat.

The horse then stepped on his legs and chest "and held him fast in the mud" until Wilford Woodruff could spring to the rescue and back the animal away. "I was fearful he was badly injured but found he was little hurt," Woodruff said.

Smith, 29, would later lead a large group of pioneers across the plains, a lengthy journey of 155 days filled with a number of disasters.

He was a tireless colonizer and became known as the father of the Mormon settlements in southern Utah. The town of St. George was named after him. In 1868, after the death of Heber C. Kimball, he became a counselor in the church First Presidency.

In the pioneer camp this night, Brigham ordered the cannon unlimbered and loaded. Thomas Tanner drilled the gun crew until dark, showing them how to use the cannon. The president was concered about the possibility of Indian raiders trying to steal the horses.

He found a way to recoup his final paycheck

Although Brigham Young told the Mormon pioneers not to take "one cent" worth of tools, iron or equipment from the abandoned missionary station where they spent the night, a way around this ban was found.

James Case, who once worked as a $300-a-year government farmer near the station, said he was fired from his job and denied his last payday when the Army commander learned he had joined the Mormons.

Under the circumstances, Brigham said Case was entitled to some of the abandoned material at the station in lieu of his pay. Other pioneers could share in it by hauling the goods for Case on a 50-50 basis.

However, the presidennt instructed Case to write former officials of the station and explain what he had done. The Mormons promptly helped themselves to some of the stoves, plows and iron bars lying about.

Brigham, always busy as a scout in addition to his leadership responsibilities, led a party of 12 men to look for a good crossing of the Loup Fork. The rest of the men repaired their wagons and graded a road to Plum Creek, which also would have to be crossed.

The scouts returned to say they couldn't find a

good place to ford the Loup, but there was a possible place about four miles away if the company wanted to chance it.

Teams were hitched up and the wagons made it over Plum Creek and another stream called Cedar Creek, although they had some difficulty in the latter crossing. They finally reached the fording place on the banks of the Loup.

William Clayton said that by the time he arrived "my feet were so hot and blistered I could not walk for some time." He had been having trouble with sore feet for several days.

The pioneers were disappointed at the crossing site because of sandbars, quicksand and a rapid current reaching waist high in places. The river was 400 yards wide and split into two streams by a large sandbar in the middle.

Luke Johnson tried crossing first after completely unloading his wagon. Even then he had great difficulty.

Orson Pratt went next with a partial load, but his horses couldn't pull against the quicksand. A number of men jumped into the river, lifted the wagon wheels and pushed until they reached the sandbar at mid-stream

Norton Jacob started over and had the same trouble. His slow-moving oxen sank in the sand and he had to leap from the wagon into the water. Ten men rushed to his rescue and used a rope to pull the wagon to the sandbar.

Pratt ventured into the second half of the river, but the quicksand mired his horses so badly that one of them fell down. Two men helped him unhitch the team and lead the animals to safety. The wagon was unloaded and the goods carried across. Then the wagon was pulled over by rope.

Two or three other wagons got over the river by the same method of unloading and being pulled by rope. Brigham finally ordered a halt because of the strenuous problems. The pioneers decided to build two rafts the next day.

Tarlton Lewis was placed in charge of building one raft and Thomas Woolsey the other.

Lewis, 41, was a southerner and a skilled carpenter. He was a bishop in Nauvoo and his 17-year-old son was serving with the Mormon Battalion. He later became a bishop in Parowan and helped settle much of southern Utah, discovering iron ore deposits and starting some of the first mines in the area.

Woolsey, 41, also a southerner, had enlisted in the Mormon Battalion and marched as far as what is now Pueblo, Colo., before being sent back as a messenger. He and others were captured by Indians on the journey and sentenced to death, but other Indians helped them escape. He arrived in Winter Quarters only three weeks before the pioneer trek west began.

The aborted crossing of the Loup Fork left six men on the far bank for the night. They were nervous because of hundreds of Indians known to be in the area and stood guard three at a time. Five men crossed by boat in the night to bolster their numbers.

"I stood guard in my wet clothes half the night," Jacob said, "and slept in them the other half."

It was a struggle to cross the Loup River

Crossing the quicksand-filled Loup Fork April 24 was a struggle, but once over, the Mormon pioneers headed southwest across barren country toward the Platte River.

They stayed near the Loup for a few days, then struck south April 27 and reached the Platte the next day near what is now the town of Grand Island.

Most of the time the pioneers tried to march parallel to a river. On a few occasions they had to go across country and complained about the dry conditions which were a hardship on the animals.

Along the Platte there were hardly any trees, but on April 30 a plentiful new fuel was discovered — buffalo chips.

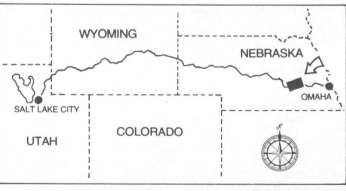

April 24-30

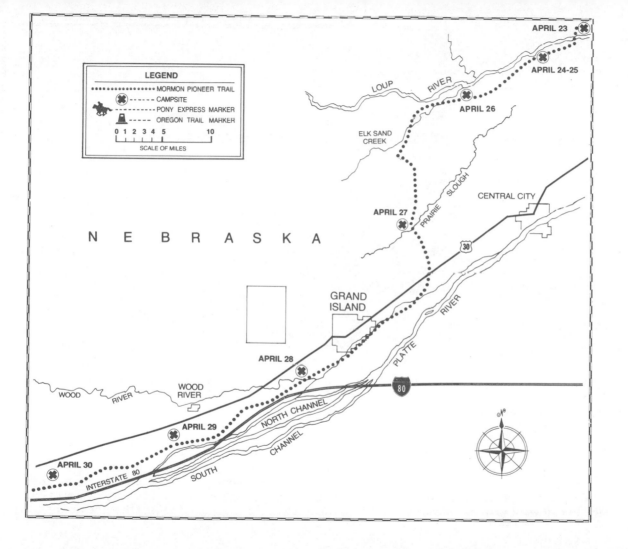

45

April 24
SATURDAY

Fording Loup Fork was a tiring endeavor

Frustrated in their efforts to ford the Loup Fork, the Mormon pioneers began building rafts to carry their wagons. But an easier approach was discovered.

Several men explored a different crossing slightly higher upstream. By unloading half the baggage in a wagon and doubling or tripling the teams, "we got across with much less difficulty."

This news caused the pioneers to abandon the raft-building project and all went to work unloading goods and hooking up teams to drive the wagons over. The unloaded supplies were ferried across by the leather boat.

As more and more wagons forded the river, the traffic packed down the sand under water and made each successive crossing that much easier. Finally, fully loaded wagons were able to be pulled through.

By 4 p.m. all had gotten over "without damage to man or beast," Wilford Woodruff wrote. The crossing was such a strenuous undertaking that the tired pioneers were deeply grateful to have the experience behind them.

The fact that no animals were injured also was a cause for rejoicing. One horse had been lost earlier that day before crossing the river. The horse, a favorite belonging to Brigham Young, had fallen into a ravine during the night. A chain around its neck was fastened to a post and the animal choked to death when it fell.

"This is a grievous loss for there are no more teams in camp than are absolutely necessary and in fact, there are hardly enough to get along very comfortably," wrote William Clayton in his journal.

While the crossing of the Loup Fork was being made, Brigham sent Clayton to explore the ruins of an abandoned Pawnee village nearby and write a description. Clayton didn't have a wagon of his own to be taken over the river.

The village had been burned by Sioux raiders once before while the Pawnee were on a hunt. The Pawnee, who were farmers and lived in lodges rather than as tent-dwelling nomads, rebuilt the entire complex. But it was burned again by the Sioux, except for one lodge.

"The Pawnee then moved to the place where we passed them a few days ago," Clayton recorded.

Thomas Bullock said the village was surrounded in part by a high dirt embankment, fronted by a deep ditch, "as if it were a fortified place." A burial ground was nearby and some of the pioneers found many human bones.

Clayton wrote a detailed description of the village and its type of construction, a report covering many pages. He noticed that the crossing of the Loup was nearly finished and rushed to join the others. He was given a horse to ride and "got over safe and only wet my feet."

Once everything was loaded back onto the wagons, the company traveled three miles and camped beside a small lake, about two miles south of the present town of Fullerton, Neb., where they would spend the Sabbath weekend.

Porter Rockwell noticed that the lake was full of sunfish. Many men gathered hooks and lines and went fishing. "We had some fine sport," Clayton wrote. He said many of the men "caught a good mess each." The fish, though small, made a good meal, he added.

Fresh Indian tracks were found on some nearby bluffs, "but the guards are faithful and we have no fear," Clayton said. However, the cannon was prepared for action in the event of an attack during the night.

The evening was clear and after dinner Clayton walked to Orson Pratt's wagon. Pratt, known as "professor" to his fellow emigrants, was a self-taught scientist. He had unpacked the telescope brought from England

Clayton took a look and "saw Jupiter's four moons very distinctly, never having seen them before."

The tired company finally settled down to bed that night, most of them probably sharing the feeling of Howard Egan: "I thank the Lord tomorrow is a day of rest."

Those Sunday rests actually gained time

As was their custom, the pioneers didn't travel on Sunday, but this wasn't really costing them time. A periodic day of rest kept the cattle in good condition.

A non-Mormon guide who crossed the plains with gold seekers many times in later years once remarked that resting every seventh day "would get you to California 20 days sooner."

That morning the cattle were taken some distance away from camp to graze where grass was better. Several men were left to guard the animals.

In the afternoon, Elijah Newman, 53, who had been suffering what the pioneers called "black scurvy in his legs" and couldn't walk without a stick, was baptised in a small lake "for benefit of his health."

After this rite and having hands laid on him for a blessing, "he returned to his wagon without any kind of help, seemingly much better," William Clayton wrote.

Newman later became one of the first settlers in Parowan and helped explore the area for coal, iron ore and salt. He served several years in Parowan as justice of the peace.

Brigham Young called the company together about 5 p.m. and spoke about the need to be alert while on guard duty and warned against conforming to "gentile customs" on an expedition of this sort.

In a subsequent meeting of the apostles, it was decided that because the company had eight horses not attached to teams, eight men would be chosen to ride them and be hunters. Another 11 were named to hunt on foot. The rest of the men in the company were to stay with the wagons and not go chasing buffalo when those animals were encountered.

During their travel before the weekend, the company had passed the place where the town of Genoa would be founded in the spring of 1857 by other Mormons.

In the fall of 1856 Brigham obtained a government contract for carrying the mail between Salt Lake City and the Missouri River. He ordered a number of way stations established to serve as rest and supply stops, Genoa being one of them.

Mormons from St. Louis, Florence, Neb., and Alton, Ill., were called to settle the community and

within a year 100 families had built rough homes and planted crops. They also erected a steam mill and started a brickyard.

In 1858 many of the people were called back to Utah because of the Utah War. The life of the little community ended in 1859 when the area became part of a new Pawnee Indian reservation.

What was left of Genoa served as headquarters of the Indian agency until 1876 when the Pawnee were removed and the Indian lands offered for sale.

Non-Mormon settlers moved in, named the town Genoa again and took up farming. Today it is a quiet little community of 1,170 persons, many of them retired farmers. The nearly empty main street has a few unhurried shops. No Mormons live in the town.

A city museum, open a few hours a week, stands on one corner. Allen Atkins, a retired amateur historian, serves as curator. Inside are a few artifacts and some old newspaper clippings about the early Mormon days, along with many Indian items and pictures of the town around the turn of the century.

''None of the people who live here know much about the town's past or early Mormon history,'' Atkins said.

The only trace left of the Mormon settlement is where a ditch and dirt wall used to be, about a mile west of town. The ditch was created when the pioneers built a dirt embankment four or five feet high to keep livestock penned inside. The openings were filled with sagebrush instead of having gates.

The dirt wall is long gone and so is the ditch, but when farmers plow that land ''you can see the different colored dirt where the ditch once was,'' Atkins said.

A historical marker giving some of the Mormon history stands in a small park near the edge of town.

Alert guards prevented Indian raid on horses

Guard duty was dreary work, but unlike some other nights, all sentries in the Mormon pioneer camp were awake and their alertness foiled an Indian raid against the horses.

About 3:30 a.m. some of the guards noticed the horses behaving nervously, so they went to investigate and heard rustling noises in the grass. Thinking it might be wolves, two of the men raised their rifles and fired.

Instead of wolves, six Indians leaped upright and ran away at top speed. The camp bugle was sounded and all the men "arose up in arms," Wilford Woodruff said. However, no more Indians were seen that night.

The company moved out about 8 a.m., the horse teams going first to break up the turf so it wouldn't hurt the feet of the oxen. The weather was hot and dry "and has a tendency to make sore lips," William Clayton said.

Ezra T. Benson discovered during the morning that one of the iron axles on his wagon had broken. He repacked the wagon load so no weight rested on the damaged axle and continued the journey.

In the evening, Thomas Tanner and Burr Frost,

two of the company blacksmiths, removed the axle and repaired it on a forge, the whole operation taking only an hour.

Norton Jacob, one of the captains of 10, followed the advice of Brigham Young given the day before and chose two men among his group to serve as cooks. Each 10 was to do the same. The cooks were excused from all other duty.

Jacob said his choices were Charles A. Harper as chief cook and Andrew Gibbons as assistant. Harper, 30, and Gibbons, 22, were not cooks by trade, but in that company they probably were as good as any others.

As they traveled parallel to the Loup Fork that day, the pioneers saw the remains of a deserted Indian village. None of the lodges appeared to be standing. The company passed within a mile of the place.

Jacob wrote in his journal that Brigham apologized for scolding some of the men, saying that Henry G. Sherwood was the only one who had a "legal right to find fault."

Whoever had a complaint must get permission from Sherwood to grumble, Brigham said, because Sherwood was formally elected to the office of "chief grumbler."

Sherwood was in charge of food and supplies for the trip and apparently took his title in good humor.

Jacob said the arrangement had "excellent effect in putting a check on some fractious persons, especially one by the name of Chamberlain, who all the time has been grumbling with his team or somebody or another. But after this he was tolerable decent."

Chamberlain was Solomon Chamberlain, 59, a maker of wooden casks and tubs. He was the oldest man in the camp and had lost his wife at Winter Quarters just before the trek. He remained a faithful Mormon until his death in Washington County in 1862.

Woodruff reported that a "tremendous alarm" was raised in camp that evening as a report flew around that Porter Rockwell and his horse had been captured by Indians.

This turned out to be a wild rumor. Rockwell was discovered safe and sound in camp. But the loss of two horses which touched off the tale was sadly true.

Joseph Mathews said he saw one of the horses going toward the river and ran to turn it back. As he did so, the horse broke into a gallop, "which made him suppose there was an Indian on him," although he couldn't see one.

Five or six men mounted up when the alarm was given and rode toward the river, but could find no trace of the horses. Another 20 armed men rode out later with Brigham at their head and also came up empty handed.

"The brethren have been repeatedly warned not to let their horses go too far from the wagons, But every time we stop they can be seen around for more than two miles," Clayton wrote in his journal.

"These are two good horses and the owners feel bad enough, but it will be a warning to others," he added.

April 27
TUESDAY

It was slow traveling over dry sand ridges

Shots were fired in the night as nervous guards heard noises in the surrounding grass. No Indians were seen and the sentries concluded the sounds were caused by wolves.

In the morning, the Mormon pioneer company turned away from the Loup River and headed across dry and sandy country toward the Platte River about 25 miles distant. The Platte was their guide and lifeline. .

"There are a great many lizards on these sand ridges, but they are of a small size," said William Clayton. Also seen were prairie dogs, rattlesnakes and owls, all living in holes in the ground.

At 2:15 p.m. the party stopped for a break. The animals were having a hard time because of pulling wagons through uneven and sandy soil and also because of the lack of water. Some teams fell behind and needed help.

While stopped, several of the men got out shovels and dug holes in a search for water, "as there is none above the surface." They obtained a little moisture this way, but not enough to give the cattle and horses to drink.

52

As the journey resumed, Wilford Woodruff, Roswell Stevens and John Brown came upon an antelope. All three fired and hit the animal. They skinned it and put it in one of the wagons.

Stevens, 37, had enlisted in the Mormon Battalion in 1846 and marched as far as Santa Fe (New Mexico) where he was chosen as one of several messengers to take back some of the battalion's army pay to families in Winter Quarters. He, John D. Lee and Howard Egan made the long trip, arriving at Winter Quarters in late November, 1846, with $4,000.

Brown, 26, had led 18 families from Mississippi and Missouri all the way to Fort Laramie (Wyoming) in 1846 in an effort to join the Mormon pioneers believed to be already on the way west. When he discovered the error, he turned south and settled the people in Fort Pueblo (Colorado) and made his way with seven other men back to Winter Quarters.

As the pioneer company traveled toward the Platte this day, Porter Rockwell, John Eldredge, Joseph Mathews and Thomas Brown rode back in search of two horses believed stolen by Indians earlier.

Near Sunday's campsite they saw movement in the grass and went to investigate. As they approached within 200 feet, 15 Indians jumped up, each with a rifle slung over his back and a bow and arrow in the hands.

The Pawnee began to advance, but the four men stood fast and raised their rifles. Seeing this, the Indians made overtures of friendship, crying out "bacco, bacco." But the men replied that they had no tobacco.

The Indians tried to lure the small band down a nearby wash, but the men turned away instead. As they did so, the Pawnee fired six shots at them. The bullets "whistled about the brethren, but no one was injured."

As they were fired upon, the men faced about and raised their rifles and the Indians fled. Rockwell and his companions did not return the shots.

"They saw the tracks of the missing horses and are satisfied the Pawnee had got them," Clayton said.

He said the Indians were some of the same ones who visited the pioneer camp when the company stopped near a Pawnee village several days ago "and proves they have followed us close ever since."

About the time the men returned to camp, the pioneers lost another horse in an accident. A loaded gun was placed inside John Brown's wagon. When Brown pulled a coat out of the wagon, it caught on the rifle and caused it to discharge.

The bullet went through a bag of clothing, starting a fire, and hit a horse in the leg, breaking the bone. The horse was one of a team pulling Stephen Markham's wagon.

"This makes four of the best horses lost in the last four days," Clayton sorrowed.

Many unnecessary deaths occurred on the frontier in those days from keeping loaded firearms about. Accidental shootings were a common occurrence.

April 28

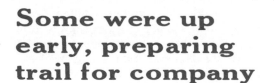

Some were up early, preparing trail for company

Some of the Mormon pioneers were up earlier than usual and spent several hours making a road to nearby Prairie Creek, which the company forded about 9 a.m.

As the wagons moved out, Luke Johnson shot the horse which broke a leg yesterday in an accidental shooting, concluding: "It was better to shoot her than to leave her alone to the mercy of Indians or wolves."

After traveling about seven miles, the pioneers neared the Platte River and once again turned to march parallel to the north bank of the familiar waterway.

From their position they could easily see Grand Island. In the days before dams and flood control made the Platte even more shallow, the island was a distinct body more than 45 miles long, lying between two channels of the river. It had been named by French trappers.

A fairly large and prosperous city now occupies part of the area where the pioneers passed. The town of Grand Island was to have its beginning in 1856 when a group of Germans from Iowa settled on the site.

They believed the capital of the United States eventually would be moved to the center of the nation — a common feeling in some circles at the time — and wanted to be among the first in the new region. Unfortunately for them, the capital stayed in Washington, D.C.

The Union Pacific railroad reached the settlement in the 1860s and a post office and flour mills were established. The community finally was incorporated in 1872 and is a major agricultural and business center belonging to the nation's wheat belt.

A historical marker, noting that the Mormon pioneers stopped near Grand Island, was once located next to gasoline pumps at a service station on Locust Street. But sometime in the last four years both the marker and service station disappeared. A floral shop now occupies the site.

Some searching produced the fact that the marker had been moved off the busy street and placed near the entrance of an exclusive residential neighborhood, where relatively few people could ever see it.

Locust Street itself is a far different sight than anything the Mormon pioneers could have imagined — a forest of garish signs on both sides of the road as far as the eye can see. Service stations, car lots, drive-ins, garages, grocery stores, shops and business concerns of every kind come together in a cluttered commercial panorama.

A few miles southeast of town is a place called Mormon Island Recreation Center — a landscaped park with a number of man-made ponds, picnic tables and an information hut.

A marker notes that several Mormon families stayed here during the winter of 1884-5 because of available wood and water. They apparently were among the last trying to cross the plains by covered wagon. By 1884, trains had been running to Salt Lake City for 15 years.

The marker said a mother and two children were left behind in graves when the group finally moved on. Local residents named the place Mormon Island. Today the site is right on the edge of I-80 and there is a nearby campgound for trailers.

All this was far in the future when Brigham Young and the pioneers with him passed by. The only thing in sight was "level prairie, green with grass," according to William Clayton. He marveled at wild onions growing in the area, "the largest I have ever seen."

The trail was extremely dusty. Wind blew dirt into the wagons "and everything is covered," Clayton said. The company stopped after making 15 miles for the day and the available grass provided good feed for the stock.

For the dry and dusty pioneers, the presence of "clear and good tasting water," was greatly appreciated. Clayton was still bothered by twinges in his jaw. He "suppered on antelope" and went to bed early.

The bugler roused the camp for an early morning start

An early start was made by the Mormon pioneer company this day because of the need to find something for the cattle to eat. All the grass near the campsite had been consumed the previous evening.

Everyone in camp was up before dawn to load wagons, harness teams and get on the trail by 5 a.m. Breakfast was postponed until later in the morning.

As usual, it was the bugler who roused the camp with blasts on his horn. The night guards generally were the ones who awakened the bugler.

The job of bugler was handled by James Craig, 26, an Irishman who later served an extended mission in England and his native land.

Craig was assigned the job of exterminating predatory animals and snakes after the pioneers arrived in the Salt Lake Valley. He helped establish settlements in southern Utah and raised cotton in Santa Clara until his death at 47.

While the pioneer company marched, William Clayton complained that "there seems to be very little rain in this country and no dew." He called the dry conditions "a drought."

After moving three miles, the company halted to let the cattle graze on fresh grass. The pioneers sat down to their own breakfasts. Clayton said his meal consisted of "cooked goose and moldy bread."

Resuming the journey, the group forded a 10-foot-wide stream after some delay and moved up a gently ascending tableland until reaching a small lake where they halted for a midday rest.

The lack of moisture and a strong south wind the past few days had parched the entire company. The pioneers, mostly from New England, were used to more moisture.

One of Orson Pratt's horses became sick and lay down several times while in the wagon harness — a worry to the pioneers because of their previous losses among the horses.

"I am not astonished," Clayton commented. The wagons and everything else are suffering because of the wind "which is perfectly dry. There is no moisture in it." He said even his writing desk was beginning to crack because of the arid atmosphere.

The wagons also were churning up the prairie turf and the resulting clouds of dust were "almost sufficient to suffocate everyone," he said.

The company camped that night across from Grand Island, a body of land about 45 miles long, which divided the Platte River into two separate branches.

Near the campsite the pioneers found a "white substance which oozes out of the ground and tastes like salt, but not so strong as common salt," Clayton said.

The cannon hauled by the Mormons brought up the rear of the wagon train. Ten men had been named as a gun crew and were responsible for taking care of the weapon and bringing it into action, if necessary. They held occasional drills, especially if Indians were thought to be around. However, the cannon was never used against Indians on the trip.

Members of the gun crew were Thomas Tanner, captain; Stephen H. Goddard, Seeley Owen, Thomas Woolsey, Horace Thornton, Charles D. Barnum, Sylvester H. Earl, George Scholes and Rufus Allen.

One of the crewmen, Goddard, 36, reportedly was the handsomest man in camp. The New Yorker had an excellent voice and often led the singing around the campfire at night. He would later become the first leader of a Mormon choir in the old tabernacle.

Travel was easy this day, but weather caused suffering

Travel was easy for the teams this day because of the level prairie, but the people in the Mormon pioneer company suffered considerably from the weather.

As they marched along, the pioneers noted that the ground was sprinkled with many patches of buffalo grass, "which is very short, thick and curly like the hair on a buffalo hide," William Clayton observed.

The wagons passed the remains of an Indian campground, apparently a large hunting party after buffalo. The number of Indians must have been huge because the campsite covered several acres.

Brigham Young, Heber C. Kimball and Amasa Lyman rode ahead as scouts. The company tried to follow an old Indian trail, but it was so overgrown with weeds and so faint that it was "scarcely discernible," Clayton said.

One of the uncomfortable things about the journey, on this and many other days, was the dust raised by the wagon wheels. It covered everything and often made breathing difficult. The rearmost pioneers had the worst of it and could barely see at times.

A cold wind came up in the afternoon and the

temperature dropped so low that "every man wants his overcoat on and a buffalo robe over it," Clayton wrote.

The camp that night was a good mile from the river and "destitute of wood and water," Norton Jacob said. Soft, moist bottom land kept the pioneers from settling any closer to the Platte River.

It took more than an hour to assemble the wagons in an "imperfect circle," Clayton said. The job took so long because the men tried to form the encampment in such a way as to have all the wagon mouths facing away from the cold wind blowing out of the north.

Only a few people had a little wood in their wagons. Most were faced with the prospect of a cold supper "and some perhaps nothing to eat because they have no bread," Clayton said.

But about 8 p.m. the lack of fuel was solved when the pioneers found a good substitue for wood in the dried buffalo dung "which lies on the ground here in great plenty." The only problem was that it tended to burn too fast.

Heber C. Kimball invented a new type of campfire. He dug a hole about eight inches deep and a foot wide. This was filled with buffalo chips. Other holes were dug at both ends of this fire pit and connected to it by small tunnels.

When the chips were set ablaze and covered with metal to create a resting place for pots and pans, the side holes allowed the fire to breathe and burn steadily. "Much cooking was done with very little fuel," Clayton said.

Luke Johnson used a buffalo skull for a chimney on his fire, creating some amusement in camp at the sight of smoke puffing out of the horns.

Because camp was so far from the river, a well was dug and "good water obtained" at a depth of about four feet, Clayton noted.

Hans C. Hansen played his violin after dinner and some of the men danced, not so much for the pleasure, but mostly as a means of getting warm in the frigid weather. Others engaged in friendly wrestling matches for the same reason.

Clayton said he went to bed early in an effort to get warm, "but having only one quilt for a covering, I suffered much from the cold."

Among those standing guard this cold night was a man with the unusual name of Datus Ensign, 21, a mechanic and carpenter. He came to Nauvoo as a teenager when his parents were converted by Mormon missionaries. His father died in Winter Quarters and Ensign himself joined the church only a few months before the exodus west. He helped settle Ogden where he died at the early age of 40.

Not far from the pioneer campsite this night was the place where the Mormon trail and the Oregon trail, coming up from Independence, Mo., on the south, both converged on the Platte River — the Mormon trail north of the Platte and the Oregon trail opposite on the south bank.

A modern-day look at the area shows mostly flat farmland with a few scattered homes, barns and silos and an occasional service station. Interstate 80 follows the same route as the Mormon corridor, staying with it for many miles.

Prairie fires made livestock feed scarce

Prairie fires burned along the pioneer route early in the week, making it hard for the Mormon pioneers to find grass for their livestock.

But this problem was forgotten May 1 near what is now Kearney, Neb., when the pioneers saw their first buffalo and engaged in a wild and successful hunt.

Later in the week rain put out most of the prairie fires, but grass for the cattle was even more scarce. The huge buffalo herds had eaten nearly everything down to the bare soil.

The Mormon pioneer trail and I-80 are almost on the identical track in this area. Motorists on the freeway are following the same route as the covered wagons.

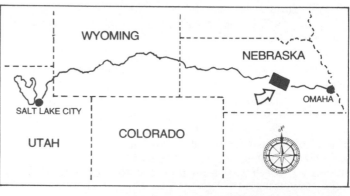

May 1-7

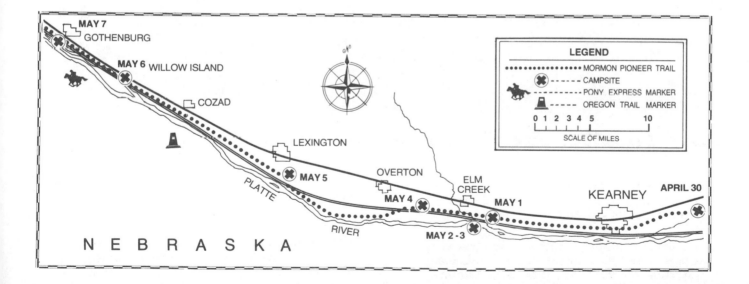

MAY 7
GOTHENBURG
MAY 6 WILLOW ISLAND
COZAD
LEXINGTON
OVERTON
MAY 5
ELM
CREEK
MAY 1
KEARNEY
APRIL 30
PLATTE
MAY 4
RIVER
MAY 2-3
N E B R A S K A

LEGEND
•••••••• MORMON PIONEER TRAIL
⊗ ----- CAMPSITE
----- PONY EXPRESS MARKER
----- OREGON TRAIL MARKER
0 1 2 3 4 5   10
SCALE OF MILES

And finally, the first buffalo were sighted

At last, buffalo are sighted!

Most of the Mormon pioneers had only heard about the large, shaggy animals. Few had ever seen them.

The camp broke early, without breakfast, because of the need to get the cattle to better grazing. Soon after starting, the company saw three buffalo on a bluff about six miles away. Mounted hunters hurriedly rode toward them.

As they rode, the men sighted a herd of more than 70 about eight miles distant. Before the hunters could get close enough to shoot, the herd began to run and was soon beyond view.

Disappointed, the pioneers continued the journey and about noon saw an even larger herd near the bluffs. Eleven hunters were chosen to attack.

"This being the first day buffalo have been seen on our journey, and the first ever seen by any except five or six of the brethren, it excited considerable interest and pleasure," William Clayton said.

The teams and wagons moved slowly and stopped frequently to watch the buffalo and the hunters.

The horsemen split into three groups. As they neared the herd, a barking dog nearly sent the buffalo stampeding away. The dog had chased an antelope right into the herd, but as the dog came close to the buffalo he apparently became frightened "at their savage appearance" and quickly retreated.

At this moment the hunters spurred their horses into a gallop and the buffalo began to run. The beasts were "very fast despite their size," Wilford Woodruff said. But a horse could gain on them.

Back at the wagon train there was some anxiety, "having read and heard so much about the mad ferocity of buffalo when hotly pursued and knowing that all the hunters were inexperienced," Clayton said.

Porter Rockwell soon was in the midst of the herd and was "enveloped in a cloud of dust." The buffalo began to scatter in all directions and the hunters opened fire.

The men quickly learned it took more than a single bullet to kill the huge beasts. They rode among the stampeding buffalo, firing pistols at close range.

One cow was wounded and separated from the rest. Heber C. Kimball, who had jumped aboard a horse and rode off to join the hunt, came close and finally knocked the animal down with a shot.

But the noise of the gun being fired right over the head of his horse sent the stallion plunging away in panic and nearly tumbled Kimball out of the saddle.

He had dropped the reins to shoot and had trouble getting hold of them again.

"The other hunters saw his situation and trembled for his safety, but could render him no assistance," Clayton said. Kimball, being a good horseman, eventually was able to recover the reins and halt his animal.

Woodruff, who had spurred his horse to get ahead of the fleeing buffalo, finally was able to turn in front of them. This was a mistake.

"They all pitched at me and gave chase," he said. "I had to be quick to get out of the way."

He managed to kill one buffalo and tried to catch some others, "but my horse had run nearly 10 miles and we gave up the pursuit."

The shooting and chasing over the prairie lasted three hours and covered many miles before the hunters began to trickle back to camp. The final tally showed they had killed a bull, three cows and six calves — "far exceeding our expectations and best hopes," Clayton said.

"The brethren's faces beamed with joy to see the meat come into camp. Some of them expressed astonishment at the size and ferocious appearance of the buffalo," he said.

Fresh meat was welcome and the pioneers were anxious to taste buffalo flesh for the first time. The animals were cut into quarters and a piece given to each company of 10.

"The meat is very sweet and tender as veal," Clayton said. Lorenzo Young said everybody in camp had a "rich repast." Others described it as a "feast."

Missing 'Nimrod' returned safely in morning

Although still excited over the rich harvest of buffalo meat, the pioneers were deeply worried. One of their number had been missing all night.

Joseph Hancock, who left camp on foot to hunt buffalo during yesterday's chase, had failed to return.

"Considerable fear is entertained for his safety," William Clayton reported, because Hancock was lame and because a prairie fire eight miles away indicated the presence of Indians.

But about 6 a.m. Hancock came limping into camp carrying a piece of buffalo meat.

He said he had killed a buffalo back on the bluffs, but because he couldn't carry the heavy animal, he stayed on the prairie most of the night to guard the meat from prowling wolves.

He built a fire and sprinkled gunpowder around the buffalo carcass. Some wolves visited during the night, but were awed by the fire. Hancock shot one

64

wolf and the rest fled. Finally, he set out for camp, but couldn't find it on the pitch black prairie, so laid down and slept.

At daybreak he made his way to camp. After telling his story, he returned to the scene of his kill with several riders. They found wolves already had gotten to the meat and eaten most of it, but some was saved.

While returning to camp, the horsemen sighted two antelope and shot both.

Hancock, 47, was such a good hunter that Joseph Smith once dubbed him, "Nimrod." Later in the trek he would once again spend all night guarding an animal he had killed while hunting away from camp.

He settled near Provo and later spent many years in California and at Council Bluffs, Iowa. He died at age 93 and was buried in the Payson cemetery.

During much of the day the pioneers were busy in camp cooking buffalo meat or building racks to dry it in the sun, or salting it down to avoid spoilage.

Some men cut the buffalo hide into narrow strips and stretched them on stakes to dry. They used the resulting thongs to "make horse halters and lariats," Norton Jacob said.

Because forage for the animals was poor, Brigham Young and some others went ahead to scout out a new camp site. They returned in the afternoon and ordered the company to move farther along the river.

The wagons traveled a few miles and the pioneers set up camp on the banks of a long shallow lake which was connected to the Platte River. Because the campsite was pleasant and the cattle needed rest, Brigham said the company would remain camped for an additional day. Some of the wagons also required repairs and several animals needed to be shod.

While camped at the new location, the pioneers saw several buffalo come down to the river to drink. The animals were less than two miles away and some of the men wanted to ride after them. But Brigham replied, "No, it's best to let them go as it is Sunday." He said more hunting could be done the next day.

Around the campfire that night, a portion of hide from one of the buffalo heads was displayed. Porter Rockwell had heard that a bullet wouldn't hurt a buffalo if fired head on at the thick-skulled creature. During the hunt he had tried it. Sure enough, the bullet bounced off.

"I found the mark where Porter shot at his head," Clayton wrote. The bullet barely cut through the outer surface of the hide, which was "near an inch thick," he said.

When the pioneers retired that night, they posted a heavy guard around the camp. In the distance they had seen the glow of a large prairie fire and felt it was meant for them.

"The Indians set fire to the prairie grass in front of us and burned over a large area," Wilford Woodruff recorded. The troubles of the pioneers with this tactic were just beginning.

May 3
MONDAY

Prairie fires continued to burn in the distance. Flames had destroyed large areas of grass in the past three days and crept within a mile of camp.

Because the fire had ruined much of the available grazing, Brigham Young ordered 15 scouts to ride ahead and examine the route. If possible, they were to find some areas of unburned grass.

The pioneers were positive the fires had been deliberately set by Indians to destroy the grass and drive off the buffalo "so we cannot subsist," Norton Jacob wrote in his journal. He said the prairie was burned over "or is still burning as far as the eye can see."

Twenty men were designated as hunters and set forth on foot and horseback, accompanied by two empty wagons. They split into two parties in search of game.

The remainder of the camp stayed put near the water and grass to rest the cattle, make wagon repairs and await reports of what lay ahead on the trail.

Indian scare alarmed pioneer hunting party

One of the hunters, William A. Empey, was chasing an antelope over a rise when he suddenly came upon what he described as "300 or 400 Indians," all of them mounted warriors hidden in a low area near the river.

Empey wheeled his horse about and retreated at full speed, giving the alarm to other hunters that a war party of of Indians was coming. "We returned immediately to camp at a pretty smart trot," Jacob reported.

Empey, 38, a Canadian who later became a missionary to England and helped colonize some areas of southern Utah, was not to reach Salt Lake Valley that year. He was among several men left behind at one point to build a ferry for the pioneers who were still coming. He entered the valley in 1848.

After the hunters returned to camp with the alarming news, other men were sent out to gather those still on the prairie, including the second party of hunters.

In this second group was Wilford Woodruff, who said he had a bad cold which had settled in his side, but who had gone hunting despite not feeling well.

He said his party had "marched 10 miles back and forth over the hills and saw no game."

The hunters were sitting on a bluff taking a rest when they saw "horsemen approaching from the camp in haste, bearing a red flag." They walked down to meet the riders and learned of the Indian alarm.

Woodruff said a large party of Indians in the area probably means they are seeking to waylay small groups of pioneers and rob them of their horses and clothing and "would take life if they could not do it without."

As the hunters and searchers returned they managed to kill three antelope and two buffalo calves and bring the carcasses back to camp.

The buffalo calves were shot when one group of hunters encountered a small herd. William Dykes dismounted from his mule to get a better shot, "a dangerous practice," according to Jacob.

In this case, the mule broke away and ran after the fleeing buffalo. One man tried to give chase, but his horse quickly tired. Stephen Markham, who had a better horse, then pursued the mule for two or three miles and finally caught it.

"Horses can be lost this way and never recovered," Jacob said. Once an animal gets mixed in with the buffalo herd, there is no way to get it back, he wrote.

The unfortunate Dykes, 31, a native Pennsylvanian, crossed the plains several more times, but eventually left the Utah territory and settled in Nebraska where he died in 1879.

While the hunters and scouts had considerable excitement and the Indian scare, the rest of the camp set up forges, shoed horses, repaired wagon wheels, continued to dry meat for jerky, did washing and other camp chores.

That night the cannon was unlimbered and made ready. It was "fired twice in the night, just to let the Indians know we were awake," Woodruff said.

May 4
TUESDAY

Brigham counseled camp on discipline

Because of the nearness of a large Indian war party, Brigham Young called the Mormon pioneer camp together and strongly counseled them to obey rules drawn up earlier.

He especially cautioned against scattering away from camp to hunt. If the men persisted, "some would be caught by Indians and if not killed, would be severely abused."

Brigham warned that the time had come that if men violate the rules and regulations of the camp, "they must be punished."

Every man must be vigilant and "seek his neighbor's welfare as much as his own. It must be so in this camp. It must be so in the whole church," he declared.

However, he cautioned that there are those in the camp who, if someone took care of their cattle for them, "would sit down and do nothing."

Brigham said the wagons should travel five abreast to more easily defend against Indian attack. The cannon should be kept ready for action and travel at the rear of the wagons. A guard will be placed around the cattle when they are turned out to graze, he said.

During the morning some horses ran away and

were chased more than six miles before being caught. In the chase, William Smoot was thrown from his horse and knocked unconscious, but soon recovered with no apparent injury.

Smoot, 19, was destined to be the last member of the pioneer company to enter Salt Lake Valley. He later helped lay out the city, driving stakes for the surveyors. He crossed the plains several times helping other pioneer parties.

Shortly after the wagons began moving, the pioneers sighted three wagons on the opposite side of the Platte River, which caused much excitement in the company.

Some of the men wanted to ride across immediately and investigate the strangers. But because the river was about two miles wide at this point and unfamiliar to anyone in the pioneer party, an attempt to ford it was vetoed.

A few hours later, one of the men from the wagons on the other side of the river rode through the shallow water and met with the pioneers. The visitor was Charles Beaumont, a French trader.

He said there were nine men in his group and they were on the way to Council Bluffs from Fort Laramie. He agreed to carry letters, but couldn't wait long. There was a rush of hasty letter writing throughout the camp.

"In about a half hour a large mail was made up to send back to Winter Quarters," William Clayton reported. He included some letters of his own.

Beaumont said the Platte could be easily forded at this point and advised the Mormon pioneers to cross to the south side. He said the road was good and the company would be away from the prairie fire on the north bank.

Some of the pioneers bought buffalo robes from the trader in exchange for foodstuffs, mostly coffee, sugar and pork. Some food also was given as payment for carrying the mail, which Beaumont gratefully received.

After bidding the trader goodbye, the pioneers pushed ahead, pausing occasionally to graze the cattle and drill the men chosen as guards.

During one of these pauses, the pioneers discussed the possibility of crossing to the other side of the Platte where good grass was available.

But it was finally decided to remain north of the river because the company was making "a permanent route for the saints still to follow — a road independent of the old emigrant trail," Wilford Woodruff said.

"Let the river separate Mormons from other emigrants so there will be no quarrel over wood, grass and water. By the time the next company comes, the grass will be better on the north side," he wrote.

The company voted unanimously to keep to the north of the river. That night they camped near a stream which Heber C. Kimball named Buffalo Creek.

Traveling the same area in 1978, the motorist sees a landscape covered by cornfields with a few cattle grazing and some power lines in the distance. Railroad tracks and an interstate highway parallel the river where the pioneer wagons once creaked along.

Platte island provided safety from fires that devastated area

Some of the Mormon pioneers became sick, a condition they blamed on all that buffalo meat.

"The change from salted meat to fresh meat is affecting a number of the company," reported Wilford Woodruff, who was one of those stricken.

After breaking camp about 7:30 a.m., the wagon train made a detour to the north to avoid a bad slough. "The horses' feet cut through the sod and the ground under appears wet, although there has been no rain for some time," William Clayton wrote in his journal.

No Indians had been sighted since the alarm two days before and Woodruff surmised the "war party" of 400 Indians was a case of mistaken identity.

"The man who saw them was frightened by a herd of antelope and supposed them to be Indians," he guessed. But the company had seen plenty of Indian signs, including freshly abandoned camps, in the past few days.

Buffalo were sighted again. However, Brigham Young directed the pioneers not to kill anything they couldn't bring into camp on a horse, which ruled out adult buffalo.

Hunters returned to the camp in the afternoon, bringing a live buffalo calf and the carcass of another calf they had killed. They said four additonal calves had been shot. Other men were dispatched to bring in the meat.

The live calf had been chased after its mother was killed and a dog finally cornered it. The calf was tied in camp that night. Dogs and some of the men teased it and were butted for their efforts. The calf learned to drink from a bucket.

Prairie fires still stretched as far as the eye could see and the flames were getting close. Brigham ordered the wagons to retreat half a mile to an island in the Platte River where "we can be secure from the fire," Clayton said.

"The prairie is all burned bare and the black ashes fly bad, making the brethren look more like Indians than white folks," he noted.

The river was easily forded and the island refuge provided some grass for the animals. The horses and cattle were beginning to suffer from the lack of feed.

Where the pioneers passed in 1847 there now stands a multi-storied farm house, painted yellow with white trim and decorated with gables and bay windows — a remarkable sight miles from any other building.

Modern-day scenery along the pioneer route is mostly empty corn fields and once in a while an advertising sign amid the stubble. The land appears flat to the horizon.

Not far from where the pioneers camped was the future sight of the town of Lexington, Neb., which got its start as a trading post named Plum Creek. It was an infamous rendezvous for gamblers, thieves and holdup men who preyed on passing miners and other travelers.

In 1867 a band of Cheyenne Indians wrecked a train near here, ransacked the freight cars and scalped the crew.

Another train carrying Mormon emigrants to a departure point for wagon travel, had an engineer at the helm who swore he would "drive the Mormons to hell." He opened the throttle and went tearing across the prairie.

But shortly after the wild ride began the baggage car caught fire. The engineer quickly stopped and backed up to the nearest watering station seven miles away. By the time the train arrived, the baggage car was in ruins.

May 6
THURSDAY

A timely light shower dampened prairie fires

Prairie fires, which had threatened the Mormon pioneers for a number of days, finally were extingished by the weather.

"During the night the Lord sent a light shower which put the fire out, except in one or two places," William Clayton reported in his journal.

The company was awakened at 5 a.m. with the usual problem of finding early-morning grazing for the cattle before doing anything else. Brigham Young gave orders to leave the island camp ground to get the animals to a place where they could have adequate feed.

A buffalo calf the hunters had brought into camp the day before was found dead, still tied to a stake in the center of the wagon circle.

Despite a desire to get started early, some of the men delayed to give their cattle some of the carefully-hoarded corn feed. Others took time to milk cows. These chores cost an hour, but once the wagons were moving, the pioneers reported the ground was hard and good for traveling.

Grass was hard to find. Where it had escaped the fire, it was eaten down to the soil by the huge herds of buffalo now surrounding the company. Horsemen had to drive them out of the wagon train path.

A young buffalo calf followed one of the hunters into camp, but Brigham ordered it placed out in the open in view of its mother because the calf was only a few days old.

But as the buffalo cow approached, two men walked nearby and the frightened animal ran away, leaving the calf alone on the prairie. Wolves soon attacked the small animal and killed it.

While stopped at noon, the pioneers discovered that some of their cows had wandered near the buffalo herd. If they once got mixed with the buffalo, that would be the last the camp would see of them because they would run with the herd.

Brigham, Heber C. Kimball and Thomas Woolsey gave frantic chase on horseback and barely turned the cows back before they were into the herd. In the excitement, Brigham lost his spyglass. Although the men hunted around the prairie for a long time, they couldn't find it.

The wagon train traveled slowly and some of the horses and oxen gave out because of the lack of feed. Wilford Woodruff said buffalo had eaten the grass to such a degree "that our cattle and horses get very little."

Green grass was available on the other side of the Platte River, but the Mormons persisted in keeping to the north bank where they would avoid other travelers. Bitter memories of persecution made them suspicious of strangers.

The company camped for the evening near some islands in the Platte. Brigham announced that no more game should be killed until further notice because "we have got as much meat in camp as can be taken care of."

This order pleased Norton Jacob who had grumbled in his journal earlier about the needless shooting of buffalo by those overcome with the zeal of hunting.

Wagon trains of emigrants going west for the gold rush often shot buffalo for sport. An eyewitness in those later years said the meat was left to rot while the Indians starved. He called it a "flagrant injustice."

Clayton said the pioneers hadn't been out of sight of buffalo all day and the largest herds still were ahead. "The prairie looks black with them," he wrote. Some said the company passed 50,000 buffalo during the day. Others thought it was more like 100,000.

This disparity in estimates also extended to the number of miles traveled each day. "Some think we have traveled 18, some 20, and some even 25 miles today," Clayton said, but put his own guess at a conservative 15. As it turned out, he was the most accurate. The scribe was pondering possible ways to keep a precise record of the miles traveled.

The Mormon campsite this night was near the place where the town of Cozad would one day be founded. Sioux Indians would attack a wagon train here in 1867, killing several men and taking a number prisoner.

A historical marker on the edge of town notes that the community lies on the 100th meridian, often termed the "line of aridity." West of this line the yearly rainfall usually is insufficient to support non-irrigated agriculture.

Brigham grouchy over spyglass loss

Ever since losing his $40 spyglass the previous day while riding after cows, Brigham Young had been in a grouchy mood. His anger over the loss of the expensive device cast a pall over the camp and caused the pioneers to tread softly.

When a search failed to turn up the glass, Brigham returned to camp and took out his displeasure on Erastus Snow for not attending to the cows.

It was Snow's turn to watch the cattle and Brigham blamed him for letting them stray close to the buffalo herd, thus forcing a frantic chase in which the spyglass was lost. Snow was unhappy at the chastisement and had words with the leader.

Rather than continue the march this day with Brigham's disgruntled disposition, a party of men felt it would be worthwhile to go back where the spyglass was lost and make one more search of the prairie.

Late in the day the persistence of the searchers was rewarded when they found the missing glass. When Brigham's prize was returned, he immediately felt much better and a lighter mood prevailed in the whole camp.

It was a wonder that the glass survived intact

because buffalo still surrounded the pioneer wagon train as it marched westward. The cattle continued to suffer from lack of feed because the buffalo had eaten nearly everything in sight.

In order to spare the teams, Brigham ordered that only one man should ride the cannon — a popular conveyance — instead of the half dozen who usually had been carried along.

The president said he had provided most of the horses so far to pull the cannon, but they were about worn out and were needed to haul his own wagon. He asked that other members of the company volunteer some of their animals for cannon duty.

As the wagon train rolled along, it was surrounded at a distance by more than 2,000 buffalo. A few of them began racing around the wagons ''running exactly as if they were racing for sweepstakes of considerable value,'' Thomas Bullock reported. When the pioneers stopped to watch, the buffalo quit playing and ran away.

The pioneers had been told to cease shooting buffalo because the company had plenty of meat. But the animals fell victims to wolves in other ways. Calves would get crushed in a stampede. Some animals became mired in mud along river banks where the soil was churned up by the endless numbers. Others simply were weakened by hunger. Many wolves prowled around the herd and immediately attacked any buffalo in serious trouble.

Because of the weakened condition of the teams, the pioneers halted for the day at 3 p.m. They had covered only six or so miles. In addition to stopping early, the company also had started late, it being almost noon before they got under way.

Part of the delay in starting was due to needed repairs on a wagon axle. Another reason was that many pioneers wanted to give their weary teams more time to graze. The emergency grain supplies for the cattles were just about depleted. The prairie would have to provide.

The Mormon campsite was on the bank of the Platte River near several small islands which offered some grass for the hungry animals.

After camp was made and everyone had a few hours rest, Brigham took five men and rode upriver a short distance to look at the country which lay ahead and to see if good grass was available somewhere.

At 6:30 p.m. he called out the company for some military drill and exercise in tactics. The arms and ammunition were inspected and found to be in good condition. There were probably several reasons for the drill. First, there was time for it; second, Brigham liked to be ready for emergencies, and third, he hated to see men sitting around idle.

During the day's brief march, the pioneers passed the future site of Gothenburg, Neb., which started as a trading post in 1854 and later became a Pony Express and stage station.

Near the station was a ranch house where riders used to gather when off duty. Mark Twain stopped there on his trip across the plains and described it in his book, ''Roughing It.''

Thousands of buffalo consumed the grass

Near what is now Gothenburg, Neb., the Mormon pioneers found their wagons surrounded by an ocean of buffalo — tens of thousands as far as the eye could see.

The Mormons' livestock suffered greatly early in the week because the buffalo had eaten all the grass, but the herds finally began to thin out.

Where the city of North Platte is now located, the river branches into north and south arms. The pioneers stayed north. Many Indian tracks were found along the trail.

By May 14 the pioneers began to encounter sand bluffs which blocked their path along the river. Climbing the hills was tough work.

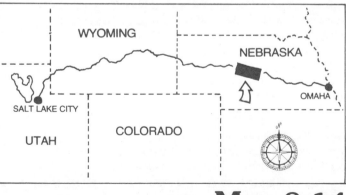

May 8-14

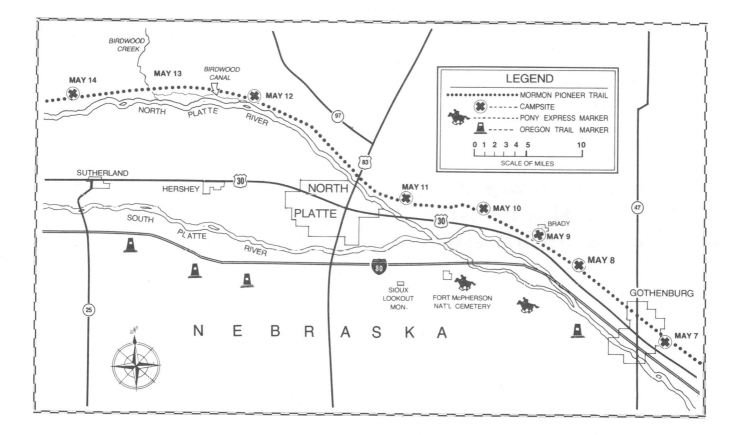

LEGEND

•••••• MORMON PIONEER TRAIL
----- CAMPSITE
----- PONY EXPRESS MARKER
----- OREGON TRAIL MARKER

0 1 2 3 4 5   10
SCALE OF MILES

BIRDWOOD CREEK

MAY 14   MAY 13   BIRDWOOD CANAL   MAY 12

NORTH   PLATTE   RIVER

MAY 11

MAY 10

SUTHERLAND

HERSHEY

NORTH PLATTE

SOUTH   PLATTE   RIVER

BRADY
MAY 9

MAY 8

SIOUX LOOKOUT MON.

FORT McPHERSON NAT'L CEMETERY

GOTHENBURG

MAY 7

N E B R A S K A

77

The awesome sight of Buffalo blackening the prairie on all sides

The Mormon pioneer wagons are like ships adrift in a sea of buffalo.

"The prairie on both sides of the river is literally black with buffalo," William Clayton said. "To try to say what number we have seen this morning would be folly."

Wilford Woodruff recorded that it appeared as if "the face of the earth was alive and moving like the waves of the sea."

Heber C. Kimball said he had heard many buffalo stories in his lifetime, but never expected to behold what his eyes were now seeing.

The buffalo are "more tame than they have been" and walk near the sides of the wagons. Horsemen have some difficulty driving them from the path ahead.

"If horsemen chase buffalo, the animals turn around and look at them as soon as the riders stop," Norton Jacob wrote in his journal.

"No pen nor tongue can give an idea of the

multitude now in sight continually," Clayton said. "Multitudes would have been killed if the president did not prohibit the brethren from shooting them only as we need the meat."

Brigham Young and Kimball explored some distance along the bluffs on foot and reported "the grass is eaten perfectly bare and the prospect of feed for our teams is poor indeed."

Clayton said hundreds of buffalo can be seen lying dead on the prairie, but added that it was unknown whether they succumbed to starvation or were killed by hunters who had passed this way recently. The stench made some pioneers ill.

Lorenzo Young said a buffalo calf wandered into camp "and seems determined to stay with us," but the company left it behind. "Before we got out of sight, a large wolf came upon it and carried it off . . . it looked very cruel."

He said his wife Harriet "has not enjoyed the day," because of a toothache. Young said he gave her a blessing "and she got better."

Clayton experienced what he called a "tedious" day. He had counted every turn of a wagon wheel trying to get an exact measurement of how far the pioneers traveled.

The company needed to know how far they moved each day and the distance between various camp grounds, water, fuel and other important points, such as creeks. The information was vital to the many wagon trains which would be following.

At first they just guessed at the distance covered, but none of the figures were the same and Clayton felt most of the estimates were too high.

"There is generally a difference of two and sometimes four miles in a day's travel between my estimation and that of some others and they all thought I underrated it," he said.

Convinced he was right, Clayton figured a way to get an accurate test of the mileage. He measured a wheel on one of Kimball's wagons and found that 360 turns of that wheel equaled exactly one mile — no more, no less.

He spent the day walking alongside the wheel and counting every turn it made. Adding up the revolutions, he figured the company had come a little more than 11 and three-quarter miles.

Others in the camp had paced the day's travel at 13 and 14 miles, "which serves to convince more strongly that distances have been overrated," he said.

Adding the new figures to his previous calculations, Clayton pounded a small cedar post into the ground and wrote on it in pencil: "From Winter Quarters, 295 miles, May 8 '47."

He said he repeatedly suggested that some device be built which could be attached to a wagon wheel and measure the distance traveled. Simply counting the turns of a wheel was enough to make a man dizzy.

Many in the camp are beginning to give serious consideration to the idea "and I hope it will be done," he wrote.

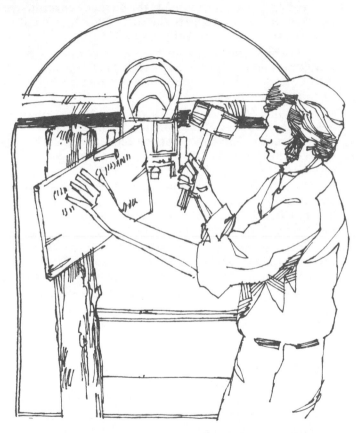

Just keeping clean provided some difficulty

Keeping clean on the trip — the ordinary tasks of washing clothes and bathing — presented difficulties for the Mormon pioneers. They had to make do ·

Some of the problems were described by William Clayton who said he walked three quarters of a mile to the Platte River "and washed my socks, towel and handkerchief as well as I could in cold water without any soap."

After taking care of those items, he undressed and rinsed in the frigid river, "which has made me feel much more comfortable, for I was covered with dust."

Clayton said he then put on clean clothing and sat on the bank of the river "and gave way to a long train of solemn reflection respecting many things, especially in regard to my family and their welfare."

He did not write down his private musings "inasmuch as I expect this journal will have to pass through other hands besides my own or that of my family."

The day, which had started very cold, turned

warm in the afternoon. Clayton calculated the company was about 300 miles from Winter Quarters, their starting point.

He searched out a piece of wood and wrote a message on it: "From Winter Quarters, 300 miles, May 9, 1847. Pioneer camp all well. Distance according to the reckoning of Wm. Clayton." The wood was nailed to a post and set up near the camp at a bend in the river.

Despite it being a Sunday, the company traveled about four miles early in the morning and camped on a sandy stretch closer to wood and water where they remained the rest of the day. The problem of grass for the animals was still very serious. Buffalo had eaten everything.

In the afternoon, Brigham Young asked the bugle to be sounded to call the camp together for worship. Among the speakers at the meeting was Erastus Snow, who commented, along with others, on the need for self-government.

He said he was particularly qualified to do so from the recent "dressing down" he received from Brigham for letting the camp's cattle wander away. Snow said he felt he deserved the reprimand and apologized for becoming angry when he was chastized.

Orson Pratt also spoke during the meeting and warned that springtime was slipping away. He said the planting season might be long past by time the pioneers reached their destination in the Rocky Mountains.

Pratt said the pioneers should be prepared for difficulties and thus "be in a condition to cope with whatever circumstances they are thrown into and make the best of it."

After the meeting, "peace, quiet and contentment seems to pervade almost every breast," Wilford Woodruff said.

Not everyone was utterly happy, however. Harriet Young, the wife of Lorenzo Young, noted that a great many dead buffalo littered the prairie. She said she had been sick all day from the smell of the dead beasts.

Another woman also had troubles. Ellen Kimball, the wife of Heber C. Kimball, tried to bake bread, "but could not because the wind blew so," Howard Egan said.

Brigham and some others rode out later that day to scout the path ahead. They found a small stream which the wagons would have to cross and saw many buffalo coming down to water.

Porter Rockwell and Phineas Young managed to get quite close to the animals in an effort to bag one, but in the whole herd "they could not find one fit to kill," Clayton said.

"They are very poor because there is no feed for them. They are so numerous that they eat the grass as fast as it grows," he added.

A cold wind began blowing that night. Egan said he had to "sleep on a chest in the front part of the wagon, crossways, and cannot stretch myself nor keep the clothes over me." Finally he gave up and shared a bed with two other men in another wagon.

They left a letter for those still to come

Sleeping on the wooden bed of a wagon was not exactly comfortable and may have contributed to a nightmare experienced by William Clayton.

He dreamed that a herd of buffalo stampeded into the camp's cattle and when he grabbed a boat and tried to row upriver for help, the paddle turned out to be a feather.

Whenever the Mormon pioneers had an especially vivid dream, they wrote an account in their journals.

Willard Richards had written a short history of the pioneer trek to this point, along with the rules and regulations adopted for the journey. A letter was drafted including this material and addressed to Charles E. Rich. It was placed at the top of a tall pole planted along the trail.

The letter was inserted into a crevice sawed into a board. The crevice was then nailed shut with cleats. The board was attached to a 15-foot pole sunk five feet into the ground. On the outside of the board, written in red chalk, were the words: "Open this and you will find a letter."

Before camp broke, Howard Egan built a fire and began baking bread. While waiting, he tried to catch up on entries in his journal. He explained he had "so little time, it accounts for my not writing much."

Egan borrowed Clayton's journal to copy some notes until his own writing was caught up. The task of keeping a journal was widely practiced among many emigrant groups, but it was a very trying job. Many scribes often complained about the problems of keeping current.

Writing was impossible while on the move during the day and camps were busy in the evening with cattle to tend, fires to build and meals to cook. Often there were no desks or writing tables. Paper and pens left something to be desired.

The pioneers began moving out shortly after 9 a.m. this day, covering two miles and then fording a small stream which Heber C. Kimball named Skunk Creek because a skunk had been killed earlier not far from here.

About this time a strange horse was sighted on the prairie. John Brown said two colts were lost last year when a company of Mormons passed this way en route to Fort Pueblo (Colorado) and "This is supposed to be the oldest of the two." Porter Rockwell and Thomas Brown gave chase, but were not able to capture the now-wild animal.

After traveling three hours the company found a place with some year-old grass and stopped to let the cattle graze. Before moving on, the pioneers set fire to the old grass so that new growth would be available for the next group of Mormon emigrants.

"It made a great fire," the camp agreed.

Meanwhile, hunters brought in a buffalo they had killed. The meat was described as good and "the fattest we have had." A deer was shot later and provided venison for supper.

In the afternoon the wagons ran into wet and soft ground. The teams began to give out because of the heavy pulling they were forced to do. Brigham Young ordered an early halt and the company made only 10 miles for the day.

Clayton, who had kept track of distance by counting the revolutions of a wagon wheel, had been pressing for some mechanical form of mileage counter and his persistence finally was rewarded.

Orson Pratt, the pioneer scientist who had been taking barometric and temperature readings each day, was asked by Brigham to give some attention to the mileage problem.

He suggested a device he called a "double screw" to be mounted on a wagon wheel.

Each six turns of the wagon wheel would cause a screw to make one revolution. The screw in turn moved a smaller wheel with 60 cogs. By the time this 60-tooth wheel made one complete turn, the wagon had covered one mile.

The first set of cogs then turned a second screw which turned another wheel with 30 cogs, each one representing one mile traveled. These were numbered and could simply be inspected at the end of a day for an accurate mileage reading instead of the tedious counting of each wagon wheel revolution which Clayton had been doing.

Pratt said the double screw device would be "simple to build and need not exceed three pounds."

Captured wolf pups provided caps for men

A wolf den was found a quarter mile from the Mormon pioneer camp. Several men took shovels and dug out the hole, capturing four pups about six to eight weeks old. They were "very vicious," but were brought back alive to camp.

The pups, about the size of rabbits, drew considerable attention. They were later killed to make caps for some of the men.

Others in the pioneer company also brought souvenirs into camp which they picked up while wandering around the prairie outside the circle of wagons.

Orson Pratt found a human skull, "probably an Indian fallen in the wars between the Pawnee and the Sioux." The skull bore the marks of an arrow wound, a tomahawk scar and other signs indicating it had been scalped.

Dr. Willard Richards picked up a buffalo horn which hornets had used for a nest. He brought it into camp to be admired by others, but it was soon thrown away.

The wagons pulled out about 9:30 a.m. and traveled five miles over a "nice, level, dry prairie," then climbed some small sand hills which came down to the banks of the Platte River from the right-hand side of the trail.

A few miles further the company forded a creek of clear water, "but this could not be very good in consequence of so many dead buffalo lying in it," William Clayton wrote.

Good grazing was still scarce. Shortly after getting started the pioneers noticed a "short sprinkling of grass on the prairie." They camped in the early afternoon on discovering an area of "much better grass for the cattle," according to Thomas Bullock.

During the day the company passed several islands with a few trees growing on them. Any trees prompted comments in the pioneer journals because there was so little wood.

"The country looks beautiful, the soil rich and is only lacking in timber," Clayton wrote.

The campsite was a half mile from the Platte River so several wells were dug. Pratt said there was plenty of cold water four feet below the surface of the sandy soil. One of the wells produced enough water to fill a pail a minute.

The camp was not an ideal place for the pioneers because of the lack of wood and being so far from water, but their first concern was good grazing for the cattle.

Appleton Harmon was working on a mileage device sought by Clayton and designed by Pratt. Clayton said he expected it to be in operation the next day, "which will save me the trouble of counting (the turns of wagon wheels, 360 revolutions to a mile) as I have done the last four days."

Keeping track of the wheel revolutions showed that the company covered eight and a half miles that day.

Harmon, 26, was an experienced mechanic. Despite being with the advance company of pioneers, he did not enter Salt Lake Valley that year. He stayed behind at a river crossing in what is now Wyoming to operate a ferry, then worked at Fort Laramie until early 1848 to earn some money.

He returned to Winter Quarters in March, 1848, and his wife burst into tears upon seeing him. Their small son had died six months earlier in his absence.

Harmon later helped build sawmills, a furniture factory and other structures in various Utah locations. He died in Millard County at age 56.

Camp duties occupied people in various ways. Bullock said he tended his cattle and did some tailoring. Howard Egan was barely able to do his chores because he "felt quite sick, having a bad cold." Heber C. Kimball and some others shared a duck killed by George Billings.

Billings, 19, was a tall youth, six feet, four inches in height. As a boy he worked on boats up and down the Mississippi River. He was a driver for one of Kimball's teams.

The lure of gold attracted him to California in 1849. He did find some gold, went to Mexico and bought cattle, intending to drive them to Utah, but the cattle took sick and all died en route. He rejoined his parents in Farmington, "poorer and wiser," according to a family biographer.

Vast buffalo herds had just melted away

Buffalo could still be seen from time to time, but the vast herds surrounding the Mormon pioneers in previous days had melted away — apparently drifting east toward better grass.

Evidence of the enormous herds was on every side, from the bare prairie eaten clean of most grass, to the bones of those who died in other years.

"The valley we traveled through this day may be called 'The Valley of Dry Bones,' because of the immense number of bleached buffalo bones," Thomas Bullock said.

During the day, Luke Johnson and Phineas Young rode up to report a recent slaughter of buffalo on the nearby prairie, apparently the work of Indians.

The hunters counted more than 100 buffalo, including many calves, lying dead on the prairie. The animals had been skinned, some of the meat removed, the tongues cut out and the bones broken to extract the marrow.

The majority of the meat was simply left on the prairie to rot — "a great waste of animal life,"

Bullock lamented. Such scenes occasionally encountered by the pioneers indicate the Indians did not always make maximum use of the buffalo they killed, as they are generally credited in most history books.

Perhaps, when buffalo became more scarce in later years because of the staggering slaughter by white men, the Indians made more efficient use of all parts of the large animals.

Norton Jacob said hunters also found carcasses of another 30 to 40 buffalo calves on the bank of the Platte River. The young animals apparently had been crushed to death during a stampede across the river while being chased by Indians.

After the Mormon pioneer company broke camp at 9 a.m. this day, the wagons crossed some "vast beds of salt, or rather dust with a salt taste," William Clayton wrote. "It looks something like dirty flour."

Wilford Woodruff, who had dismounted from his horse to look around the bluffs north of the trail, had to give chase on foot when the animal trotted away.

While running after the uncooperative horse, and possibly muttering under his breath, he discovered the abandoned remains of a big Sioux Indian camp. There were ruins of several hundred lodges and many pieces of buffalo robes and other animal skins.

Woodruff left his gun in the empty camp in order to better chase the horse, which finally was caught with the help of another pioneer on horseback. On his return he picked up the rifle and also "a good dressed white wolf skin."

The company camped that night some distance past the junction where the Platte River divided into north and south branches, gradually bearing away from each other.

"We traveled 12 miles according to Clayton's roadometer," Bullock said.

This device had been finished by Appleton Harmon and mounted on a wagon wheel, thus relieving Clayton of the wearisome task of counting revolutions of a wheel to keep accurate track of how far the pioneers marched each day.

The campsite for the pioneers this night was northwest of the future site of the town of North Platte. The community began when a trading post was opened in 1866 to serve the railhead. The place quickly acquired a population of more than 2,000.

But it suffered the same fate as many railhead boom towns. As the rails pushed further west, most of the town went with it, buildings and all. Only 20 structures were left in 1867. The community later became a division point on the Union Pacific railroad and grew steadily despite a disasterous prairie fire in 1893.

Just west of North Platte is the former home of William Cody, popularly known as Buffalo Bill. He got his famous nickname by killing 4,280 animals in 17 months as part of a contract to deliver meat to railroad construction workers in Kansas just after the Civil War.

Cody later went on the stage and then created a wild west show which toured much of the world and made him a celebrity. He did much to create the legend of the American cowboy. His old home is now the Buffalo Bill Ranch State Historical Park.

May 13
THURSDAY

Some took time out to visit Indian village

Brigham Young ordered the bugle blown at 4 a.m. so the camp could get an early start, but despite this pre-dawn stirring, it was five hours before the wagons were rolling.

Some members of the camp took time after breakfast to visit a nearby abandoned Sioux village. The empty settlement contained more than 400 lodges.

The Mormon pioneers marveled that the Indians had left so much behind. There were pieces of buffalo robes, furs, moccasins, horse halters and other items. It was as if the Indians had newly outfitted themselves and thrown away many of their older goods.

Those who visited the Indian camp collected many of the odds and ends, either for their personal use or as souveniers. Like tourists in years to come, they were always on the lookout for small items to carry away as keepsakes of their journey.

The morning weather was raw and cloudy. It was cold enough that most of the pioneers donned overcoats and buffalo robes. The wind was blowing strongly from the north.

Hard feelings were evidenced between two men in the company as a result of an incident the night before. Thomas Tanner had arrested Aaron Farr and put him under guard part of the night, apparently for being too boisterous when the camp was called for prayer.

"Perhaps Aaron was a little out of order in conversing loud after the horn blew for prayers, but I think Brother Tanner's angry spirit more blameable," William Clayton confided in his journal.

At 8 a.m. the pioneers began rounding up their livestock, but it took another hour before the wagon train could start moving westward again. As they traveled they noticed the grass was beginning to improve, probably because the buffalo were not as plentiful as in previous days.

During the day the pioneers came upon a river about 100 feet wide flowing from the northeast. They were unable to find any reference to it on their charts. "There is no mark on the maps showing that such a river flows," Thomas Bullock said.

The pioneers forded the stream with difficulty because the bottom was mostly quicksand. Three wagons became mired while crossing, but teams were doubled and with the help of men pulling ropes, the wagons were dragged free. The men got very wet.

On the other side, high sand hills reached all the way down to the Platte River and blocked the route. Scouts rode ahead and found a way through the bluffs without a major detour. A mile out of the way the pioneers discovered a valley leading through the obstacle

Brigham and the other leaders decided to camp at the stream they had just crossed and tackle the trail through the sand hills the next day when the teams were more rested. Sand always was the worst terrain for the animals, making the work of pulling the wagons extra hard.

While waiting for the report of the scouts, Bullock said he found "a very pretty green snake which I played with on the end of a stick. I was afterwards told it was one of the most poisonous of snakes."

The sand hills harbored a large population of snakes and they were a real hazard for the unwary.

Brigham and Heber C. Kimball sighted a large rattlesnake while on a scouting expedition and said it was the largest they had ever seen.

The pair were among the most active horsemen in the entire company, always out in front of the wagon train to find the best route and locate midday resting places and camp sites for the night. Because of the cold wind, both were nearly frozen for their efforts this day.

Only 10 and three-quarter miles were gained by the pioneers by the time they made camp, but the feed for the cattle was an improvement over previous places. The only fuel for fires was buffalo chips. No trees were to be seen anywhere among the sand bluffs.

That night Wilford Woodruff had some observations about the nearby Platte River. He said it was a very unusual river because it was so broad (almost a mile wide) and yet so shallow that the wind pushed the water around.

On windy days the river ebbs and flows like the sea, he said.

"When the wind blows hard from the south, the water all rushes to the north shore and the depth on that side suddenly increases. When the wind is from the north, the water rushes to the south shore," he said.

In times when the wind blows hard, as it did this day, the water is pushed so far to one side "until one can walk across two-thirds of the river bed on bare ground," Woodruff marveled.

May 14
FRIDAY

On a cold morning Wilford Woodruff missed close shot

Cold weather from the previous day continued into the night and the livestock in the Mormon pioneer camp "suffered considerably," according to Orson Pratt.

However, scientist Pratt measured the temperature later in the morning and found it not too terrible at 38 degrees.

Several herds of buffalo were sighted in the distance, but they were fewer in number and getting harder to bag. Wilford Woodruff hid himself on the bank of the Platte River in the early morning and waited for 17 bulls to come down to drink. He ambushed them, but in the excitement, missed a fairly close shot.

"I fired at the youngest one, but missed him," he reported ruefully to other hunters in the camp.

Before the company could get the wagons rolling, a violent thunderstorm swept across the prairie. "I nearly got wet through," Thomas Bullock said. "All took to their wagons for shelter until it was over."

Norton Jacob said he fed the last of his corn supplies to his team that morning. The feed was depleted because of the lack of grass the previous week. However, after making a zig-zag six mile march through the sand hills during the day, the pioneers discovered "better feed than we have had for some time."

Pratt climbed one of the highest bluffs where "a beautiful and extended prospect opened on every side." He said he could see both forks of the Platte River from his vantage point. The south fork was some distance from the pioneer route along the north fork.

Many Indian tracks were found along the banks of the Platte River, all of them quite fresh. The signs indicated a large group, including women and children. "But we are satisfied the Lord hears the prayers of his servants and sends them out of the way before we come up to them," William Clayton said.

An earlier report of 32 Indian ponies grazing on the far side of a bluff caused some alarm among the Mormons. But it turned to laughter against John Higbee, who made the report, when it was discovered they were "our own horses that a few of the brethren had taken over the hill to graze," Bullock said.

The company continued for several miles until another high range of sand hills blocked the path. Here the pioneers halted again until scouts could seek possible routes through the barrier.

Heber C. Kimball finally reported no trail led through the bluffs without going many miles out of the way. Brigham Young decided to camp on the spot and climb the bluffs the next day by doubling up teams.

Accordingly, camp was formed at 5:30 p.m. after having made only eight and three-quarter miles for the day. The sand hills were making it difficult to travel very far with having to seek possible detours.

Clayton said the sand in the hills was "like large drifts of snow" in some places. In other spots there were "deep chasms as if wasted by heavy rains." Wild flowers grew in the sandy soil, "not unlike the violet and very rich."

The weather warmed during the day, much to the relief of the pioneers. A light shower fell about noon, but the company paid scant attention to it.

Hunters for the pioneer camp had considerable success in the afternoon, shooting two buffalo, three antelope and a badger. It took until after dark to bring all the meat into camp. Higbee also wounded an antelope, but said it got away while he was reloading his rifle.

Pratt noted that Indians apparently were aware of the Mormon camp "and are lurking around trying to steal horses." There was music around some of the campfires that night "as usual," he said.

After the pioneers retired for the night, the Indians made a move. A shot was fired by a guard to foil an attempt on the animals. The camp was roused and all horses, which had been staked outside the wagons, were brought into the circle for the rest of the night.

As a result of the alarm, the company cannon was loaded and prepared for quick action. Many of the men in addition to the sentries were awake part of the night, but all remained quiet until dawn. The cannon was unloaded again in the morning.

An early odometer measured the distance

Accurate measurements of how far they traveled each day became available to the Mormon pioneers this week.

A gear box mounted on a wagon wheel kept track of the distance down to fractions of a mile. Previous guesswork proved to be too high most of the time.

A boatload of pioneers crossed the Platte River May 20 to confirm that Ash Hollow had been sighted. The river was so shallow the boat was dragged over by hand.

Ash Hollow, on the south side of the river, was a popular stopping place for emigrants on the Oregon trail.

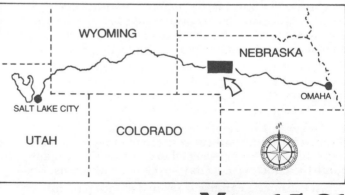

May 15-21

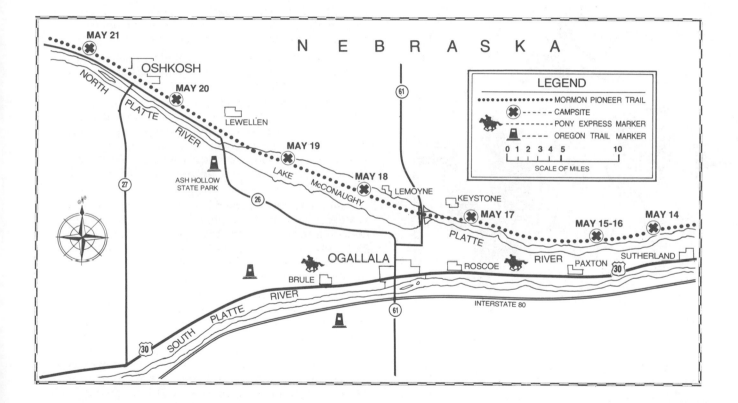

Soft sand was hard pulling for the oxen

More than 18,000 square miles of sand hills cover west-central Nebraska and the Mormon pioneers began finding these hills a frequent obstacle.

Since early in the trek they had traveled along a corridor with the Platte River on the left hand and bluffs and sand hills marching along the right hand.

But recently the sand hills closed the corridor from time to time by reaching all the way down to the bank of the Platte River, forcing the pioneers to make their way between and over the grass-covered, but sandy, rises. The hills generally weren't too steep, but the soft sand nearly wore out the teams trying to pull wagons through it.

The company camped in front of a series of bluffs yesterday. During the night a guard, Rodney Badger, noticed movement in the grass and went to investigate. A team of nearby mules pricked up their ears and snorted. Badger fired into the grass "and a man jumped up and ran away."

The shot roused the camp and all men were asked to check their own animals. The cannon was loaded, but not fired. Badger, 23, was a strong frontiersman. Before reaching the Salt Lake Valley, he was sent back to assist following wagon trains and was reunited with his wife. They entered the valley in October, 1847. He became a bishop and six years later was drowned while saving four of six children whose wagon capsized while crossing the Weber River.

At daybreak the pioneer camp found it a very cold morning, "more like January than May," according to William Clayton. The climb over the sand hills was delayed about an hour by rain, finally beginning at 9 a.m.

The company "took a wandering course through a mountain of sand, which was hard pulling for the oxen," Thomas Bullock wrote.

Where the teams descended from the sand hills "it was steeper than most house roofs and we went down in almost a jump," Bullock added.

Crossing the bluffs required travel of more than a mile and rain began to fall again. Perhaps the rain helped, but the wagons made it without doubling the teams. "We got over without difficulty, much better than we had anticipated," Clayton reported.

Norton Jacob, still worried about feed for his teams, said the prospect for "warm, grass-growing weather was not very flattering." But a short time later the company came upon an area of rich grass, "the most of anyplace this journey," according to Bullock.

"The cattle soon fill themselves, which is a comfort and blessing to the camp," Clayton said.

The pioneers also had a good supply of food. "Buffalo, deer, antelope, geese and ducks are plentiful," Orson Pratt said, noting that the hunters have provided an abundance of meat.

Not all the hunters were successful. Wilford Woodruff tried a long shot at a buffalo. His 480-foot shot struck the beast in the shoulder, but the wounded bison refused to go down and "hobbled away with the herd and I did not get him."

While food was plentiful, fuel to cook it was harder to acquire. Some pioneers scouted along the banks of the river and obtained a few sticks of driftwood. The rest gathered buffalo chips for their fires.

The dried buffalo dung "abounds everywhere," Clayton said, "but the rain has injured it some for burning."

Once again the way ahead was barred by a range of sand hills and the company decided to camp because it appeared impossible to get over the bluffs before dark. A cold and damp wind made things uncomfortable that night.

As they traveled that day the pioneers saw more Indian signs, including temporary camp sites. The Sioux apparently also used buffalo chips for fuel. They dig up the sod and pile it in a circle around the fire to provide seats, Clayton said.

"We have passed a number of these temporary little camping spots this afternoon," he said. Among the tracks are footprints and moccasins of children, making it plain that "whole families are amongst their number."

The pioneer trail at this point followed the north branch of the Platte River. Modern Highway 30 and I-80, as well as the Union Pacific railroad tracks, run parallel to the south branch of the river a few miles away.

A buffalo fat candle aided journal keeping

When darkness fell on the prairie, it was really dark. Except for campfires, there was no artificial light and most activity had to cease.

Those Mormon pioneers keeping journals, for example, could only write during the day, when much else was going on.

Thus William Clayton was highly pleased with a significant gift from Edson Whipple — a sleek candle made from buffalo fat. Whipple had managed to make two candles and gave one to the scribe.

Writing by the flickering light of the candle that night, Clayton reported it burned "very clear and pleasant" and the tallow smelled "sweet and rich" and was more pleasant than the tallow of domestic cattle.

Whipple, 42, had lost his entire family after the flight from Nauvoo, burying his mother, his wife and his baby daughter on the banks of the Missouri River.

He crossed the plains again to bring another pioneer company to the Salt Lake Valley. Later he helped settle Iron County, laid out the city plan for Parowan, served on the city council and built the first threshing machine run by water power. He died in the Mormon colony in Mexico at age 89.

It being Sunday, the pioneer company remained in camp this day. Thomas Bullock called it a "day of purifying, with nearly all engaged in washing."

When the bugle was sounded to call the camp together for worship, Eric Glines was on guard duty. He sighted some buffalo wandering toward the camp's grazing horses and went out to drive the buffalo away.

As he approached, one of the buffalo "did not seem much disposed to move," so Glines shot him. The wounded animal staggered away and was hit three more times. It finally fell dead after running more than 600 feet.

The beast was judged to weigh 700 to 800 pounds and provided considerable meat for the camp.

Glines, a 24-year-old Canadian, did not enter the Salt Lake Valley that year, but was among several men sent back to act as guides for following companies. He later helped settle the Sacramento Valley in California.

The whole episode of the buffalo shooting took place in full view of the camp, which had assembled for Sunday worship. Heber C. Kimball, who preached that day, made a comment about hunting on the Sabbath, but was mild in his remarks.

He added that he had never traveled with a group

generally better behaved than this company.

Kimball said the Lord had answered the pioneers' prayers and turned aside the Indians so the company was not molested by them. In fact, this had been so effective that he had a "curiosity to see a Sioux, but couldn't get an opportunity."

Earlier that day, Wilford Woodruff reported he had been sick and arose two hours later than usual. He found his horses still tied while all other animals in the camp were grazing. This caused him to mutter darkly about one of the men in his group who was "destitute of the spirit."

Scouts rode ahead to find the best path through another series of sand hills blocking the route. They returned after several hours to say they discovered a four-mile passage through the difficult bluffs.

During the day Clayton put up another sign post estimating the distance from Winter Quarters as 356 miles and noting the last 70 miles of that were accurately measured.

"We shall continue to measure and put up guide posts as often as circumstances will permit throughout the journey," he said.

Final touches were completed on the "roadometer," the gear device designed by Orson Pratt and built by Appleton Harmon. It measured the turns of a wagon wheel and gave an accurate count of miles traveled.

The whole thing was encased in a box connected to the axle of one of Kimball's wagons. The box was 18 inches long, 15 inches high and three inches thick.

May 17
MONDAY

Range of sand hills made traveling difficult

Breaking camp always was a busy time. Cattle had to be fed and watered, fires built, breakfasts cooked, teams hitched and wagons reloaded.

As the pioneers bustled about in preparation for resuming their march after a two-day rest, they could see another range of sand hills lying in front of them.

Twice in recent days they had to struggle up such hills, wearing out the animals in pulling through the soft sand. The bluffs ahead seemed higher than previous hills.

Wagons began rolling out of camp about 8:30 a.m. and soon reached the hills a mile and a half distant. During the climb the pioneers "passed quite a number of small streams," Orson Pratt reported.

There were several steep places of descent on the other side of the bluffs. "However, all the teams got over safely," William Clayton said. Once across, the company found much water and considerable good grass.

"The whole of this bottom seems full of springs and we have to keep near the bluffs to make a good

road to travel," Clayton wrote. Even close to the bluffs the ground was soft and springy. One of the streams crossed by the wagons was named Spring Creek by Brigham Young.

During a noon halt, after traveling more than six miles, one of Brigham's horses became mired in the soft ground. "A number of men collected and with a rope dragged it out, washed and rubbed it and all was well again," Clayton said.

About two and a half hours later the trek resumed. The pioneers crossed a low range of sand hills and forded a wide, but shallow, stream to reach level prairie once again. The ground was still soft even on the prairie.

Unlike the cold weather of recent days, conditions were pleasant and "It looks as though we might have spring return again," Norton Jacob wrote.

Hunters rode into camp and reported they had killed three buffalo. Men were dispatched with the leather boat to skin the animals and bring back the meat. Meanwhile, the company continued the journey and finally stopped for the day about 6 p.m. after finding some dry bottom land.

Soon after camp was established, the boat brought back the buffalo meat, but "Brigham was not pleased with it as we had so much meat in camp already and they (the hunters) went out without counsel," Wilford Woodruff said.

In addition to the buffalo, the hunters also bagged an antelope. The meat was cut into quarters and distributed evenly throughout camp. "It appears some have already got more than they need and feel unwilling to take a good forequarter," Clayton noted in his journal.

A fawn was captured and brought into camp by Roswell Stevens, who decided to try to raise the animal.

The pioneers had been traveling along the north side of the north fork of the Platte River and the south fork ran parallel a few short miles away. But now the two branches began to spread farther apart.

Modern roads, I-80 and Highway 30, follow the south fork. For motorists on these routes, the Mormon trail is about six miles to the north. Highway 26, north from Ogallala more closely follows the trail.

The pioneer campsite on this day in 1847 was northeast of the future site of Ogallala, which got its name from a tribe of Sioux Indians.

After the Civil War the ranchers of Texas were anxious to find new markets for their cattle. They rounded up their herds and drove them north. Because of the railroad, Ogallala became an important cattle shipping point. The first herds arrived in 1867.

For many years the town was a wide open place full of cowboys celebrating the end of long cattle drives. In mid-summer there were sometimes as many as 15 outfits camped near Ogallala at the same time.

In later years the town calmed down, but it still boasts a wild west decor in some places and puts on a big rodeo and western show for tourists. Even buffalo steaks can be had during the tourist season.

Brigham admonished party for over-hunting

Hunting had been good. Too good. There was more meat in the Mormon pioneer camp than could be profitably used. The continued shooting of game had upset Brigham Young.

Early in the morning, Brigham called the captains of 10 together and spoke sharply to them.

"Some members of the company have left meat on the ground and would not use it because it was not a hind quarter," he growled. "God has given us a commandment that we should not waste meat, nor take life unless it is needful."

There are some in camp who "would kill all the game within 100 miles if they could, without one thought of who created it or formed those great pastures for the wild animals to feed in," Brigham charged.

"Some men will shoot as much as 30 times at a

rabbit if they did not kill it and are continually wasting their ammunition. But when they have used all they have got, they may have the pleasure of carrying their empty guns to the mountains," he declared.

"We now have enough meat to last some time if we take care of it," the president said.

Brigham then turned his wrath toward the mounted horsemen. He said only Heber C. Kimball, Wilford Woodruff and Ezra T. Benson take the trouble to scout out a good road for the wagons during the day.

All the others seem to care about is to "wait until their breakfast is cooked for them and when they have eaten it, they mount their horses and scatter away," he said.

Then if an antelope comes across the track, "the whole of us must be stopped perhaps half an hour while they try to creep up near enough to kill it," he said.

"But if we come to a bad place on the route, all the interest they have is to get across the best they can and leave myself and one or two others to pick out a crossing place and guide the camp," Brigham said.

He called on the captains to lead the camp by their example and teach their men proper behavior. The meeting was dismissed and a chastened group dispersed.

After breaking camp, the wagons moved across "a very hard prairie and good traveling," according to William Clayton. Soon they reached a creek more than 20 feet wide with about 18 inches of water in the channel.

Brigham's horse nearly stepped on a large rattlesnake and when Thomas Woolsey came walking by moments later, the snake coiled and struck at him, missing his foot by scant inches as he jumped aside, Thomas Bullock reported.

John Higbee shot the head off the snake and the serpent was thrown into the creek, which Brigham then named Rattlesnake Creek.

The company crossed several other streams during the day and finally camped on the west bank of an eight-foot wide creek after traveling 15 and three-quarter miles. The Platte River to the south was described by Clayton as "very wide" and there was plenty of driftwood for fires.

The bluffs come within a quarter mile of the river bank and Orson Pratt said the pioneers were pleased to see rock ledges in the sand hills, which may mean a change in the geography and less of the troublesome sand.

This portion of the Mormon trail has disappeared beneath a modern reservoir. Even the north fork of the Platte River is gone. The river, the trail route and the bluffs are now all under water.

The trail is in the midst of Lake McConaughy, a 20-mile long reservoir created by the construction of Kingsley Dam. The lake is a vacation and fishing spot.

Highway 61, which can be reached by driving north out of Ogallala, Neb., crosses the dam and gives a good view the length of the waterway. Somewhere at the bottom lies the path followed by the early Mormons.

May 19
WEDNESDAY

Another uncomfortable day of heavy downpours

Rain fell most of the night and at daybreak "it still looks gloomy," William Clayton said. He didn't know it, but this would be one of the most uncomfortable days for the Mormon pioneers thus far.

Despite the wetness, the camp was in high spirits. Because of the need for better grazing, it was decided to move out without breakfast. A race soon developed.

Early in the trek the camp had been divided into two groups and it was the second division's right to lead the way this day. But some of those in the other division were ready first.

"They rushed on their teams and drove fast," Clayton reported. Those of the second division were left behind and had to "run their teams" across the prairie to catch up and take their rightful place at the head of the company.

After traveling more than three miles and splashing across several small streams, the pioneers halted for breakfast at 6:20 a.m. Orson Pratt described the region as "marshy, with many lakes and streams and many ducks about."

Another range of tiresome sand bluffs rose ahead of the pioneers. They slowly worked their way up the sandy hills, "the most difficult of any climbed so far," Pratt said. While struggling through the sand, a heavy rain drenched the wagons, teams and pioneers.

Finally, at 10:30 a.m., the company halted and everyone took cover "to wait for more favorable weather," Clayton wrote. The wagons had covered six miles "over the worst road we have had since Winter Quarters, rendered worse by the heavy rains," he added.

As the rain poured down and the pioneers huddled in the wagons in their soggy clothes, Howard Egan went out to get some of the harness and saddles out of the wet. He found R. Jackson Redden (invariably called "Redding" by everybody in camp) was already going around storing away equipment.

"Redding is a faithful, praiseworthy man who works for the good of the camp," Egan wrote later in his journal.

In mid-afternoon the rains ceased and the wagons jolted forward once more. They had barely started when rain poured down once more. After two difficult miles, the pioneers decided to give up for the day and established camp.

"The rain still continues to pour down heavily and this has been the most uncomfortable day we have had and the hardest on our teams," Clayton said. However, "the brethren feel well and cheerful," he added.

Earlier in the day, Heber C. Kimball had a brush with some mean-looking wolves. While scouting ahead a mile from camp, he rode into a deep hollow and saw two very big wolves looking at him, "one of them as large as a two-year-old steer."

He turned around and saw several others watching him from the other side. This alarmed him, especially since he didn't have any weapons.

He made a noise to scare them away, "but they still stood." Kimball concluded he had best move away as soon as he could. After he told the story to Brigham Young, they decided to name a nearby stream Wolf Creek.

Kimball rode out several times that day to seek an easier route for the wagons and became soaked to the skin. Egan said Kimball was "pretty near sick, but his ambition and the care he has for the camp keeps him up."

Before they left Winter Quarters the Mormon pioneers obtained maps prepared by John C. Fremont during his famed explorations of the west in the early 1840s.

Now they wanted to draw their own route on the Fremont map, but Clayton found the famous chart "does not agree with my scale or Pratt's calculations." It was finally decided to collect all the necessary data and make a whole new map of the pioneer route at the end of the journey.

Several people who visited the pioneers in Winter Quarters or met them on the trail spoke of the Salt Lake Valley. Some of them later claimed to have been the source of the Mormon decision to settle in the desert area.

But Brigham had the Fremont maps long before the exodus and talked often of a new home in the Rocky Mountains. He knew where he was going before the first wagons started.

May 20
THURSDAY

Company passed the Ash Hollow landmark

Invention of the so-called "roadometer" by the Mormon pioneers made it possible for them to accurately know how far they traveled each day — probably the only emigrants able to do so.

Unfortunately, the device built by Appleton Harmon broke down just after starting this day and forced William Clayton to resume his tiresome and dizzying job of counting each turn of a wagon wheel to keep track of the miles traveled.

To make the job a little easier, he tied a red rag on one of the wheel spokes. He also drafted some of the younger pioneers from time to time to take his place at counting. The roadometer was repaired the next day.

As they followed the north fork of the Platte River, the pioneers noticed rocky bluffs on the opposite side instead of the usual sand hills. A ravine led into the bluffs and a grove of ash trees could be seen.

Some of the company thought it might be Ash Hollow, an emigrant landmark where the Oregon trail joined the north fork of the Platte, although on the opposite side of the river from the Mormon route.

If this actually was Ash Hollow, the pioneers would know for certain how far they were from Fort Laramie, according to the maps of John C. Fremont,

which they were using. They could test the distance to see if the maps gave the correct mileage.

"We have already discovered his (Fremont's) map is not altogether correct in several respects," Clayton wrote, "especially in showing the windings of the river and the distances of the bluffs from it."

The pioneers launched their reliable old leather boat to cross the Platte, but the water was so shallow and swift that paddles were useless. One of the men in the boat, John Brown, jumped out of the craft and was "obliged to drag it most of the way over."

The four men sent over the river soon confirmed that this indeed was Ash Hollow. The site offered several acres of fairly level ground amidst the bluffs. It was a popular stopping place for people on the Oregon trail, although the bluffs were hard to cross.

One of the rocky bluffs was known as Windlass Hill because wagons had to be winched down its steep slope. Early accounts often mentioned accidents and injuries on this hill. Indians also liked to ambush emigrants here while everyone was busy with the wagons.

Brown, who had come this way a year earlier with a party of Mississippi Mormons, knew the place well. He found the grave of an Oregon emigrant he had help bury the previous season.

After exploring the hollow, Brown and the others recrossed the Platte and joined the pioneer company which had waited for them. None of the others visited the famous camping place. The journey westward was soon resumed.

Many small creeks and springs flowed across the pioneer route and Thomas Bullock said the ground was very soft, which made his wagon "rock like a cradle" instead of the usual jolting.

The rocky bluffs south of the river became "more bold and prominent and relieve the monotony of the scenery," Norton Jacob said. Wilford Woodruff thought some of the rock formations resembled old castles like those he had seen in England and Scotland.

Although he admired the scenery, Woodruff's mind was occupied by troubles. He said Joseph Egbert earlier had run a wagon tongue "into the back of my wagon," knocking in the end board and allowing rain to dampen the load.

Then on this day, John S. Fowler "ran into it again." But when Woodruff spoke to him about it, "he denied it, which caused some words between us."

The order of march in the pioneer wagon train changed each day. Every morning a different group of 10 was assigned to lead "so as to divide the chore of breaking the road," Jacob said.

While traveling this day, the company passed a solitary tree on the prairie, the only one for miles. Tied in its branches was the body of an Indian child, wrapped in a buffalo robe.

Bodies of dead Indians often were placed in trees, when timber was available, to keep wolves from getting at the remains. This somber sight was encountered several times by the pioneers during the trek.

May 21
FRIDAY

A phenomenon of the West: How far you can see

Most of the pioneer company was made up of New Englanders, emigrants from Canada and Great Britain, and a few southerners. The country they were seeing was new to nearly all of them.

As they admired the scenery, they constantly were surprised at how far they could see, a phenomenon often experienced by easterners visiting the West for the first time.

"Objects can be seen at double the distance they could be seen in the Mississippi Valley," Norton Jacob said. As a result, "we are very liable to be deceived by distance."

For example, hunters often would shoot at animals which seemed to be fairly near, only to see the bullets kick up dirt before reaching the target, he said.

"While I think about it," Jacob wrote, "the brethren have been quite orderly about shooting since they got such a dressing down (earlier in the week from Brigham Young)."

Before starting this day, William Clayton put up one of his guide boards for the Mormon wagon trains following. The sign said the estimated mileage from

Winter Quarters was 409 miles and from Ash Hollow, eight miles.

The wagons rolled rather slowly across the prairie and many in the company strolled about, keeping an eye on the cattle and otherwise sightseeing.

Some of these discovered a large bone, apparently the "leg bone of some mammoth," Orson Pratt said. It was petrified, was 18 inches long, 11 inches wide in places and weighed 27 pounds.

'It is a curious specimen of ancient zoology and, if circumstances would permit, worthy of preservation," Pratt said. But the big bone had to be left on the prairie.

Scouts sighted two Indians, a man and a woman, late in the afternoon. "The squaw fled to the bluffs as fast as her horse could go, but by signs made to them, they gathered courage and came up," Clayton said.

When the Indians were first seen, the forward wagons halted until those in the rear could close the ranks and provide better defense, if necessary.

As the two Indians approached the wagon train, the pioneers saw others "peeping over the hill," Thomas Bullock wrote.

"The man has got a good cloth coat and appears well dressed," Clayton said. The horses ridden by the Indians were described as work horses, "which makes us suspect they have been stolen from travelers," he added.

Brigham was friendly to the Indians, who represented by sign language that they were Sioux, but he gave orders not to bring them into camp. The two soon rode into the hills.

While scouting ahead during the day, Brigham and Heber C. Kimball came upon a nest of wolf cubs. They caught two and killed them with sticks. Four or five others escaped into a hole in the ground. The men "tried to dig them out, but were unsuccessful," Bullock said.

The pioneers disliked wolves intensely and killed them whenever possible, although they did not go out of the way to hunt them. Snakes also were destroyed when they got in the way, but Clayton reported one exception.

As he was walking along, looking over the river, "I heard a rattlesnake. Looking down, I saw that I had stepped within a foot of it. It rattled hard," but seemed inclined to wriggle away without attacking. Some men threw it from the track without killing it.

When the pioneers made camp that night they had covered 15 and a half miles for the day. "The feed is very poor, not much but old grass," Clayton said. The campsite was about a mile from the river and some of the men dug a well to get water for cooking.

On the south side of the river were some trees, "the first timber we have seen for more than a week," except for a few cedar trees and the ash trees in Ash Hollow the previous day.

Because the prairie was so bare of timber, anytime the pioneers caught sight of trees it was occasion for comments in their journals. The lush forests of the east would not be repeated in their new western homeland.

Some different Indians, and Chimney Rock

An encounter with some Sioux on May 24 was memorable for the pioneers because they saw a kind of Indian they hadn't known before — clean, attractive and well-dressed.

An exciting landmark was in sight most of this week. It was Chimney Rock, the psychological half-way point of the long trek, although in actual miles it wasn't quite halfway.

On May 26 the pioneer wagons drew even with Chimney Rock, which loomed high on the other side of the river.

One of the pioneers planted some corn May 27 near the site of what is now Scottsbluff, Neb., just to see if it might grow in prairie soil.

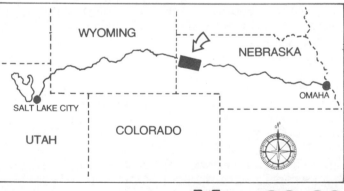

May 22-28

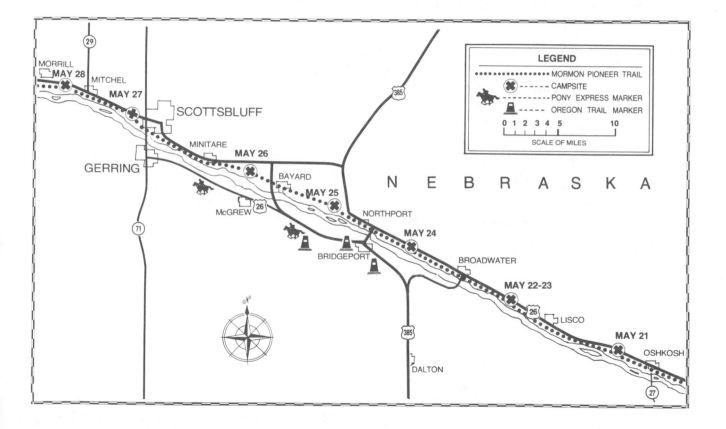

109

Porter Rockwell brought exciting news to company

One of the great landmarks on the emigrant trail was Chimney Rock, so named because its slender pillar rising above the bluffs resembled a giant chimney.

The rock was on all early maps and the Mormon pioneers were anxious to see it, both because of its fame and because it would give them a chance to check the accuracy of their maps.

After breaking camp this day, the company crossed several dry creek beds "where heavy streams run at some seasons of the year," William Clayton wrote.

The pioneers also waded through a very shallow stream and a large crab was seen. They promptly named the stream Crab Creek on their charts.

While ascending a high hill, the company conducted a rabbit hunt parallel to the line of march, Thomas Bullock said.

During a midday halt Porter Rockwell rode into camp with some exciting news. He said he climbed atop a high bluff a mile distant and had seen Chimney Rock, "which appeared a long distance off."

This aroused Clayton's curiosity and "in order to satisfy myself, although my feet were very blistered and sore, I determined to take my telescope and go on the bluff."

The bluff was rocky and steep, but Clayton made it to the top where there was a quarter of an acre of level ground. With a piece of red chalk he left a little graffiti — his name and the date. Taking a seat, he then viewed the surrounding countryside through his telescope.

"At the distance, I should judge about 20 miles, I could see Chimney Rock very plainly," he said. It "very much resembles the large factory chimneys in England."

Standing on that same bluff in 1978, Chimney Rock is not visible to the naked eye – a tribute to the eyesight of Rockwell, who wasn't equipped with field glasses.

Other bluffs in the area attracted Clayton's attention and he went exploring among them, heading in the general direction where he could meet the wagons, which had resumed the march westward.

The wagon train crossed more dry creeks and the pioneers found "a great many petrified bones, some very large," Clayton wrote. In addition, he reported a great variety of shrubs, plants and flowers, "all new to me" and "many of which have a very plesant smell."

In some places the air seemed thick with the "rich odors from these plants," he said.

During the march Amasa Lyman rode his horse up a large steep rock and did an impersonation of "Napoleon Bonaparte crossing the Alps." The pioneers thought it was very good, Bullock wrote.

A range of bluffs reached down to the river and the wagon train clung to the foot of these hills on a winding course, several times marching in the bed of a dry creek.

The wagons pulled into a circle after making 15 and a half miles for the day. The camp was near the foot of a "stupendous mass of rocks, almost perpendicular."

From below, the summit seemed barely large enough for one man to stand on, but when the pioneers climbed to the top they found a flat area with enough room to seat 20 persons.

The bluffs in this place "look more like ruins of an ancient city, with castles, towers and fortifications on all sides," Clayton recorded. Some of the pioneers climbed other bluffs and found a lone tree atop one.

Because of their appearance, these bluffs were named Ancient Ruins Bluffs.

That night the pioneers played music and danced. They also held a mock trial, one of their favorite pastimes, and charged James Davenport with blocking the highway and forcing ladies to detour around him. They found it quite amusing.

Solomon Chamberlin was voted by the company as the most even tempered man in camp — "invariably cross." The other pioneers took his disposition lightly, a kind of standing joke.

Rattlers a constant peril, finally one struck home

For several days the pioneers had been seeing many rattlesnakes. They had a number of close calls, but nobody was bitten. Today, while halted for the Sabbath, their luck ran out.

Nathaniel Fairbanks, 24, a New York stonecutter, was scrambling down one of the bluffs near camp when a rattler struck him on the calf of the leg. Within two minutes his tongue "began to prick and feel numb."

He made it back to camp, but by that time his hands were prickling and had lost some feeling, much the same way a hand or foot reacts when the circulation is cut off.

Fairbanks began suffering pains in the stomach, complained of dizziness and dimness in the eyes. The bitten leg began to swell. The pioneers tied a mixture of tobacco juice and turpentine on the snake bite. They also fed him a drink of alcohol and water, causing him to retch.

The leaders in the camp laid hands on the stricken man and gave him a blessing, then made a bed for him. "He suffered a great deal," they said. Fairbanks would recover, but he was destined to have only six more years to live.

He was drowned in 1853 when he was thrown from a mule while crossing a river near Sacramento, Calif., during a cattle drive from Salt Lake City to the west coast.

His was not the only encounter with a snake that day. Thomas Bullock was climbing in the rocky bluffs when a rattle sounded at his feet. He yelled in fright and leaped into the air, landing to the far side of the snake.

Luke Johnson turned at the cry and saw Bullock flying through the air. "If that's the way you fight, my friend, I take his (the snake's) part in the battle," he laughed.

During the day the apostles and some others climbed the largest of what they called Ancient Ruins Bluffs. Orson Pratt measured the bluff as 235 feet high. The climbers took a buffalo skull with them to the summit and wrote their names on it and left it in the southeast corner.

They also climbed another bluff during the exploring excursion and discovered a lone cedar tree. Some of the men carved their names in the bark. Both the skull and the tree have long since vanished.

That afternoon, Brigham Young called the camp together for worship. He urged the pioneers to seek after knowledge, each learning what he can in his own sphere.

Brigham said some in the company had expressed fears that they wouldn't reach their destination in time to plant crops.

"Well, suppose we did not," he said. "We traveled as fast as our teams were able to go. When we had done all we could, I would feel just as satisfied as if we had 1,000 acres planted in grain. The Lord would do the rest."

The president said he was satisfied with the general conduct of the camp and was pleased "to see so much union and disposition to obey counsel."

Howard Egan described the session as "a first rate meeting" and said Brigham "gave us some glorious instructions, which done my soul good."

After the meeting, Heber C. Kimball and William Clayton went out on the prairie to pray. While they were kneeling, a strong gust of wind carried Kimball's hat away.

They quickly finished the prayer, but the hat was out of sight. The two followed the direction of the wind and soon saw the hat "at a distance on the bottom of the prairie, still flying swiftly." They gave chase and finally recaptured it after running more than a mile.

Rain and hail followed the wind that night and the temperature dropped sharply, which worried Wilford Woodruff. He said that a year ago, on the same day, a group of trappers was traveling along the north fork of the Platte River when a similar storm arose. That night 16 of their horses froze to death.

Woodruff put blankets on his animals and stayed up much of the night with them. Next morning the horses shook with cold, but when let loose "ran to warm themselves."

An encounter with a different kind of Indians

Although the Mormon pioneers had seen plenty of Indian signs and foiled individual attemps to steal horses, they hadn't met any large parties of Indians since early in the trek.

This day they were to have such an encounter. But it was a meeting with a kind of Indian they seldom had seen before and they were deeply impressed.

The day began very cold, but traveling was good and the wagons covered 10 miles before halting for a break about 1 p.m. For the past few days an Indian dog had attached himself to camp and trotted along with the company.

While the pioneers were halted, two Indians came to camp and in sign language asked for food. They were fed with "bread, meat, beans and coffee." Thomas Bullock said. "They gave signs they were camped on the other side of the river."

The Indians tarried for awhile and then went away, "taking the dog with them," William Clayton said.

In mid-afternoon the march resumed, but the horses gave out after a few hours and the company pitched camp around 6 p.m., having traveled 16 and a half miles for the day.

Clayton said the oxen appeared to be thriving and

the mules were taking the journey well. Only the horses were a problem and couldn't stand up to the day in and day out strain.

Just before making camp, the scouts for the company sighted Indians on the opposite side of the river. The wagons were drawn into a circle, then Brigham Young sent some men down to the river bank with a white flag.

When the Indians saw the white banner, they held up a U.S. flag and began to cross the river on their ponies, "some of them singing," Howard Egan said. They were about 35 in number and included some women and children.

A few of the party came into camp while the rest waited outside. Until now, most of the Indians familiar to the pioneers were poor, unkempt and lived in what the whites considered savage and primitive conditions. They were usually suspected of trying to steal anything they could lay their hands on.

But these Indians, who described themselves as Sioux, "were all well dressed," Clayton said. Norton Jacob said they were "noble looking fellows." He added that some of the women "are pretty brunettes." Lorenzo Young said the Indians appeared "quite intelligent."

Clayton reported that some had "good, clean blankets" and others wore "nice robes artfully ornamented with beads and paintings." They wore beads and shells suspended from the ears. Their moccasins were white and decorated with beads. They appeared to fit very tight to the feet.

"All appeared well armed with muskets" and for cleanliness and neatness "they will vie with the most tasteful whites," Clayton wrote.

The Indians presented letters "written in French and signed by trappers at Fort Laramie," Jacob said. The pioneers managed to make out the French, which attested that the Indians were friendly and peaceful.

Food was sent to the group and some were escorted around the camp, the pioneers making sure they were shown several of the repeating revolvers and the cannon. The gunners went through a mock loading and firing of the cannon several times, "which seemed to please them (the Indians) much," Clayton said.

That night the elderly Indian chief and his squaw came to camp and indicated they would like to stay for the night. A tent was fixed for them and they were given supper.

"The old chief amused himself very much by looking at the moon through a telescope for about 20 minutes," Clayton noted. The rest of the Indian party made beds for themselves outside the circle of pioneer wagons.

The weather was dry, but so cold that wet clothing laid on the prairie to dry, soon froze stiff.

Guards were especially alert during the night because of the Indians close at hand. But all was quiet. The Indians "were very good and stole nothing," Wilford Woodruff said. Egan added that they behaved themselves "better than any Indians I ever saw before."

Indian visitors behaved themselves

The pioneers were up early. So were the Sioux Indians who had camped outside the circle of wagons while their chief was an overnight guest with the Mormons.

"They marched around, mostly trying to obtain something to eat," William Clayton reported. Some of the pioneers traded food for moccasins, robes and other items.

John S. Higbee had a mule which was foundered and unable to work. He traded this animal for an Indian pony. The pony was to give the pioneers trouble in the next two days.

Before taking leave of the Mormons, the Indians wanted a written recommendation from the pioneers, "which they deserved," Thomas Bullock said. He wrote out a paper for them over the name of Willard Richards.

The paper said, in part, that the Indians had behaved themselves "civilly and peacefully," were "very friendly" and "the best behaved Indians we have yet seen." The Sioux appeared pleased with the letter and the two groups waved to each other as the pioneer company moved off. The Indians crossed to the other side of the river and were soon lost from view.

The weather had been cold the last two nights. Bullock said he left some damp clothes out overnight and awoke to find them covered with a thick frost.

Perhaps because of the cold, a number of pioneers were ailing. Bullock said he was sick and was fed a drink of "tea and cayenne pepper to warm me."

Wilford Woodruff complained he was suffering from "rheumatism of the shoulder, back and teeth." He had to stay in his wagon all day and passed the time during the rough ride by reading about California and Oregon.

The wagon train climbed a low bluff to avoid a large ridge of sand and then halted to let the animals graze. By this time the sun was hot "and the roads sandy and hard teaming," Clayton said. At 1 p.m. they had covered seven miles and stopped again to rest the teams.

After a two-hour respite, the wagons moved forward once again, making good time for a while. But the path became very wet and soft due to recent rains and "many small ponds of water are all around," Clayton wrote.

That night the ground at the campsite was still damp. "We have camped on a wet spot, but the feed being poor where it was dryer, we decided to stay for the benefit of the teams," he said.

Hunters for the camp had to work harder than in the past because "we have see no game for several days except a few antelope and hares," Clayton said. "The buffalo appear to have left this region and, in fact, there are little signs of many having been here."

The pioneers did take time to destroy some of those creatures they found distasteful. Bullock blasted away at a rattlesnake until he finally killed it and Porter Rockwell shot two wolves while he was out hunting for game.

Rockwell also managed to bag two antelope which were skinned and brought to camp. The meat was divided equally among all in the company.

Chimney Rock, the famous landmark, had been in sight for several days and appeared to the pioneers to be only two miles distant, although they admitted it probably was farther away than that. They had been fooled by distances before.

For supper that night, Brigham Young dined on some bread baked by his wife in Nauvoo nearly a year and a half ago. "It was still very good," Bullock wrote. Lorenzo Young and his wife found some pigweed on the prairie and "picked a mess for greens." They said they "relished well."

During the day the company passed a formation on the south side of the Platte River known as Courthouse Rock, so named because an earlier St. Louis traveler thought it resembled the courthouse in his home town.

A smaller formation nearby was named Jail Rock by later cowboys who figured a jail was often the closest building to any western courthouse.

The pioneers were approaching an area where a Mormon woman would be buried five years later and whose grave would be one of the few to survive the passing of the years.

On Aug. 15, 1852, Rebecca Winters died of cholera while crossing the plains and was buried near present-day Scottsbluff, Neb. A friend of the family took the time to carve "Rebecca Winters, Aged 50 years" on an iron wagon tire to mark the grave.

Fifty years later the grave was found by railroad surveyors who slightly rerouted the tracks to miss the grave. Relatives in Utah then erected a marker and protective fence around the plot.

Chimney Rock was 'halfway' landmark

Excitement reigned among the Mormon pioneers today. They reached a point directly north of Chimney Rock, the psychological halfway mark of their long trek to the West.

The landmark had been sighted some days earlier and was thought to be 20 miles away. But the company traveled more than 41 miles before they were opposite the tall column rising from a rounded base.

The pioneers marched about five miles after breaking camp before drawing even with Chimney Rock looming on the opposite side of the north fork of the Platte River.

Orson Pratt estimated the height of the shaft at 260 feet. The column has changed since pioneer times due to weathering of the soft volcanic ash, clay and sandstone which make up the formation.

Chimney Rock was named by Joshua Pilcher in 1827, although it was well known to travelers before that time. Indians called it The Teepee. A group of whites who passed by in 1842 amused themselves by shooting away small projections at the top and carrying off the pieces as souveniers.

Some excitement was caused in the pioneer camp this day when an Indian pony acquired in a trade was used to haul a wagon.

While crossing a soft place, the wagon came unhitched and the whipple tree struck the horse in the lower back legs. The frightened animal bolted. This caused several other teams to panic and run some distance with their wagons before they could be stopped.

The running Indian pony caused the team and wagon of John S. Fowler to leap ahead. Wilford Woodruff said the Fowler wagon "darted by my carriage like electricity and came within one inch of a collision with my wheels."

If the wheels had locked, "we would have been a wreck," he said. "A person can hardly conceive of the power that is manifest in animals, especially mules, when in a fright."

The runaway pony finally was caught after a mile chase and brought back to the wagon train and hitched once more to the wagon. No damage was done, but the pioneers thought that was a miracle. It took some time to get the wagons organized again.

The experience gave them food for thought as to what might happen if a band of screaming, yelling Indians were to suddenly charge the camp and frighten the animals.

The wagons covered more than seven miles before making a mid-day stop, commonly called "nooning." The path was "very straight and hard, excepting a few spots where the water stands, caused by late heavy rains," William Clayton said.

The march was resumed in mid-afternoon after the ususal two-hour rest. When camp was pitched at 5 p.m. the company had covered a total of 12 and a quarter miles for the day.

Norton Jacob said the pioneers "camped near the river in a most delightful spot."

Porter Rockwell, the most successful hunter in camp, brought in two more antelope. Two others were killed by Joseph Hancock and John Brown. The meat was divided in the usual fashion — equal shares for each company of 10.

A few days earlier, some men had captured a young eagle and Carlos Murray was trying to rear the bird. As the company set up camp, he put the eagle under a wagon, but someone came along later and backed up the wagon. The wheels ran over the eagle and killed it.

Murray, whose age is not known, was one of the youngest men in camp and was a nephew of Heber C. Kimball. Murray and his wife were to be killed nine years later. They were slain by Indians in 1856 while traveling near the Humboldt River in what is now Nevada.

Thomas Bullock, one of the scribes for the camp, nearly lost his precious ink bottle this day. While standing near a well dug for water, the bottle fell from his pocket and splashed into the four-foot deep hole.

"I went to work, emptied the well, descended into it, and after groping some time in the mud at the bottom, I found it again safe," he said.

May 27
THURSDAY

The Mormon pioneeer company broke camp in the morning amidst "scenery truly delightful beyond imagination," according to William Clayton.

Chimney Rock was visible to the southeast, bluffs of various shapes and sizes were across the river and Scott's Bluff lay to the southwest.

For the pioneers, who had spent many weeks laboring across the open prairie and sand hills, these features were cheerful and pleasing to the eye.

Nebraska bluffs provided 'truly delightful' scenery

Scott's Bluff was the name given to a large hill rearing 750 feet above the prairie. Later, the same name was applied to an entire range of rocky bluffs which Clayton described as "majestic and sublime."

The pioneers were unacquainted with the vast Rocky Mountains which were still ahead. Those mountains would make the Nebraska hills look like sandpiles by comparison. But for now, they were impressed with the long range of bluffs.

The bluffs at this place were named after an unfortunate early trader named Scott. He and his party lost their supplies and weapons when their canoes overturned in the Platte River. They subsequently suffered much hunger and Scott fell sick.

His fellow travelers came across a fresh trail left by white men and abandoned the ailing Scott in order to overtake the men ahead. When they reached help, they told their rescuers that Scott had died.

Next year they returned to the same area and found Scott's bleached bones some 60 miles from where they left him. One theory holds that the doomed man crawled all that way on his hands and knees before dying, because he was unable to walk.

The nearby town of Scottsbluff, Neb., was first laid out in 1899. It became an agricultural and shipping center, with sugar beets one of the main crops.

In the spring of 1905, Scottsbluff was dubbed the "Venice of the West," not because of artistic excellence, but on account of its Main Street which lay under a foot of water. Plank sidewalks 10 feet wide ran along both sides and frogs splashed in the street.

Citizens finally dug up sod from some nearby corrals and raised the street to the level of the sidewalks so pedestrians could walk from one side of Main Street to the other without wading. The town is now one of the major cities in Nebraska.

Wilford Woodruff spent much of the day scouting the trail for the Mormon pioneer company. He said of his efforts: "It should be understood that we are piloting a road for the House of Israel to travel for many years to come."

Thomas Bullock took time to plant three grains of white corn "to show the next camp some Indian corn growing on the prairie." Records do not indicate if the corn survived or was seen by other pioneers.

The trail in the afternoon was very dusty. Heavy rains seen by the pioneers in previous days apparently had not come this far west. Although rain was uncomfortable for the travelers, often soaking them to the skin, it wet down the dust and made things more pleasant in that respect.

Clayton and Heber C. Kimball rode together for a time in Luke Johnson's wagon while Clayton read aloud what he had written in Kimball's journal. The scribe had been asked to keep a daily record for Kimball, in addition to his other duties.

As a result, the apostle's diary and Clayton's journal sound very much alike.

Hunters were out during the day, according to their usual assignment. They managed to kill four antelope which were skinned on the spot and brought back to the wagon train.

Among the hunters was Lewis Barney, 38, a New Yorker who joined the Mormons in 1840 after he became curious about why they were being persecuted.

He brought his family across the plains in 1852 and set up a lumber business in Provo. He was called to help colonize a number of Sevier County communities and later walked all the way to Arizona where he lived for a year. He finally died in Colorado at age 86.

The day's march for the pioneer company ended at 4:45 p.m. when the wagons were formed in a circle near the river. They had come nearly 14 miles during the day.

Many of the pioneers commented on the broken bluffs on the other side of the Platte River. The rocks resembled towers, walls and castles, all jumbled together.

May 28
FRIDAY

Leaders frowned on some of the activities

Some of the recreation and activities occupying the time of the Mormon pioneers were beginning to draw criticism from their leaders.

Travel was delayed by a morning rainstorm which lasted until nearly 11 a.m. During the wait for the weather to clear, Heber C. Kimball noticed some of the men playing cards and was greatly displeased by the sight.

He told them they shouldn't be spending their time in games, dancing and holding mock trials and especially criticized the "profane language frequently uttered by some."

Kimball "reasoned with them on the subject," according to Clayton, and said it "would lead from bad to worse if persisted in, until the consequences would become serious."

As the company traveled during the day, the wagons crossed a stream blocked by beaver dams and containing a great number of speckled trout. The trout were the first seen by many of the men since they were in England.

Along the way a number of elaborate ant hills were sighted. These hillocks consisted mostly of small pebbles which the ants had laboriously hauled into place. Among the tiny rocks were Indian beads. The insects had found them and they added a colorful decoration to the ant hills.

Also seen were dandelions, pigweed, pepper grass and various other growths. A plant, which some called dogwood, gave off a strong perfume. Prickly pears grew on the prairie in great abundance and some were picked by the pioneers.

They had "a good flavor and with sugar could be made into a substitute for fruit," Thomas Bullock said.

That evening the pioneers camped near the river. The feed for the livestock wasn't especially good, but there was a "tolerably plentiful" supply of driftwood for fires, Clayton said. There also were the remains of two large trees cut down by previous emigrants.

Bullock confided to his journal that he had been through a hard day and the strain of his work was keeping him from doing the job he wanted with his diary.

"I wanted to have the best and fullest journal of this mission," he sadly wrote."

Concern about Indians still was very real. Thomas Brown and Porter Rockwell came across footprints of Indian ponies, indicating that a hunting party was near. After a time they sighted five or six Indians a quarter mile away, but there was no attempt to communicate.

In camp that night, Brigham Young noticed some of the men playing dominoes and remarked that "the devil seems to be getting power over the camp the last several days."

He met with some of the apostles around a campfire and talked of the "careless manner" being exhibited by many in camp, including "levity, loud laughter, whooping and halooing among the elders."

Brigham, who was to be known in Salt Lake City for favoring dancing and amusements, said no harm would arise from merriment or dancing "if the brethren know when to stop." But if indulged in too far, such activity "leads the mind away from the Lord and they forget the object of the journey."

The leader warned, as Kimball had earlier, that if continued, things would get much worse. If the pioneers travel with the same kind of behavior for another 550 miles "it will lead to the shedding of blood," he said.

Brigham said the people in the company weren't just going west for themselves. They were the "pioneers for the whole church of God on the earth, seeking for a place to establish the kingdom. But we have not found it yet."

Across the Platte to join the Oregon Trail

The Mormon pioneers were much subdued in the early part of this week. Brigham Young had given them a vigourous tongue-lashing and called for more saintly attitudes and behavior.

By June 1 the company reached the river bank opposite Fort Laramie. Next day the men began ferrying the wagons across the Platte.

The change to the south bank was made because the northern route was impassable.

Being on the south side of the Platte put the pioneers on the famed Oregon trail and brought them into contact with many other emigrant companies which were on the move in 1847.

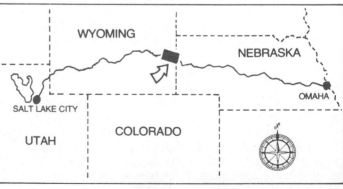

May 29-June 4

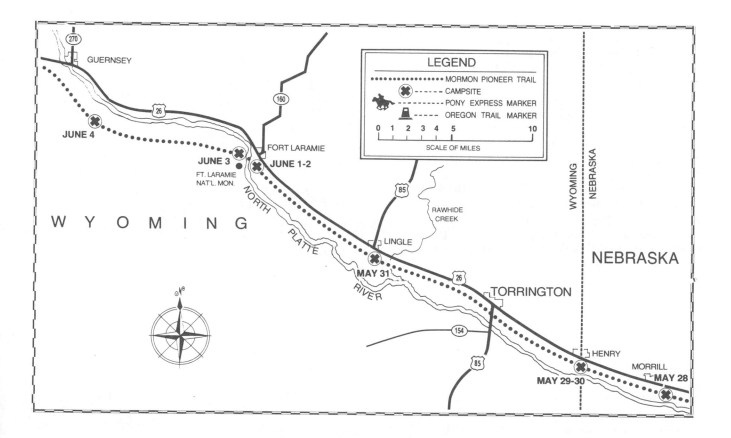

LEGEND

········· MORMON PIONEER TRAIL

⊗ ---- CAMPSITE

🏇 ---- PONY EXPRESS MARKER

🪦 ---- OREGON TRAIL MARKER

0 1 2 3 4 5 ——————— 10

SCALE OF MILES

GUERNSEY

JUNE 4

FORT LARAMIE

JUNE 3   JUNE 1-2

FT. LARAMIE NAT'L. MON.

W Y O M I N G

NORTH PLATTE RIVER

RAWHIDE CREEK

LINGLE

MAY 31

TORRINGTON

NEBRASKA

WYOMING / NEBRASKA

HENRY

MORRILL

MAY 29-30   MAY 28

Brigham lectured pioneers on behavior

For several days Brigham Young had been troubled by the attitude and behavior of many in the Mormon company. He was about to unleash a scathing rebuke on their heads.

Morning dawned cold, wet and cloudy and the company delayed travel until the weather cleared. About 10:30 a.m. things improved and the bugle sounded to prepare for the march.

After the teams were hitched, Brigham climbed into the leather boat, using it as a platform in the midst of the circled wagons. He summoned the entire camp and asked that the roll be called.

Without wasting time on preliminaries, he stunned the camp by declaring that he refused to travel any further with the pioneers because of the spirit they were showing.

Since marching into the western wilderness, the Mormons had left behind their persecutors, he said. "We are beyond their reach, we are beyond their power, we are beyond their grasp. What has the devil now to work upon?" Brigham asked.

"Upon the spirits of the men in this camp," he answered. "And if you do not open your hearts so that the spirit of God can enter . . . you are a ruined people and will be destroyed."

He told the camp that unless there was a change and a different course of conduct, "I go no further. I am in no hurry.''

Brigham said he could perhaps understand some of the behavior if the company were composed of men new in the church. In that case he would preach to them, watch over them and tell them what to do each day.

But the camp is made up of men experienced in the church, holders of the priesthood, and they do not have enough faith to get rid of a quarrelsome spirit, he said.

''When I wake up in the morning, the first thing I hear is some of the brethren jawing at each other and quarreling because a horse has got loose in the night. I let the brethren dance and fiddle night after night to see what they will do. But I do not love to see it,'' Brigham said.

He said some offer the excuse that they need to dance for a little exercise to pass the time in the evening. But he told them to walk beside their wagons during the day, carry their rifles, bring wood to camp, and help others over rough spots if they aren't getting enough exercise.

He also criticized gambling, card playing, checkers and dominoes, declaring that the men involved want to engage in such things every night, all the time, while the spirit of the Lord is neglected.

''Joking, nonsense, profane language, trifling conversation and loud laughter'' were condemned and Brigham said he was ashamed to see it. ''You don't know how to control your senses,'' he told the assembled group.

The president said every man in camp should ''repent of his weakness, of his follies, of his meanness, and every kind of wickedness, and stop your swearing and profane language.''

He called the camp forward, according to rank in the priesthood, and asked them to signify by raising hands if they were willing to repent.

''All covenanted with uplifted hands without a dissenting vote,'' William Clayton wrote.

Brigham noted there were a few non-Mormons in the camp (three blacks and Benjamin Rolfe) and said they would be protected in their rights as long as they conducted themselves well. Otherwise they would be left on their own.

He singled out Rolfe for praise and said his conduct had been exemplary during the trek. Rolfe would later join the church after reaching the Salt Lake Valley, as would Green Flake, one of the blacks.

Heber C. Kimball, Wilford Woodruff, Orson Pratt and Stephen Markham also spoke briefly and agreed with all Brigham had said. The meeting was then dismissed and all returned to their wagons for a few hours of meditation.

A much-subdued company resumed the march about 1:30 p.m. and traveled about eight miles before halting in a downpour of rain.

''No loud laughter was heard, no swearing, no quarreling, no profane language, no hard speeches to man or beast. It truly seemed as though . . . we had emerged into a new element, a new atmosphere and a new society,'' Clayton wrote in his journal.

May 30
SUNDAY

Prayers dominated a peaceful, quiet day

A quiet and sobered camp remained settled for the Sabbath, still feeling the effects of the previous day's tongue lashing from Brigham Young.

More attention was paid to religious matters and there was less of the usual activity and camp bustle as most pioneers stayed near their tents and wagons.

"I never noticed the brethren so still and sober on a Sunday since we started," William Clayton observed. "There is no jesting, nor laughing, nor nonsense. All appear to be sober and remember their covenants, which makes things look far more pleasant," he said.

About 9 a.m. most of the men gathered at a spot just south of camp and had a prayer meeting for more than an hour under the direction of Tarlton Lewis. They expressed thanks for divine help and confessed their own shortcomings.

Lewis, 42, a southerner and a skilled cabinet maker and carpenter, was a bishop in the young church. His eldest son, 17, was with the Mormon Battalion. The rest of his family was living in a covered wagon at Winter Quarters.

He returned for his family after the pioneers reached the Salt Lake Valley. Later he was a leading explorer and colonizer in southern Utah. He died at age 86 in Teasdale, Wayne County, widely known as "The Grand Old Man."

The prayer meeting was dismissed to allow the pioneers to take care of their cattle, but the same group reassembled about noon to partake of the sacrament.

"All conducted themselves peaceably and quiet today," said Howard Egan. "They seem to have profited by the instruction we got on Saturday."

Lorenzo Young said his mind "was weighed down and it was a day I shall long remember."

The apostles and some others later walked to the nearby bluffs and found a level spot surrounded by hills. In this secluded place they dressed in temple clothing and Brigham offered up prayers "for ourselves, this camp and all pertaining to it, the brethren in the army, our families and all the saints."

Taking part in this prayer circle were Brigham, Heber C. Kimball, Willard Richards, Orson Pratt, George A. Smith, Wilford Woodruff, Amasa Lyman, Ezra T. Benson, Phineas H. Young, John Pack, Charles Shumway, Shadrach Roundy, Albert P.

Rockwood, Erastus Snow and Clayton.

Albert Carrington and Porter Rockwell also went with the group, but did not participate. Instead they stood guard a short distance away to prevent any interruptions in the solemn occasion.

"We all felt well and glad for this privilege," Clayton wrote, although he, himself, wasn't in the best of health, suffering from stomach pains.

As the group started toward the bluffs, a heavy black thundercloud loomed from the southwest and threatened to pour rain any minute. But rather than postpone the ceremony, Clayton said the men were 'willing to take a wetting."

However, the rain held off until after the prayers were finished and the group changed clothes. A heavy downpour drenched the area as they returned to camp.

Everyone stayed in their tents or wagons until the rain ceased just before 5 p.m. Taking their telescopes, Brigham and a few others hiked about three miles to a high point among the bluffs where they watched the setting sun and scanned the surrounding landscape. Sand hills stretched as far as they could see.

Those hills had plagued the pioneers for some time. Every time such a bluff had to be crossed, it nearly wore out the animals pulling through the heavy sand.

Some idea of the difficulty of the pioneers was experienced in a trip over portions of the trail in a modern vehicle. Despite four-wheel drive, the vehicle nearly became stuck in the sand several times.

May 31

MONDAY

Pioneers entered what is now the state of Wyoming

As they traveled across the empty prairie, the Mormon pioneers this day crossed the future dividing line between Nebraska and Wyoming.

The prairie was bare and devoid of grass. There were no special landmarks in sight. The north fork of the Platte River was still on the left of the wagon train, the sand bluffs to the right.

The end of the month of May on the plains caused William Clayton to muse in his personal journal that there was "a better feeling, a more noble spirit, a more general desire to do good, than we have before witnessed."

This improvement was caused by the strong rebuke issued two days earlier by Brigham Young against what he termed the frivolity, profanity, quarreling and improper spirit among the pioneers.

During their morning travel the Mormon company came across a wagon trail "which evidently leads direct to Fort Laramie," some 25 or 30 miles away. Following the track, the pioneers encountered some trees on their side of the river, the first since May 10.

In that time they had traveled 215 miles "without wood for fires, except driftwood, and much of the time nothing but buffalo chips," Clayton said.

He described the prairie as "naked" with only a few weeds and wild garlic, which some of the men "picked considerable to eat."

Wilford Woodruff liked the prickly pear which grew in abundance on the prairie in certain places. When the skin of thorns was peeled away, the pears were "delicious and pleasant to eat, although a little tart."

One of the hunters, John S. Higbee shot a deer with a long tail. Clayton said the animal was "the first of its kind I ever saw."

Following the present route of Highway 26, the pioneers traveled across uneven ground, much of it very sandy, which caused a strain on all the teams. After covering an unusually large number of miles —

17 for the day — the company pitched camp on the banks of a stream which was only 10 feet wide and very shallow.

The pioneers entered what is now Wyoming by following a prehistoric Indian trail. This also was the route used by expeditions from Astoria in the Oregon Territory as they made their way to St. Louis in 1812. Along the way the Mormons passed the site where the town of Torrington, Wyo. would one day be built. Torrington was named after a town in England.

A trading post was built near the site soon after the pioneers passed. In 1850 a party of non-Mormon emigrants was attacked by Sioux. They fought off the Indians from inside the post, but some black slaves in the company were killed. The bodies were buried beneath the floor of the trading post after the battle.

The Mormon campsite of May 31 was the location of a major incident in 1854, touched off when a party of Mormon emigrants lost a lame cow. It wandered into a Sioux camp. The pioneers didn't go after the cow, but reported the loss when they reached Fort Laramie.

A young lieutenant fresh from West Point took 28 men and went to the Indian camp to demand return of the animal. When he learned it had been killed and eaten, he wanted to arrest the culprits. The Indians refused and he ordered his men to fire into the tents.

The Sioux returned the fire, killing the officer and five men. The rest of the soldiers fled, but were overtaken and killed on the prairie. For some time afterwards Fort Laramie was in a virtual state of siege.

June 1
TUESDAY

·Pueblo Saints waited at Ft. Laramie

After more than seven weeks on the trail and little contact with anyone except Indians, the pioneers were about to have a joyful reunion with other Mormons.

The morning dawned warm and pleasant "and a feeling of peace, union and brotherly love seems to dwell in every breast," William Clayton noted.

As the camp prepared for the day's march, Clayton pondered on past persecutions of the Mormons and said "the idea of dwelling with my family in a land of peace, in the midst of the saints of God, is better felt than described."

Travel was fairly slow this day as the company made only 12 miles, but in mid-afternoon a cry went up from some of the pioneers. They had sighted Fort Laramie about four miles to the southwest on the opposite side of the river.

Advance scouts for the group saw some men come down to the river from near the fort. The men identified themselves as part of a company of Mississippi Mormons who had crossed the Nebraska prairie ahead of Brigham Young in 1846. They had spent the winter at a settlement in Pueblo in what is now Colorado

Known as the Mississippi saints, the group originally consisted of 14 families, including some persons from outside Mississippi. They had expected to meet Brigham's company on the trail in 1846 and traveled all the way to Fort Laramie before discovering that the main party never left Winter Quarters.

The group then turned south and settled in August, 1846, at Pueblo on the Arkansas River where they spent a mild and fairly comfortable winter. Several months after their arrival they were joined by sick detachments released from the Mormon Battalion and the settlement grew to about 275 men, women and children.

A few of the Pueblo Mormons made their way back to Fort Laramie the next spring and had been waiting about two weeks for Brigham's company to appear.

"It caused us much joy to meet with brethren in this wild region and also because we should have some news from the brethren in the army," Clayton wrote.

How the Mississippi saints got out in front of Brigham's company makes a story all its own.

Briefly, John Brown and some other men and their families left Nauvoo in January, 1846, on orders from Brigham to gather Mormons living in a Mississippi settlement.

The instructions were to travel west after collecting the Mississippi saints, enter the prairie from Independence, Mo., and meet up with the Nauvoo Mormons somewhere in Indian country.

Brown did the job asked of him and took the Mississippi saints on a 640-mile march from their homes to Independence where the company was joined by the Robert Crow family from Illinois and the William Kartchner family from the Nauvoo area.

Setting out over the Oregon trail, they traveled to the Platte River where they expected to meet the Nauvoo Mormons, but not finding them, "We continued our journey up the river," sticking to the Oregon trail on the south side of the Platte.

In July they met a group of travelers near Chimney Rock, nearly halfway to the Rocky Mountains, "by whom we learned there were no Mormons on the trail ahead of us," Brown said. Some wanted to turn back, but they pushed ahead to Fort Laramie and were advised to go south to Pueblo for the winter.

After getting his people settled, Brown and others headed back east. He returned to his Mississippi home and then made his way to Winter Quarters. He was named a captain in Brigham's company and in April set out once more across the plains.

The reunion near Fort Laramie brought news that some members of the Mormon Battalion had died. The sick detachments were expected to receive their mustering out pay and start for Fort Laramie in two weeks.

The pioneers formed their wagons in a V arrangement at the river. On the other side of the river was the abandoned ruin of Fort Platte. Fort Laramie was two miles further west.

June 2
WEDNESDAY

No traveling was done this day. The Mormon pioneers stayed in camp while their leaders visited nearby Fort Laramie (or Fort John as they knew it) to learn more about what lay ahead.

The Platte River was more than 100 yards wide at this point. Fort Laramie was on the other side. Brigham Young and others crossed in the leather boat in what appeared to be deep water.

On the south side of the river they made a brief inspection of old Fort Platte, which had been abandoned some years before in favor of Fort

A cordial welcome at old Fort Laramie

Laramie. "The outside wall is still standing, but the inside is in ruins, having been burned," Howard Egan reported.

The walls were made of adobe brick, "being large pieces of tempered clay dried in the sun and apparently laid one on another without mortar or cement," William Clayton wrote.

Brigham and his party then moved on to Fort Laramie, also built with adobe brick. Originally it was a wooden fort, but it burned down seven years earlier and was replaced by the brick structure. First called Fort William, it was later known as Fort John and finally took the name of the stream where it was located, Laramie Fork.

The fort was a trading post rather than an army station. "There are many souls at this fort, mostly French, half-breeds and a few Sioux Indians," Clayton said. Others in the Mormon party counted 38 persons living at the fort.

The brick walls surrounding the post were 168 feet by 116 feet. The enclosure contained 18 buildings.

Camped near the fort were some of the Mississippi Mormons who had come up to intercept the pioneers. Brigham and his group "tarried with them" for a time, sharing stories of their adventures.

Entering the fort, Brigham and his party were kindly received by James Bordeaux, a Frenchman who was in charge of the post. He told them they could not continue west on the north fork of the Platte because bluffs block the trail four miles ahead. He said these bluffs could not be crossed with loaded wagons.

Bordeaux offered to rent the Mormons a good flatboat to ferry their wagons to the south side of the Platte. The price was $15 to bring the entire company over the river. Brigham accepted the offer.

The Frenchman said the Mormons' old enemy, former Missouri governor Lilburn W. Boggs, who issued the infamous extermination order against them in Missouri, had been on the Oregon trail and recently stopped at Fort Laramie.

Boggs made all kinds of derogatory comments about the Mormons and cautioned people at Fort Laramie to watch their horses and cattle when the pioneers neared, Bordeaux said.

Boggs and company were continually quarreling, Bordeaux reported, and many deserted the ex-governor. The fort superintendent said he told the Missouri group that the Mormons "could not be worse than he (Boggs) and his men."

During the lengthy conversation the pioneers learned that Fort Bridger was 350 miles distant. After the talk with the superintendent, the Mormons visited the fort trading post.

The owner said he dealt only with Sioux Indians because Crow Indians in the area were untrustworthy.

The pioneers priced items in the store and noted that a pair of moccasins sold for $1, as did a lariat and a knife. A pound of tobacco was $1.50, buffalo robes were $3 to $5 each and a gallon of whiskey was $32. Calico and cotton was $1 a yard, flour was 25 cents a pound, a cow cost $15-$20 and a horse about $40.

The Mormons thought the prices were rather high. No sugar or spices were to be had because supplies had not yet arrived from Fort Pierre on the Missouri River, some 400 miles away.

Taking the flatboat, Brigham and his men floated down Laramie Fork to the Platte River, "a pleasant ride of about three miles, the current being very swift," Clayton said. The boat was then towed to camp for use the next day.

It was decided to send several men to the Mormon colony at Pueblo to hurry the people there to Fort Laramie so they could follow in the wake of the pioneers.

Those chosen for the trip were Amasa Lyman, Thomas Woolsey, John H. Tippetts and Roswell Stevens.

June 3

The pioneers began ferrying the Platte

Since leaving Winter Quarters two months earlier, the Mormon pioneers had followed, more or less, the north bank of the Platte River. Now they were leaving it.

The Platte would continue to be their guide, but the route along the north bank had become impassable. It was necessary to use the south bank, a switch the pioneers had avoided as long as possible, even when the traveling was easier and the grass better on the south side.

They were trail blazing for other Mormon companies to follow and wanted to have a route where there would be as little contact — and trouble — with other travelers as possible.

The south side of the Platte was the Oregon Trail and was heavily traveled. From now on, the Mormons would find themselves jockeying for campsites with other emigrants headed for California and Oregon.

An example of the numbers of people headed west that spring was reported by three men with pack horses who reached Fort Laramie that morning. They said they had seen more than 2,000 wagons on the road from Missouri.

"We are satisfied the report is exaggerated,"

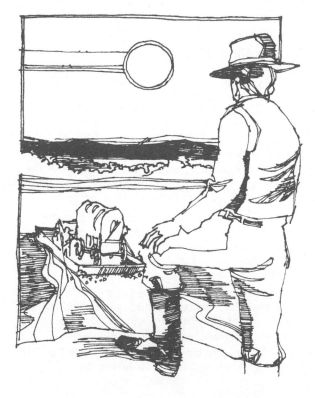

William Clayton said, but obviously, a considerable number of non-Mormon emigrants were using the Oregon trail.

A company of 18 wagons was camped three miles from the Mormons and a man in that party came to the fort to say that his group counted 500 wagons on the trail. His company lost four horses to Indians recently, he added.

The pioneers began rafting their wagons across the Platte at 5 a.m. on the boat rented from Fort Laramie. One wagon was moved to the opposite shore every 15 minutes. A strong wind blowing up the river "made it easier crossing," Howard Egan said.

In addition to getting across the river, Brigham Young gave some thought to the 250 Mormons living at Pueblo to the south in what would later become Colorado. They included sick detachments of the Mormon Battalion who had dropped out of the historic infantry march.

Four men were picked by Brigham to travel to Pueblo and get the people there on the road to Fort Laramie and thence on the trail to the Salt Lake Valley. These Mormons would arrive in the valley just a few days behind Brigham's company.

It was typical of Brigham that he issued orders to the Mormon Battalion detachment at Pueblo, even though they hadn't been discharged yet and technically were still in the U.S. Army. Their discharges were due soon and Brigham figured they might as well be moving.

Amasa Lyman, Thomas Woolsey, John H. Tippets and Roswell Stevens were chosen to go to Pueblo. They left camp about 11:15 a.m., accompanied a short distance by Brigham and others who held a brief meeting, knelt down, dedicated the four to God, and blessed them.

At 1:30 p.m. a violent storm arose. Rain and hail lashed the pioneers and lightning split the sky. The job of ferrying wagons over the river was halted while the storm raged for two hours.

Most of the horses already were across the river and were housed in the ruins of Fort Platte near the crossing site. Fort Laramie was about two miles farther away.

At 3:30 p.m. the storm ceased and once again wagons were boated across the river. By 5 p.m. all the first division were over. The second division worked even faster, averaging a wagon every 11 minutes. One crossing was accomplished in 10 minutes. The fastest time for any wagon in the first division was 13 minutes.

But the storm broke out again at 7 p.m. and the pioneers were forced to give up for the night, leaving about 15 wagons still to get over the river.

During the afternoon, Wilford Woodruff and some others had visited a nearby Indian and French burying ground. As was their custom, the Indians laid out their dead on a platform about 10 feet above ground.

The French were buried in graves, each with a "strong picket around and a cross at the head, they being Catholics," Woodruff noted.

Company was praised for behavior, discipline

The pioneers arose long before dawn and started ferrying wagons across the Platte River at 4:40 a.m. All but 15 had been rafted over the previous day.

By 8 a.m. "the last wagon was over," William Clayton reported. Now the company was ready to resume the trek to the Salt Lake Valley.

A number of men walked two miles to Fort Laramie to bid farwell. They deposited a package of letters which traders at the post promised would be sent along to Winter Quarters. Other mail was left for pioneers to collect as they reached the fort.

James Bordeaux, the fort superintendent, praised the Mormon pioneers for their behavior and discipline. He said that "never before had such a company passed Fort Laramie."

While at the fort, the pioneers heard more reports that the Oregon trail was getting crowded. A traveler from St. Joseph, Mo., said he passed hundreds of wagons coming from Missouri.

One of the traders gave the Mormon leaders "a very favorable account of the Bear River Valley" in what is now Idaho. He said it had plenty of timber, good grass, an abundance of fish and winters without too much snow. This was interesting information, but not vital. The pioneers knew they weren't going to the Bear River Valley.

Luke Johnson, who had studied some medicine and served as the camp physician, did a little doctoring among the people at Fort Laramie during the Mormon stay and was paid with moccasins and animal skins.

Just before noon, a group of 17 Mormons from Pueblo, who had met the pioneers on their arrival at the fort, joined their five wagons to the company. This raised the number of people in camp to 161, not counting the four men dispatched to Pueblo.

The newcomers included Robert Crow, Elizabeth Crow, Benjamin B. Crow, Elizabeth Jane Crow, John McHenry Crow, Harriet Crow, Walter H. Crow, George W. Therlkill, Matilda Jane Therlkill, Milton Howard Therlkill, James William Therlkill, William Parker Crow, Isa Vinda Exene Crow, Ira Minda Almarene Crow, Archibald Little, James Chesney and Lewis B. Myers.

The Crow company also brought with them 11 horses, 22 cows, three bulls and seven calves. But some members of the party were low on food supplies.

Addition of the animals raised the total livestock in the company to about 300 head, not counting chickens and dogs. The large number of animals was the reason the pioneers always were worried about grazing places for cattle.

After leaving Fort Laramie the company marched about eight miles and descended a very steep hill. "All the wagon wheels had to be locked and we had some time getting down," Clayton said.

Ropes were attached to the back of the wagons and men strained to keep the wagons from running out of control down the steep slope. The place later became known as Mexican Hill, but the source of the name is unknown. Once they were down safely, the pioneers moved a half mile and camped for the night.

Fort Laramie was purchased by the U.S. government in 1849 and became a real military post. Troops were stationed there. Soldiers used to shoot at buffalo which wandered near and one officer is reported to have fired a cannon into a crowd of the beasts, killing 30 at once.

The fort was a popular rendezvous for many Indian tribes, but became a hot spot in the decade from 1867 to 1877 when white settlers began invading the Sioux lands guaranteed by treaty.

East of the fort the Sioux maintained a tree burial ground. The dead were tied in trees, as was the custom. One giant box elder was known as the "papoose tree" because it was big enough to hold the bodies of as many as 40 Indian children at once.

Fort Laramie is now a historical site. A few old buildings dating from the 1850s have been preserved around the post parade grounds.

Encounters with old enemies from Missouri

The Mormon pioneers began having encounters with their old enemies, the Missourians, who were on the trail in great numbers.

As the Oregon trail veered away from the Platte, the pioneers and various Missouri companies continually leap-frogged each other, seeking to be in front for the best campsites.

June 9 was one of the best days of the entire trek for the Mormons as they covered 19 miles. Their camp was near Ayers Natural Bridge, which some of them visited.

At Deer Creek, on a return trek to Winter Quarters in August, Brigham Young and others were chased by a grizzly bear.

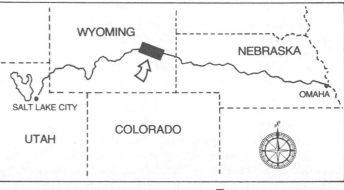

June 5-11

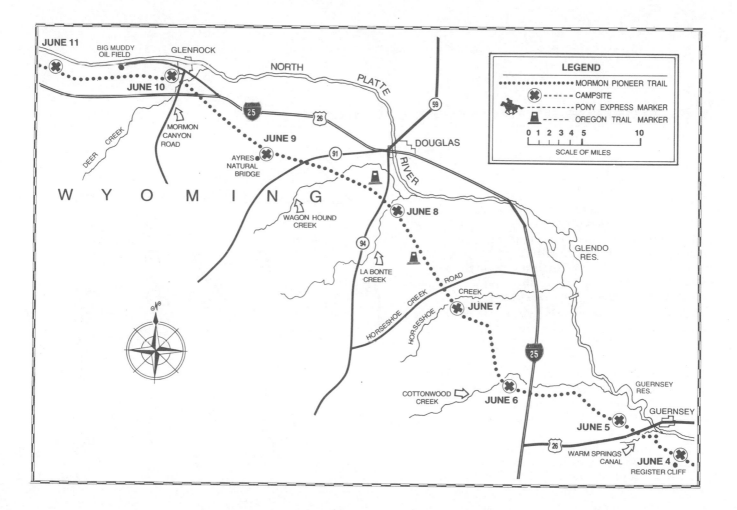

JUNE 11

BIG MUDDY OIL FIELD

GLENROCK

JUNE 10

NORTH

PLATTE

59

DEER CREEK

MORMON CANYON ROAD

JUNE 9

DOUGLAS

RIVER

26

91

AYRES NATURAL BRIDGE

W Y O M I N G

WAGON HOUND CREEK

JUNE 8

94

LA BONTE CREEK

GLENDO RES.

HORSESHOE CREEK ROAD

HORSESHOE CREEK

JUNE 7

25

COTTONWOOD CREEK

JUNE 6

GUERNSEY RES.

GUERNSEY

JUNE 5

26

WARM SPRINGS CANAL

JUNE 4

REGISTER CLIFF

LEGEND

• • • • • • • • • MORMON PIONEER TRAIL

⊗ - - - - - CAMPSITE

🏇 - - - - - PONY EXPRESS MARKER

🗿 - - - - - OREGON TRAIL MARKER

0 1 2 3 4 5   10

SCALE OF MILES

June 5
SATURDAY

Wandering oxen delayed early start

Since leaving Winter Quarters in April, the Mormon pioneers had been alone and unmolested. But now they were on the well-traveled Oregon Trail and found that their old enemies, the Missourians, also occupied the trail in great numbers.

The camp for the previous night was near Register Cliff, a favorite graffiti stop for emigrants. Thousands wrote or carved their names in the soft rock of the cliff over the years, although the Mormons with Brigham Young apparently did not.

The bugle was blown early, but travel was delayed until 8:30 a.m. when it was discovered that several oxen had wandered off in the night. The animals finally were recovered.

While the wagons were being hitched, Heber C. Kimball lectured George Billings, a 19-year-old teamster, for "abusing his team and kicking them." William Clayton thought Kimball gave the young man "some very good advice."

The surrounding bluffs, which had been mostly sand hills for the past weeks, began to give way this day to a more rugged landscape. "The peaks and hills are more lofty," Wilford Woodruff wrote in his

journal.

The pioneers began to see signs they were entering "elk, bear and mountain sheep country," he added. But no record was made of ever seeing any of those animals the rest of the trip. In fact, the Mormons made special note that they didn't see any bears.

As the company traveled, the trail became "hard, uneven rock, which shakes and jars the wagons very much," Clayton said.

At a sharp turn near the bottom of a hill, Robert Crow's wagon turned over. "However, it was soon righted and no injury done to anything." This was the first of a number of accidents to plague the Crow family in the coming weeks.

At noon the pioneer band halted near a large warm spring noted on Fremont's maps. The spring, which became known as the "emigrant's laundry tub," was used often by travelers to wash their clothes in the 70-degree water.

Emigrants usually were grimy and ragged due to conditions on the trail. Wood for fires to heat wash water was scarce and most washing had to be done in cold water, if at all.

The warm springs are just south of what is now Guernsey, Wyo. Until this point the pioneer route is paralleled today by Highway 26, but near the springs the pioneers left the Platte River and headed across country, still on the Oregon trail.

While the company was halted at the warm springs, two men on mules approached the Mormon camp. They identified themselves as Missourians and said their company of 11 wagons was nearby and headed in the same direction.

The strangers said two other companies of travelers arrived at Fort Laramie this same day with news that another three groups were within 20 miles of the fort. Most of the people in all these companies were from Missouri, including areas where the Mormons had been severely persecuted in the previous decade.

This was disquieting news.

In the afternoon the pioneers resumed their march over rocky terrain, although the trail improved somewhat later in the day. Camp was set up in the evening on the bank of a small stream, the wagons having come a good 17 miles despite the rough travel. The Missourians were camped just a little to the east of the Mormons.

After things were settled, Brigham and some others went to nearby high ground, taking their telescopes. They said they could plainly see Laramie Peak, still covered with snow.

The pioneers had been two months on the prairie and amid sand hills. Now real mountains were looming ahead.

East of the campsite was the future location of Guernsey, a town named after a local rancher. Just outside of the community is a famous reminder of the emigrant days — wagon tracks worn deep into solid rock. The wagons had to climb a hill at that point and the thousands of wheels over the years gradually wore ruts several feet deep.

A meeting with a company of Missourians

Life was rather leisurely in the Mormon pioneer camp on Sunday. The company had no plans to travel this day, although that would change in a few hours.

About 8 a.m. a group of 11 wagons, driven by Missouri emigrants who had spent the night nearby, passed the stationary Mormon camp. The two parties generally ignored each other as far as any conversation.

"We heard a young child cry, which is quite a novelty to us," Thomas Bullock said.

An hour later some of the men assembled a little way from camp for a prayer meeting. "It was a good and lively meeting," Bullock reported. Not all joined in. "Many kept about their wagons, some washing, some at other things," William Clayton noted.

Just as the meeting ended, four men on horseback rode up and said they were part of another Missouri company of 19 wagons on the trail just behind the Mormon encampment.

"Some of these (riders) are recognized by the brethren. They seem a little afraid and not fond of our company," Clayton said. Remembering the persecutions suffered at the hands of the Missourians, "I feel to wish that their fears may follow them even to Oregon," he added.

Norton Jacob said some of the riders were known to have been "engaged with the mobocrats heretofore." The term "mobocrat" was applied to those who had persecuted the Mormons in Missouri and other places.

After the horsemen had moved on, the camp assembled once more for a religious meeting. The pioneers sang a song, had prayer and were about to start the preaching when a heavy storm broke and poured water upon them.

Also they noted the Missouri company approaching and Brigham Young ordered the Mormon cattle to be moved out of the way. It was decided to cancel the meeting and the brief session ended with another prayer.

The Mormon camp watched as the Missouri emigrants marched by, noting that most of the wagons were pulled by five yoke of cattle, instead of the two used by the pioneers. "They have many cows, horses and young cattle with them," Clayton observed.

An Oregon guide was leading the company (the Mormons never used professional guides, preferring to "trust in the Lord.") and he stopped long enough to inform the pioneers that there was water available about six miles ahead and then no more for another 15 miles.

At this news, the company decided to travel some distance despite it being Sunday, because they wouldn't be able to get all the way to the second water supply the next day. Accordingly, they hitched up the wagons and moved forward about five miles and camped again.

During the trip they passed the 19 Missouri wagons which had passed them earlier. The Missourians had halted in some timber alongside the trail.

Several men from the Missouri company visited the Mormon wagon train as it slowly rolled by. They wanted to look at the mileage counter, "having heard from some of the brethren that we had one," Clayton said.

"They expressed a wish to see inside (the box which covered the device) and looked upon it as a curiosity," he said.

In the late afternoon the Mormons pitched camp a short distance between the two Missouri companies which had passed them earlier in the day.

One of the men in the second company of Missouri wagons told George A. Smith that he had broken the spring in his carriage "and seemed much troubled to know what to do to get along," Clayton said.

"He asked if there was any man in our company who could fix it. Burr Frost set up his forge and welded the spring and had it ready to put on before dark," Clayton said.

Most emigrant companies on the trail were not equipped with a blacksmith and a forge, but the Mormon pioneers had three and were ready for all emergencies.

Some more brushes with Missouri parties

Most emigrants who used the Oregon trail were concerned about their own fortunes and cared nothing about those who might follow. But the Mormon pioneers knew thousands of their co-religionists were coming and did all they could to make the road easier.

Before they started this day, the Missouri company behind them was on the move and passed by once more. A third Missouri company, made up of 13 wagons, also bypassed the Mormons while they were halted for a noon rest.

The leapfrogging of various wagon trains was due partly to a desire to be out in front and thus have first choice of camp sites. Those following often would have to travel further to find decent grazing for their cattle.

William Clayton spent the morning with Orson Pratt, learning how to use the sextant. The two men also discussed "astronomy and philosophy" as they walked together alongside the wagon train.

The company climbed a bluff and crossed a rocky ridge. While getting down the other side, the wheels were locked to keep the wagons from getting ont of control on the steep downgrade.

"The descent was rendered unpleasant by the many large stones scattered in the road," Clayton said. "Many of the brethren threw them out of the way as we went down and the road is much improved."

Many other travelers had passed the same way, but none had taken time to improve the route. The pioneers "also dug down some places and leveled others, which will make the road much better for other companies," Clayton noted.

At 3:30 p.m. the company halted for the day, having covered 13 miles. They stopped early because of a fine campsite near Horseshoe Creek in the midst of a grove of trees. Sage and mint seemed to "perfume the air."

Wilford Woodruff said the camp had "the most splendid feed we have met with on the entire journey," a sentiment echoed by many others in the company.

Near the camp, Heber C. Kimball discovered a large spring of water, which he named after himself.

The exact location of Heber Springs became lost to historians over the years, but a recent trip over the trail by the writers of this series may have pinpointed the long-missing spring.

While traveling on a back road near Horseshoe Creek, we hailed a man in a pickup truck to inquire if he knew anything about the Mormon trail route. The name Heber Springs came up and the man, Grover Thompson, said he was born on a nearby ranch and all

his life had heard his father talk about "Heber Springs" on their property.

Thompson pointed out where the old Mormon trail came through a gap in the hills near his ranch. He then guided us through several gates on his ranch until we reached a spring with a few trees around it. "This has been known as Heber Springs since before my father's time," the 55-year-old rancher explained.

The spring was covered with green scum and some nearby trees had been bulldozed down. It bore no resemblance to "one of the clearest and largest springs of water I have seen for a long time," as Clayton described it. But it seemed to be in the right place and a lot of changes can occur in 130 years.

While camped near the springs, the pioneers had another accident involving Robert Crow. Earlier one of his wagons overturned. Now his legs became entangled in a rope as several men were trying to yoke two steers.

One of the steers fell "and he fast with it," Clayton reported. However, the ropes were cut "and he was liberated without injury."

Some of the pioneers were a little upset with the Crow family when a hunter for the group killed a deer and refused to divide it equally with the rest of the camp, according to the rules.

But Clayton later learned that the Crow family did not have any supplies and had to depend on their hunter, Lewis B. Myers, "for what they had to eat."

That night a strong wind shrieked through the trees, "so much that I could not write," Clayton said.

June 8
TUESDAY

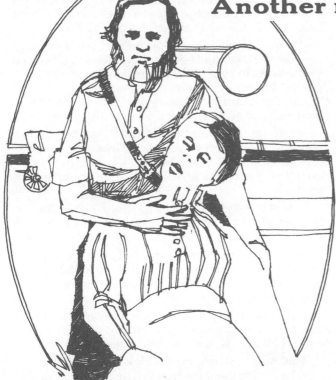

Another mishap for Crow family

Since Robert Crow and his party of 17 joined the pioneer company at Fort Laramie, the family had suffered several accidents. Now they were about to become victims of still another mishap.

The weather was cool when the Mormon pioneers broke camp at 7:30 a.m. They crossed the narrow Horseshoe Creek and began to climb a steep bluff.

"We found this ascent the worst we have ever had, being three quarters of a mile up and seven very steep rises in that distance," William Clayton wrote. By doubling the teams the pioneers managed to pull the wagons to the top.

Shortly after getting down the other side, Harriet Crow was run over by one of the wagons. She stood on the wagon tongue to get a drink from a water bucket and the team moved suddenly, throwing her to the ground.

She fell under one of the wheels, "which passed over her leg below the knee and downwards, rolling over her foot near the toes," Clayton said.

"She screamed and appeared in great agony," he

said. At first it was feared the foot was broken, but apparently it was only badly bruised. Her foot was washed with camphor and she was laid in one of the wagons.

After a noon halt, the company resumed the journey. A group of men went ahead and "cleaned up the road of stones, using pickaxes, bars and spades," Wilford Woodruff said. "It was a great help to our weak wagons."

John S. Higbee, riding ahead as a scout, sighted the Missouri companies which had passed the Mormon wagon train a day earlier.

"They had such strife one with another in trying to start first that they did not stop to milk their cows. In cleaning up breakfast they strewed meal, salt, bacon, shortcake, beans and other things upon the ground," he said.

When the pioneers reached the area where the Missourians had camped, they found three wolves feeding upon the fragments of breakfast left upon the ground.

"I picked up a pocketknife and a spoon," Woodruff said.

The Mormon pioneer company climbed some more bluffs during the afternoon in the face of a strong wind. "It was so cold that we suffered some," Clayton said.

He noted that the mileage measuring device on one wagon was not working properly, "which made me pay more attention to it." The distance traveled that day was measured at 15 and one-half miles.

Just before stopping for the night, the company crossed a stream 30 feet wide and two feet deep, "with a very swift current," Clayton said. This was shown on the Fremont maps used by the pioneers as La Bonte Creek.

The pioneers camped on the west bank of the creek in a stand of timber. Porter Rockwell came in with a deer he had killed and said the Platte River was about four miles to the north of the campsite.

A group of eastbound traders camped near the pioneers that night and several visited the Mormon camp to exchange news. "We got some information on the Salt Lake country," Woodruff said.

Thomas Bullock said the traders were friendly and noted that they described the "Utah country" as "beautiful." This interest by the pioneers indicated that they knew exactly where they were going in the Rocky Mountains.

The traders agreed to carry some mail east and many of the pioneers seized the opportunity to write quick letters to their families at Winter Quarters.

The pioneer camp was a few miles south of what is now Douglas, Wyo. The town was established in 1886 when it was announced that a railroad station would be built at that place. A community sprang up almost overnight, but it was a wild town the first year with 25 saloons.

Fort Fetterman, an army post, was the first settlement in the area. It was founded in the 1870s near where Douglas would later be built. The fort served as a supply point for the many cattlemen in the region.

Advance party sent ahead to salvage boat

A group of traders who camped near the Mormon company the previous night said they left a makeshift boat at the Platte River some distance ahead. They told the pioneers they could have it.

The boat was constructed of three buffalo hides and was left hanging in a tree. Possession of the skimpy craft might save some time in crossing the river.

However, three companies of Missouri emigrants were on the trail ahead of the Mormons and probably would reach the river — and the boat — ahead of the pioneers.

It was decided to send a party ahead and attempt to pass the Missouri companies. In addition to securing the traders' boat, this group was assigned to build a substantial raft for a ferry, kill game and do other advance work.

"Nineteen of the best teams and wagons with 49 men were sent ahead," Howard Egan reported. They broke camp and started a half hour before the remainder of the company.

Shortly after the rest of the wagon train began the day's march, the pioneers entered a strange landscape — "a valley full of red sand," Thomas Bullock said. "It may properly be called the Red Valley."

William Clayton said "most of the rocks and bluffs are of the same red color, (as the sand) only a deeper red. It affected my eyes much from its brightness and strange appearance."

In the midst of this red landscape, the pioneers crossed a stream about 10 feet wide with shallow water. But the banks of the creek were very steep and "most of the teams required assistance to get up," Clayton said.

The red valley was about four miles in length and the pioneers seemed glad to leave it behind and once more enter familiar terrain.

Other travelers were on the trail. In the morning the Mormon company was passed by four mysterious riders with pack horses and mules. Every time they talked to someone they gave a different account of where they were from and where they were going.

One of their stories was that they were from Santa Fe and they told the pioneers that "the Mormon Battalion was in California," Wilford Woodruff said.

At the noon halt, Egan reported the ground was "literally covered with large crickets." They were so numerous that "to walk without stepping on them is almost impossible," Clayton added.

By 2:30 p.m., having rested about two hours, the wagon train was on the move again and found the route "much better, not being so uneven," Clayton said.

The improved traveling conditions resulted in faster movement. The pioneers covered more than 19 miles during the day, one of the best performances for the entire trip so far. Camp was established on the banks of a small stream the pioneers identified as "A La Pierre." The creek is known today as the Le Prele. The pioneers had some trouble with French.

"There are still some high bluffs around, but the country west appears much more level," Clayton said. One of the Missouri companies was visible, "notwithstanding their exertions to get ahead of us," Woodruff said.

Also ahead were creeks and canyons where the pioneers would find coal and where several of the leaders would later have a close call with a grizzly bear.

After settling the pioneers in the Salt Lake Valley, Brigham Young, Heber C. Kimball and others turned around 33 days later and headed once more for Winter Quarters. It was near here, on Deer Creek, where they had the encounter with the bear on the return trip.

They were walking up the creek bed, which was only partially filled with water, when they suddenly met a mother grizzly bear and her cub. The bear showed no respect for the priesthood and charged. Kimball stood his ground and fired a shot when the animal was within 35 feet, but to no effect.

All fled for their lives and reached safety by frantically scrambling up some rock cliffs on the banks of the creek. A recent look at the site indicates it would have been very difficult climbing, but the group appears to have been highly motivated.

June 10
THURSDAY

A good day on the trail, company covered 18 miles

For several days the Mormon pioneers had been out of contact with their familiar guide, the Platte River, but they were about to join it again.

During their cross-country journey south of the famed river the company had been making exceptionally good mileage and they did so again this day.

The pioneers broke camp at 7:30 a.m. and marched quickly. An hour later they caught sight of one of the Missouri companies three miles ahead of them.

Not far from where they had camped the previous night, the Mormons found a natural arch under some rocky bluffs. A stream was flowing beneath it — "a tunnel formed by some strange feat of nature," William Clayton said.

The arch, 30 feet high and 50 feet wide, later became a small state park, named after the Ayers family who donated the land which had been part of their ranch.

As the pioneers traveled this day, the Platte River slowly came into view. It was their first glimpse of the waterway since they left its banks several days and 77 miles earlier and took a course more directly west.

By the time they established camp that night, the pioneers had covered 18 miles, nearly matching their record pace of 19 miles the day before. Along the way they had found a grave heaped over with stones. The name, "J. Umbree, 1843," was marked on one rock.

The company camped in a lush stand of trees where "birds sang merrily and enlivened the grove," Thomas Bullock said. Because of good feed the past few days, the cattle were prospering.

Wilford Woodruff went fishing and sat on the bank of a creek for half an hour, musing alone and as unconcerned as if he were back home. "Suddenly I heard a rustling in the bushes near me."

For the first time, he said, "the thought flashed across my mind that I was in a country abounding with grizzly bear, wolves and Indians. I was a half mile from camp and had no weapons. Wisdom dictated for me to return to camp."

The somewhat alarmed Woodruff beat an immediate and hasty retreat. He never did find out what was in the bushes.

Others also tried their hands at fishing in the nearby stream and all had success. Most of the haul was catfish. Clayton caught "24 nice fish which would average over a half a pound each. Some weighed more than a pound."

If the fishermen could have had the camp fishing net, "we might have caught enough for all the camp," he said. Unfortunately, the net was with those men who had been sent ahead to a fording place on the Platte.

The pioneer camp was near the future site of the town of Glenrock, Wyo. The town got its start when Mormons built a way station in the early 1850s where emigrant companies could rest and feed their livestock.

The collection of snug cabins near Deer Creek was abandoned in 1857 during the Utah War. The buildings were promptly taken over by an Indian agent and the site became a military fort in 1861, serving as the nucleus for a town.

Building of a railroad line in 1886 brought life to the area. The town was moved to its present location. One of the factors stimulating growth was the development of nearby coal mines — a resource found by the pioneers with Brigham Young.

"Some of the brethren discovered a rich bed of stone coal where any quantity might easily be dug. It is said to look good and is a fine quality," Clayton wrote.

To the south of Glenrock is Mormon Canyon where Brigham sent men to found a small settlement in 1853 to help feed emigrants bound for the Utah Territory. The settlers moved out in the late 1860s when emigrant trains gradually declined as railroad transportation became more available.

June 11
FRIDAY

Day for hunters as marksmen bagged 8 antelope

Early morning often was the best time of the day. The weather was comfortably cool, everyone was rested, and another day of unknown adventure lay ahead.

William Clayton, who arose at 4 a.m. to try some more fishing, was enchanted by the scenery around the camp, saying "it reminds me of England."

The air was calm and "the warbling of many birds, the rich grass, good streams and plenty of timber make it pleasant," he said. The only drawback was that the fishing wasn't as exciting as the night before. This time he landed just four of them.

The Mormon company began moving about 7:30 a.m., leaving behind the attractive campsite on Deer Creek. They traveled four hours, then stopped to rest the teams, having made more than nine miles in that time.

Hunters had considerable success during the day, shooting eight antelope and bringing the meat to camp. Among those who felled animals were William Empey, Charles Barnum and Seeley Owen.

Empey, 38, a Canadian, did not reach the Salt Lake Valley with the pioneer company. He was one of a group left to operate a ferry not far from where he shot his deer. He entered the valley in 1848, later served a mission to England, and helped colonize southern Utah.

Barnum, 47, another Canadian, was a skilled stonemason who worked on the Nauvoo temple. When it came time to abandon that city, his family refused to accompany him. He remained a faithful Mormon all his life, dying in Salt Lake City at age 94.

Owen, 42, a Vermonter, lost his wife in the tragic winter on the banks of the Missouri before the trek west. He had a small daughter who was brought to the Salt Lake Valley by relatives. He built a home near Provo and later moved to Arizona where he was killed in an accident at age 76 while working on the Atlantic Pacific railroad.

As the pioneer company moved along, men on horseback continually tested the Platte River, seeking a fording place. But the river was swollen by melting snow and no acceptable crossing was located.

The area being traversed by the pioneers would one day be rich oil country boasting many wells and vast refinery complexes. But all the Mormons could see was that they had to cross several creeks and the wagons had a difficult time because of the steep banks and soft clay lining the sides.

The company had another good day's travel, covering 17 miles and approaching the site of what would one day become Casper, Wyo. In 1847 it was just a good place to cross the North Platte River.

The pioneers pulled to a stop when they overtook two Missouri companies preparing to cross the Platte. The best place was still 12 miles away. An advance party of Mormons already was there, waiting for the others to catch up..

"There is no camping place beyond (the Missourians) unless we go some distance," Clayton said. So the pioneers settled down near the river, just behind the Missouri party.

The Missouri emigrants were attempting to raft their wagons across at this point and had gotten one load over. Other members of their party had gone ahead to the other crossing place.

Thomas Bullock said the Missouri camp was a half mile from the Mormons, "but made 10 times more noise than the whole pioneer camp."

The brethren "could clearly hear their bawling and profanity," he noted.

Ferrying the North Platte cost valuable time

The longest delay of the the entire trek took place this week as the pioneers constructed rafts to ferry their wagons over the North Platte River.

After long marches on June 11 and 12, they reached the site of what would one day be Casper, Wyo. Here they had to cross the 100-yard-wide river, swollen by spring runoff.

The crossing was slow, not only because the pioneers rafted their own wagons over, but they also did a booming business for other emigrant companies who paid a fee for ferry service.

Five days were spent at the river. When the pioneers were safely over, they left nine men to operate the profitable ferry and help future Mormon companies.

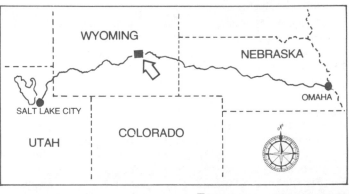

June 12-18

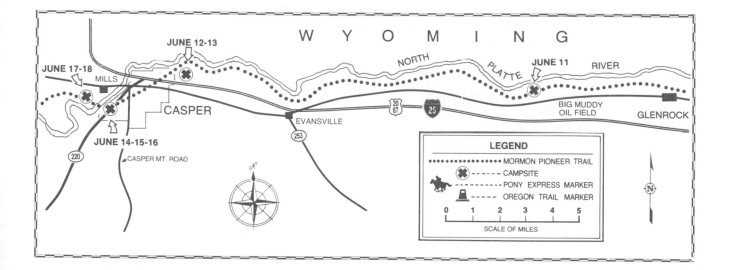

June 12
SATURDAY

The leather boat proved handy, and profitable, again

An advance party of Mormon pioneers was sent to the Platte River crossing in an effort to get there ahead of Missouri companies on the trail in front of the pioneers.

The fast-moving advance group reached the river near what is now Casper, Wyo., before the Missourians.

The pioneers were equipped with a leather boat which they had used often during the trek. Now they were about to make some profit from it.

When the Mormons and the Missourians arrived at the river crossing, they found the water was higher than usual and loaded wagons could not be taken over

the waterway.

Upon noticing that the pioneers were equipped with a boat, the Missouri emigrants offered to pay the equivalent of $1.50 a load to have their supplies ferried to the other side of the river. Payment would be made in flour valued at $2.50 a hundred pounds, corn meal at 50 cents a bushel or bacon at six cents a pound.

The leather boat, christened the "Revenue Cutter," could carry more than 1,500 pounds at a time. It made about 24 crossings with Missouri supplies. For this work the pioneers received $34 worth of flour (more than 1,300 pounds), some corn meal and a little bacon.

"This is a great blessing to the camp inasmuch as a number of the brethren have had no breadstuff for some days," William Clayton said.

Rodney Badger traded wagons with one of the Missourians and "got a horse, 100 pounds of flour, 28 pounds of bacon, and some crackers to boot," Howard Egan said. "The horse and provisions alone were worth as much as his wagon," he noted.

Blacksmiths with the advance party also set up their forges and did some repair work for the Missourians, which was greatly appreciated.

During the ferrying, one Missourian tried to swim across the river, which was 100 yards wide. When he reached the swiftest part of the current, the swimmer realized he wasn't going to make it and "began to moan," Clayton said.

The Mormons in the boat went to his rescue and "arrived in time to save his life," an act which brought considerable friendliness from the formerly hostile Missourians.

The emigrants put away their weapons which they previously had kept on display and invited the Mormons to share in some hot food prepared by the Missouri cooks.

While talking to the emigrants, the pioneers heard a blood-curdling tale about the fate of a former benefactor at the hands of a Missouri mob.

Bill Bowman, a guard at the jail where Joseph Smith, his brother, Hyrum, and others had been imprisoned in Missouri in the mid-1830s, apparently was involved in letting the Mormon prisoners escape.

Bowman's father was camped with the emigrants at the Platte. He said the Missouri mob, heading by Obadiah Jennings, suspected his son of allowing the Mormon prisoners to flee the state. They rode Bowman "on a bar of iron until they killed him," the father said.

Jennings was the same man who reportedly led the mob which slaughtered 17 Mormon men and boys in an attack on the village of Haun's Mill.

This story about the fate of Bowman did not make the Mormons feel any friendlier toward Missourians in general, but relations between the two groups camped at the Platte were calm.

After their supplies were ferried across the river, the Missourians swam their empty wagons through the fast water with the aid of guide ropes. Several of the wagons rolled over in the swift current.

Tunis Rappleye and Artemus Johnson went hunting and failed to return by dark. Search parties were sent out, but both men got back safely late that night.

Rappleye blamed his problems on confusing distances. He set out for the "nearby" bluffs, only to find they were about 10 miles away. Johnson simply got lost.

Meanwhile, the main body of pioneers marched more than 11 miles, struggling over a number of ravines and creeks, and reached a point not far from the advance party's camp.

June 13
SUNDAY

Partial day of rest as they faced Platte again

For 600 miles the Platte River had been a constant companion to the Mormon pioneers, serving as both their guide and source of water. Now they were preparing to leave it behind.

This fording of the Platte came to be known among the pioneers as the "last crossing." The bustling oil town of Casper later grew up along the banks of the river.

Once across the broad river, the pioneers would strike west across a dry and barren wasteland. They were aiming for the Sweetwater River to serve as their next guide and beyond that, other streams necessary for survival.

Also ahead lay the forbidding Rocky Mountains — a rugged country far different from anything the New England experience of the pioneers had offered. As one historian put it: "The easy part of the trek was over."

On this Sunday the pioneers enjoyed at least a partial day of rest as they girded themselves for crossing the Platte. In addition to resting the cattle, they gathered for the usual Sunday prayers and sermons.

Heber C. Kimball was the first speaker, exhorting the group to be watchful and humble. He urged every man to be as clay in the hands of the Master Potter and let their lives be molded toward exaltation and glory.

"His remarks were very touching and appropriate to our circumstances." William Clayton observed.

Brigham Young spoke next about the "liberty of the gospel" and said it guarantees a fullnes of liberty to every man. But that does not mean the laws of God can be freely broken or the works of God's hands killed and wasted.

Brigham said there was a great difference between the behavior of the pioneers and the Missouri emigrant groups sharing the same trail. He said the Missourians would "swear and rip and tear."

The Missouri persecutors have sought to deny the saints a place on the earth, but they themselves would be "swallowed up and go to the land of forgetfulness."

On the other hand, the faithful Latter-day Saints, while they might suffer some privations, eventually would "increase in dominion and power."

Orson Pratt gave the final sermon and warned the camp to avoid folly of every kind because such behavior would disqualify them "from the society of just men and angels."

After the meeting, camp leaders met at Brigham's wagon to discuss the crossing of the Platte River. It was agreed to send a number of men and wagons to cut timber in the nearby hills. Wooden poles would be used to lash wagons together and keep them from turning over in the rough water.

The pioneers had seen several of the Missouri wagons capsize in the river as they crossed earlier.

Howard Egan was sent across the river with a half dozen men "to build a raft" for carrying provisions.

In preparation for crossing the river, horses were ridden into the water and the boat was rowed over, all checking the depth of the stream. It was found to be four to six feet deep for most of its 100-yard width.

With these and other assignments, "the brethren are gone to work and are diligently preparing to cross the river tomorrow," Clayton noted.

The supplies of flour, meat and bacon paid by the Missourians for being ferried over the river were distributed equally throughout the camp. Each person received five and one-half pounds of flour, two pounds of meat and a piece of bacon.

"It looked as much a miracle to see our supplies replenished in the midst of the black hills as it did to have the children of Israel fed with manna in the wilderness," Wilford Woodruff observed.

Clayton noted the day had been hot, "more like summer than any we have had yet on the journey."

All around the campsite, "the ground seems to be alive with very large crickets. A person who has never seen them could form no idea of the vast numbers of crickets in this region," he said.

Crossing Platte a difficult chore

Fording the Platte River proved to be a difficult problem for the Mormon pioneers. They had hoped to cross in a single day but finally resigned themselves to using the better part of a week.

All the wagons were unloaded and the supplies shipped across in the leather boat and on a raft built the day before. However, the current was so strong that the raft was abandoned after two trips.

To get the wagons across, it was decided to float them. Two wagons were lashed side by side and a guide rope stretched across the Platte at the narrowest point.

The wagons floated along all right, but "when the wheels struck the sand on the other side, the current was so strong that it rolled them one over the other," Howard Egan said.

The bows holding the canvas covering were broken and other damage done. One of the wagons belonged to John Pack and when it rolled he lost a plow, two bars of iron and some horseshoes which had not been removed from the wagon bed when the crossing began.

The battered wagons finally were pulled from the water. For the next attempt, four wagons were lashed together with ropes and poles.

One of the vehicles belonged to Norton Jacob. He said the poles "broke under my wagon and it turned up sideways, but was righted and got ashore without much injury."

Two abreast didn't work and four abreast had problems "so we thought we would try one wagon alone," Egan said.

"Some of the brethren thought if one person would get in the wagon and ride the upper side, It would prevent it from turning over. I volunteered," he said.

Soon after Egan pushed off, Andrew Gibbons, 22, "jumped into the river and caught hold of the end of the wagon," apparently to aid Egan.

"When we got out about the middle of the river, the wagon began to fill with water and roll from one side to the other. I got on the upper side and held on for a short time, when it rolled over, leaving me off," Egan said.

He saw he was in danger of getting hit by the rolling wagon, so he swam away, but not before "one of the wheels struck my leg and bruised it some." He made it to shore holding his hat in one hand.

Gibbons also swam to shore. He later became a missionary to Indians and helped colonize southern Utah and parts of Nevada and Arizona. He and his wife became the parents of 15 children, but eight of them died in childhood.

After the upset of the single wagon approach, the pioneers "thought it safest to take the wagons over on a raft," Egan said. This had been done with one wagon, but was "very slow and will take three or four days" to move all the wagons, he said.

While the slow, hard work of crossing was in progress, a thunderstorm broke and rain "poured down in torrents, accompanied by hail, and the wind blew a perfect gale," Egan said. William Clayton said it was the "strongest wind I ever witnessed."

The rain and hail beat through the wagon covers and "the river rose rapidly," Thomas Bullock said. Many supplies were out in the open and became soaked.

Working the rafts was suspended while the storm lasted. Afterwards the men "labored mightily," many of them up to their armpits in water. "All were very weary when the work was done," Wilford Woodruff said.

A total of 23 wagons were gotten over the river "after a very hard day's labor," Clayton said. There was no trouble with the supplies. "One man can carry (freight) in the cutter faster than all the rest of the camp can get the wagons over," he said,

Woodruff, who spent part of the day chasing horses which ran away in the storm, probably expressed the feelings of most when he wrote: "I went to rest weary, but had pleasant dreams."

June 15

Strong wind hindered the crossing and the pioneers lost a horse

Getting wagons across the swift Platte River continued to be a struggle, hampered by strong winds, high water and the accidental drowning of a horse.

Two more rafts were built and put to work, along with the one already being used. On one of the new rafts, "we put oars to it. This worked better than running with poles alone," Norton Jacob said.

But the wind blew so hard the rafts "could not get along very fast," William Clayton reported. Despite a long day's work, less than two dozen wagons were ferried over.

During the afternoon, animals belonging to the Robert Crow family were driven into the river to swim them to the other side. One of the horses promptly ran into trouble in midstream.

"They forgot to take the rope off one of the horses and after he got out in the middle of the river, they discovered he was drowning," Howard Egan said. A boat was rushed to the rescue and pulled the stricken horse to shore, "but he was dead."

The pioneers figured the rope had become entangled in the horse's legs, making it impossible for him to swim. The rope also may have "pulled his head under" when it wrapped around his legs, Thomas Bullock said.

For the Crow family, it was another in a series of accidents which had plagued the party ever since they joined the pioneer company at Fort Laramie.

After loss of the horse the pioneers hesitated to drive their cattle across. "The current was very strong, the wind high and the river rising, which made it look dangerous," Clayton said.

However, it was decided to go ahead. The cattle were driven into the river and all got over safely. Twenty wagons were ferried across the Platte during the day, for a total of 43 in two days — a little more than half the wagons in the pioneer company.

Many of the men were soaked to the skin from working in the river. Wilford Woodruff said he felt "somewhat unwell" because of the wet and cold and strenuous labor.

The pioneers already had ferried supplies across the river for one company of Missouri emigrants. Other groups arriving at the river expressed interest in paying for ferry service by the Mormon boat and rafts.

Brigham Young decided to leave 10 men at the ferry site when the company resumed its march to the west. The main purpose of this crew would be to

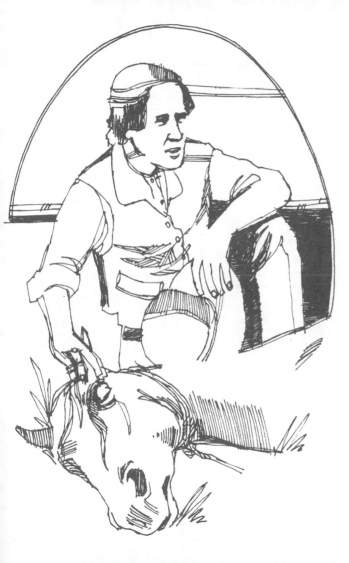

operate the ferry for subsequent Mormon travelers from Winter Quarters.

In addition, the ferry apparently could do a nice business with "gentile emigrants." By this means the men probably could "make enough to supply a large company with provisions," Clayton said.

Egan was asked by Heber C. Kimball to take a wagon, six mules and some men to collect two large logs from the nearby hills. These would be hollowed out to form canoes which could serve as the base for a heavy raft — more sturdy than the ones already in use.

Brigham's decision to continue operation of the ferry had some bearing on the eventual founding of the town of Casper, Wyo., at this site.

The ferry continued operation for a number of years and became the major reason many emigrant companies chose to cross the Platte at this point.

In 1850 Kit Carson noted there were so many wagons waiting to be ferried over that people had to register and wait their turn. Sometimes it would be a week before they could be carried across.

Tent stores sprang up to do business with the waiting crowds. In 1859 a man named Louis Guinard built a 1,000-foot toll bridge of timber, resting on stone pillars. Indians often raided the site and troops eventually were stationed there.

In 1865 a young lieutenant, Caspar Collins, was killed near the bridge with some of his men in an Indian fight. Fort Casper was named after him, although the name was misspelled.

Work progressed on heavy raft to be operated as ferry

Work was pushed by the pioneers on a heavy new raft to serve as a permanent ferry for the Platte River. It would carry both Mormon emigrants and non-Mormons — the latter a handy source of cash and supplies.

A group of men was sent into the hills to chop down and hollow out two large logs. These would serve as canoes, or pontoons, to float the raft.

Just before dark the men returned "with two good canoes, each 25 feet long and nearly finished," William Clayton said. Other men set to work cutting slabs to serve as the deck of the new ferry boat.

When the timber for the planking arrived, Brigham Young "stripped himself, went to work with all his strength . . . and made a first-rate white pine and white cottonwood raft," Thomas Bullock said.

One raft being poled across the river provided temporary excitement during the day. James Craig, the camp bugler, and William Wardsworth were on board with a wagon when Craig's pole became stuck in the river bottom and flipped him overboard.

He swam safely to shore, but Wardsworth was left

alone to battle the swift river and could not control the raft. Despite all his exertions, the raft was carried two miles downstream before he could get it to shore.

At the close of the day, not all the pioneer wagons were across the river. The number brought over "could not be easily counted on account of their being scattered all along the banks of the river for about a mile," Clayton observed.

He said the Mormon leaders had completed plans to leave some men behind to operate the ferry, taking "gentile" companies over the river for $1.50 a wagon.

"They will thus earn a good stock of provisions for themselves and be prepared to set the brethren of the next company over without delay," Clayton explained.

There was no shortage of customers. A train of 19 wagons arrived at the south side of the river and offered what seemed to be a standard price of $1.50 per wagon to be taken across. "Another camp five miles away also asked to be ferried over," Bullock said

The pioneers' leather boat was being used to carry supplies across the Platte, but even that had its problems. One group set out in the loaded boat and "filled it half full of water and came near sinking," Wilford Woodruff said.

Woodruff took time to do some hunting and downed an antelope with a lucky shot. The bullet cut the animal's throat "and he fell dead in his tracks." The hunter said it was the first antelope he had ever killed.

The town of Casper, which would one day grow up near the site of the ferry, got its real start when the Chicago and North Western Railroad extended a branch line into the area in 1888, making Casper the terminus.

Because the railroad was not a main line, growth was slow. But Casper was a wild town nonetheless. About 1900 the mayor shot and killed a man in a Main Street gunfight.

Oil was discovered in the nearby Salt Creek area in 1890 and Wyoming's first refinery was built at Casper five years later. An oil boom began in 1916 and more large refineries were constructed.

At the height of the boom the town was so crowded that garages and sheds rented for astronominal prices. Some people walked the streets all night because they had no place to sleep. Businessmen closed their shops and doctors and lawyers gave up their practices to buy, sell and trade oil stocks.

New companies were organized every day, land grabbers flourished, and even members of the President's cabinet were mixed up with shady characters. One incident, known as the Teapot Dome scandal, sent the nation's secretary of interior to prison.

But the big-spending times ended in the 1920s and the depression of the 1930s dropped the population of Casper to half what it had been at the peak.

The town has boomed again in the modern emergy era. Oil refineries stretch for miles and the Mormon ferry site is swallowed up in the city, the location known only approximately.

Missouri groups ask for help

For five days the Mormon pioneers had been stalled on the banks of the wide North Platte River. Ferrying their wagons across the swift water had proved difficult and time-consuming.

The delay was the longest halt of the entire trek. Additional complications arose from Missouri emigrant trains. They asked the pioneers to provide them with ferry service.

The emigrants preferred to use the existing Mormon ferry — even at a price — because building a raft to navigate the broad river wasn't easy, as Brigham Young found a few days earlier.

A plan was adopted for a raft which Thomas Grover, an experienced boatman, didn't think would work. When Brigham insisted on going ahead, Grover told the president he had "forgotten more about water than you ever knew," a comment which angered the leader.

Next day the raft was built and launched. Grover said it would sink and it did so almost before the words were out of his mouth. Brigham sighed, turned to him and said, "Brother Thomas, now what is your plan?"

Now, after several days of back-breaking work,

the pioneers "got our last wagon over safely, a matter of rejoicing to all the camp," William Clayton said. The heavy cannon was the last piece of equipment hauled across the river.

In the meantime, two more companies of Missourians arrived at the river and offered $1.50 in supplies for each wagon rafted across.

A contract was agreed upon with one group, but the second company offered an extra 50 cents per man (for the 10 men operating the ferry) if they could go first.

Albert P. Rockwood had made the contract with the first Missouri company "and did not like to break it," Clayton explained. But then it was pointed out that today was Stephen Markham's day to command the raft "and he had a right to take the last offer if he chose."

Using this reasoning, the ferry crew took the higher offer and went to work rafting the second party of Missourians over the swift river. They worked "all night until daylight" and moved many wagons from both companies to the opposite bank.

"The brethren suffered much working in the water for it is very cold," Howard Egan said.

In addition, pushing the raft with poles was hard labor. Each crossing carried the raft more than a half mile downstream before it reached the other side. This made it necessary to have a team of oxen pull the ferry back upstream to the landing site.

Among those taking turns working with the ferry were John S. Gleason and Levi Kendall. Most men in the company had a hand in the project one way or another.

Gleason, 28, would work in the Utah Territory as a farmer, a miner, a school teacher, an operator of a sawmill, and hold various political and military offices. He was a gifted orator. Brigham Young once said of him: "If John were as good a financier as he is a speaker, he would be a wealthy man."

Kendall, 25, a New Yorker, was adopted by Brigham after the pioneers arrived in the valley. He lived for a time in Springville, crossed the plains again to help other Mormon emigrant companies, and lived to see the 20th century. He died in 1902 at age 80.

Some of the Missourians being carried over the river on the Mormon ferry indicated plenty of other business was en route. They said ,"one thousand wagons are between Fort Laramie and this place." Wilford Woodruff noted that companies "are arriving daily at fording places along the river."

While the Mormon pioneers were getting their own people across the river the past few days, their wagons were strung out for a distance on both shores. Now Brigham ordered them drawn into the usual protective circle for the night.

Thomas Bullock said he was "glad to get to bed" that night, "having traveled 24 miles during the day after stray oxen." However, sleep was difficult, even for the exhausted, because of swarms of mosquitoes. "They are more numerous than anyplace on the route so far," he said.

Ferrying the 'gentiles' became thriving business

Although they had their own wagons safely across the North Platte River, the Mormon pioneers still were hard at work "ferrying over the gentiles," Wilford Woodruff said.

The ferry operation was exceedingly popular with non-Mormon emigrant companies and did a booming business from dawn to dark and sometimes beyond.

Another large company of emigrants arrived at the river during the day and immediately asked to become customers.

Work was still being done on a larger ferry boat which a Mormon crew would continue to operate after the others in the pioneer company pushed on to the Salt Lake Valley.

Brigham Young and the other apostles decided to postpone the departure one more day. The men would finish construction of the bigger raft and also take provisions to be paid by the Missourians for ferry service.

Bullock was aggravated when he arose in the morning after a long day chasing oxen and found the animals had wandered away again in the night. "I waded five or six miles through wet grass and found a group of stray cattle, among which were two that I tied up last night."

He previously had suffered a bad cold from getting wet feet "and this morning's jaunt will, I am afraid, bring it back," he wrote in his journal.

Bullock and Porter Rockwell visited the Missouri companies which had been rafted across the river and collected the pay due for ferry service.

From the Ashworth company they received a bushel of beans, 153 pounds of flour, one heifer and $6.55 cash; from the Peck company, five and a half bushels of meal, 916 pounds of flour, a peck of beans and some honey; from the Kerls company, 226 pounds of flour, 117 pounds of soap, six plugs of tobacco and one cow.

After this business was completed, Bullock and Rockwell were invited to breakfast by the Missourians. They were served bacon, warm biscuits, light fried biscuits, milk and coffee with sugar.

"Eating a good breakfast from a woman's cooking is a remembrance of past times and renews the desire for such times to come again," Bullock said.

While much of the camp was otherwise engaged, Clayton took time to go fishing with John Pack. He said he had good luck and "caught 65 very nice ones." They proved to be too many to carry all at once, but Thomas F. Cloward came along and helped bring the catch back to camp.

Cloward, 23, was a shoemaker and made the first shoes produced in the Salt Lake Valley just after the pioneers arrived. Heber C. Kimball's wife had worn out her footwear on the journey, so he took an old pair of boot tops and made her some shoes. He later settled in Utah County where he ran a shoemaking shop. He died in 1908.

Brigham held a council meeting and named nine men to stay at the Platte River and operate the ferry. Those selected were Thomas Grover, captain; John S. Higbee, Luke Johnson, Appleton Harmon, Edmund Ellsworth, Francis M. Pomeroy, William Empey, James Davenport and Benjamin F. Stewart.

Eric Glines also wanted to remain behind, although Brigham asked him to continue with the pioneers. Glines offered arguments to back up his desires and eventually stayed at the ferry site, much to Brigham's annoyance.

The president said that when he gave a man counsel, he did not want that man to reject the advice or bring up many arguments trying to alter it. "I will turn on my heel and leave him."

Brigham declared that the Lord is determined to establish his kingdom in the last days and "he will have a faithful and obedient people."

The Mormons had suffered much, the apostle said, but it was for their own good. "If we had not been naked and afflicted, but always been in prosperity, we would have been lifted up in pride . . . and not gathered together and built up Zion."

Across wasteland to Sweetwater River

Once across the North Platte River the pioneers moved southwest to the Sweetwater River, a three-day journey through a barren wasteland.

Just before reaching the Sweetwater they passed Independence Rock, a famous landmark. This turtle-shaped rock and nearby Devil's Gate were major points of interest for all west-bound emigrants.

Staying close to the south side of the Sweetwater, the Mormons found an underground ice spring June 24. Brigham's best horse was accidentally shot this day.

On June 25 the pioneers found many unmelted snowbanks along the route, making the nights very cold

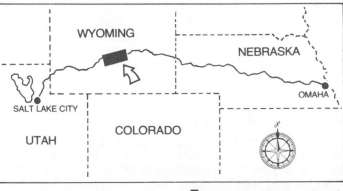

June 19-25

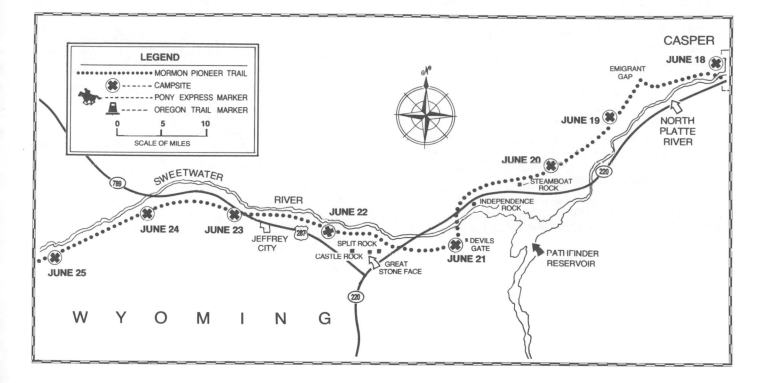

173

Pioneers moved on after river crossing

For six days the Mormon pioneers had been engaged in crossing the Platte River near what later became Casper, Wyo. But they were once more on the march.

The pioneers broke camp just before 8 a.m. in high spirits, glad to be moving again. The lengthy halt had done their cattle a world of good.

"It was remarked by several that their stock had fattened so much while stopping at the ferry that they hardly knew them," William Clayton said.

Traveling was easy for about six miles, but the trail suddenly turned up a high bluff and teams had a long, hard pull to the summit. The descent on the other side was "rough, crooked and uneven," Clayton said.

This bluff is near what is today known as Emigrant's Gap. The route of the 1847 pioneers can be followed by taking Poison Spider Road west from town.

The pioneers had been told there was a body of water supplied by a spring about 12 miles from the ferry. Clayton said they "could see the water boil up out of the mud in several places."

After watering at the spring for an hour, the company pushed on and finally camped in a barren spot surrounded by bluffs. The halt was made at 7:40 p.m. after an especially long day in which the wagon train covered 21 and one-half miles — "the longest distance we have traveled in one day since leaving

Winter Quarters," Clayton reported.

The excellent mileage was due to the good condition of the cattle, plus the desire of the pioneers to get across a barren wasteland and to the Sweetwater River as quickly as possible.

None of the pioneers were happy with the campsite. Two small streams were nearby, but bad water flowed in one of them. Grass was scanty and there was no wood.

"This camping place was the most wretched of any we have found on the way," Wilford Woodruff said. "The water tasted as though it had run through a bed of salt and sulpher. It was nauseous and horrible."

In addition to the bad water, the banks around the streams were so soft that an animal "cannot go down to drink without sinking immediately overhead in thick, filthy mud," Clayton said.

He called the area "one of the most horrid, swampy, stinking places I ever saw. A guard was posted to keep cattle away from what Norton Jacob described as "a perfect mire hole."

Jacob said the whole place had a "forbidding aspect" and was very unusual with mire holes in the mountains, frost in the summer, salt water in the streams and no wood. In addition, the mosquitoes were extremely bad.

Despite the guard, an ox became mired in the mud about 9 p.m. "He was nearly covered, but got out again" when the camp came to the rescue, Clayton said.

Hunters were out as usual and Porter Rockwell, nearly always the most successful, reported he had killed a fat buffalo two miles away. A team was sent to bring in the meat.

Lewis B. Myers, the hunter for the Robert Crow party which had joined the pioneer company at Fort Laramie, killed two buffalo, "but took only the tallow and tongues and left the rest to rot upon the ground," Clayton wrote.

Two other hunters, John Norton and Andrew Gibbons went out. "Gibbons has not been seen or heard of since," Clayton said.

This day was part of an 11-day period in which Thomas Bullock, the camp scribe, was unable to make entries in his journal. In catching up later, he said he merely kept notes during that time.

He complained it was "almost impossible for me to do justice in writing the journal, besides a team to drive, a cow to look after, fetch water, hunt and carry wood, load and unload the wagon, look after oxen, stand guard, etc."

Bullock said "almost every man in camp has more or less time to spare, but I have no time allowed to fulfill the very office I was brought along to fill, namely keep the camp journal."

He also was discouraged because of ill health which had bothered him part of the way. He spoke to Brigham Young, "who told me I had proved faithful, I should enjoy better health and this journey would prove as good as a little fortune to me."

Missouri trick fails to deter pioneers from reaching camp

Despite this being the Sabbath, the Mormon pioneers were not anxious to remain camped near the poisonous and swampy streams where they had spent the night.

Two more oxen were found almost buried to their heads in the mud around the water "and all hands appeared wishful to leave this place," William Clayton said.

Teams were hitched up and the wagons rolled out at daybreak without anyone waiting for breakfast. The first mile was rough with many steep places. Some men were sent ahead with picks and shovels to improve the route.

After covering nearly four miles, the company halted near a clear stream of water with good feed for the cattle. Most fixed themselves breakfast, using sagebrush for fires because no wood was available.

Heber C. Kimball and Ezra T. Benson were scouting ahead the evening before and rode near this place, but not close enough to discover the water.

While they had been riding slowly along, six men wrapped in blankets and giving "every appearance of being Indians" jumped up from the grass at the side of the road in an apparent attempt to frighten the two Mormons.

The six mounted horses which had been hidden nearby and rode away parallel to the road, trying to discourage Kimball and Benson from continuing.

But the two simply pushed ahead. The "Indians" then rode out of sight. The Mormon scouts reached a high ridge in time to see them enter a Missouri camp.

Kimball and Benson said they were satisfied the "Indians" were really Missourians who tried to trick the Mormons into turning back and keep them from reaching a good campsite where the Missouri wagons were halted.

"It is considered an old Missouri trick and an insult to the camp," Clayton said. "If they undertake to play Indian again, it is more than likely they will meet with Indian treatment," he added.

Aware of several Missouri companies in front of them, Brigham Young decided to "press on and crowd them up a little."

The pioneers also had some contact with a company of emigrants following them and learned that Andrew Gibbons, who was missing while hunting, had finally appeared. He had made his way to a previous campsite only to find the pioneers gone and a group of Missourians there instead.

He told the Missourians about a buffalo killed earlier and helped them bring the meat to camp, afterwards staying with them for a meal.

Meanwhile, the Mormon pioneers pushed ahead, sighting a vast range of hills with snow-covered peaks. By 8:20 p.m. the company halted, having covered 20 miles for the day.

"We had been in the hopes of reaching the Sweetwater River, but it appears we are yet some miles from it," Clayton said. He noted the entire surrounding country was "destitute of timber, not a tree to be seen or a brush larger than the wild sage which abounds in this region."

Clayton said there was "some anxiety in camp" about Wilford Woodruff and John Brown who had been sent ahead 15 miles to find a campsite and wait for the wagons. No trace has been seen of them.

"It is supposed they have fallen in with some of the companies either forward or back and have concluded to tarry with them overnight," he said.

Because of concern for the missing men, a large fire was built of sage to serve as a beacon. The camp cannon "was fired at midnight to let them know our whereabouts," Thomas Bullock wrote.

Woodruff and Brown had, in fact, joined a Missouri company ahead and had supper with them, enjoying bacon, buffalo meat, cornbread, coffee and milk. Afterwards they slept on the open ground "but did not rest well."

Woodruff said there was a great difference between the Missouri company where he spent the night and the Mormon camp. He said the Missouri men, women and children were "all cursing, swearing, generally scolding and finding fault with each other."

The Independence Rock took some scouting

"We can see a huge pile of rocks to the southwest a few miles. We have supposed this to be the rock of Independence," William Clayton wrote in his journal.

Going ahead of the rest of the pioneers, he took a closer look at the famous landmark — almost always a stopping place for wagons on the Oregon trail.

Clayton guessed the rounded rock was 400 yards long, perhaps 80 yards wide and 100 yards high "and the ascent is difficult all around." His estimates were fairly accurate, except that the rock wasn't that high.

Travelers appear to have climbed it often. He noted at the southwest corner that visitors had left "hundreds of names, both male and female . . . with red, black and some with yellow paint."

Clayton climbed to the top of the bare rock and found a number of pools of water, apparently collected during heavy rains. "Some of the pools are up to eight inches deep and taste like rain water," he said.

Getting down the sloping surface was more difficult than climbing up. The descent was "hard and slippery, with nothing to hang onto," he said.

Independence Rock was named by the first white travelers to see it in 1812 and is considered a remarkable example of geologic erosion.

Clayton noted other bare ridges of granite rock in the region and said they looked as if "giants in by-gone days had taken them in wheelbarrows of tremendous size" and simply dumped them on the ground.

The scribe thought he might have been the first Mormon to climb Independence Rock, but it actually had been visited earlier in the day by Wilford Woodruff and John Brown as they tried to find their way back to the pioneer company after spending the night with Missourians.

Both men had climbed the rounded rock and took the occasion to kneel in prayer on behalf of Brigham Young, the pioneers, their wives and families and the scattered church wherever members might be found.

As they finished their prayers the two men noticed a burial being conducted by a nearby group of emigrants for a 25-year-old woman who died in the night. The victim, they learned, was the third member of her family to die on the trail.

Standing atop Independence Rock, Woodruff and Brown sighted the approaching Mormon pioneer company and set out to rejoin their companions.

Before reaching Independence Rock the pioneer company found a bed of what they called "saleratus" — a kind of bicarbonate or leavening salt "said to raise bread equal to the best bought in eastern markets." Lorenzo Young gathered a bucketful to try out.

Norton Jacob visited a similar find at nearby Soda Springs. He described it as a pool of clear water about 400 to 500 yards in diameter with the "taste of strong lye," The shore around the pool was covered up to three inches thick with a white substance. He took a bucketful.

The pioneer company reached the Sweetwater River about noon and rejoiced after a 49-mile march across what was often a barren wasteland since leaving the Platte River.

Clayton described the river at this point as 120 feet wide and three feet or more deep. "The current is very swift and the water a little muddy, but pleasant tasting."

The pioneers forded the Sweetwater, the first of many times they would cross the winding stream in coming days. They stopped briefly at Independence Rock to put up a wooden marker with the date and distance from Fort Laramie (175 miles).

A few miles further and the pioneers reached the Devil's Gate, another Oregon trail landmark. The gate was a chasm 330 feet deep with the Sweetwater River running between the cliffs for about 200 yards.

The river at the bottom of the chasm narrowed to less than 50 feet "dashing furiously against huge fragments of rocks" and making a roar "which can be heard plainly in the camp," Clayton wrote.

The pioneers camped a short distance beyond Devil's Gate and many of them walked back to get a better view. Thomas Bullock called it "a romantic spot." Many agreed with his description.

Alone on the prairie with broken axle, Harriet Young got help

The pioneers had been making very good progress the past week or so — about 20 miles per day despite increasingly rugged country.

After breaking camp at 7:20 a.m., the company crossed three small creeks within a few miles of each other. The last stream was only a brook two feet wide, but it proved too much for the wagon of Lorenzo Young.

While jolting over the banks of this small obstacle, Young's wagon broke an axle.

The Youngs had fallen behind the rest of the wagon train by nearly a mile because of problems with their animals when the accident struck them.

"One of our axletrees broke on the naked prairie without a stick of timber or anyone to help us," Harriet Young, the wife of Lorenzo, said.

Young rode after the rest of the company to get help, leaving his wife with the wagon. "I was alone and felt somewhat lonesome," she said, "but Brother Henry (William Henrie) came back and stayed with me."

Henrie searched the prairie and found a piece of wood. The rear of the wagon was unloaded and raised up. The wood was lashed to the broken axle "and we started for camp."

One of the Missouri companies following the Mormon pioneers had come up to the stranded Young wagon and helped out by taking the load from the damaged wagon into their own.

Despite the distrust and suspicions between the Mormons and the Missourians, they often helped each other when there was trouble along the trail.

Henrie, 47, who went to the aid of Mrs. Young, was to become a leading explorer in the Utah territory. He helped colonize several areas, sent his sons on missions and pledged his goods to the poor.

In 1856 he was called on a mission to Panaca in what is now Nevada. Perhaps feeling he already had sacrificed much, he refused to go. His wife and sons went without him and suffered extreme hardship for the next six years, finally moving to Panguitch.

Mrs. Henrie became a school teacher, the first Relief Society president in Panguitch and established a cooperative mercantile store.

Henrie stayed alone at his home in Bountiful where he died in 1883. His will left all his earthly goods to the church to be used as the leaders saw fit.

While Young was having trouble with his wagon, the rest of the pioneer company went ahead until the noon halt. Brigham Young then turned back to aid his brother, but learned he was coming with the Missouri group.

Brigham told the pioneers to get moving so they wouldn't be overtaken by the Missouri company. "However, they passed us," William Clayton said.

The Missourians told the pioneers of a death back at the Mormon ferry on the Platte River. They said an emigrant tried to swim his horse across the river and fell off. He was drowned in the swift water.

After camping that night, Thomas Bullock was called to guard duty, an assignment that caused him some bitterness because again he couldn't write in his journal.

"If I must guard, the camp must do their own writing," he said, referring to his job as scribe — a task he was having trouble doing properly.

"I have too many commanders. It is hard for me to do everything," he grumbled in his journal later.

A grave on the trail brought solemn reverie

Shortly after breaking camp this day, the Mormon pioneers found a grave and wooden marker to the left of the trail where a woman had died in July, 1846.

The sight of the grave caused a number of solemn thoughts by William Clayton.

"Some of the numerous emigrants, who probably started with a view to spend the remainder of their days in Oregon, fell by the way and their remains had to be left by their friends far from the place of destination," he wrote.

"I felt a renewed anxiety that the Lord will kindly preserve the lives of my family, that they may be permitted to gather to the future home of the saints," he said.

"And when their days are numbered, their remains may be deposited at the feet of the servants of God, rather than be left far away in a wild country," he said.

For some Mormon emigrants, an unmarked grave in the wilderness was to be their fate.

Not far from where the pioneers traveled this day was the site of a major tragedy in 1856. A handcart company of 576 English emigrants headed by Howard Martin was delayed and caught in early winter storms. More than 100 died in nine days and were buried in a trench. The survivors were rescued by a wagon train rushed from Salt Lake City.

The site of the tragedy has since become part of the Sun Ranch. Martin's Cove, a hollow at the foot of some cliffs where the emigrants sought shelter, is invisible from the road. Cows now graze and drink there.

Not far to the west was where the James G. Willie handcart company also came to grief the same winter. Their supplies were nearly exhausted when the 500 emigrants were trapped in blizzards and sub-zero weather. Dozens died and were buried in mass graves.

The Mormon pioneers of 1847 struggled through sand at the foot of rocky hills near what is now Jeffrey City and Highway 287. Much of the pioneer route has since been blocked by a uranium mill. Portions of the trail are under water due to construction of a tailings pond.

Those parts of the trail still accessible were traveled in 1978 by a four wheel drive vehicle and the powerful machine nearly became stuck in the sand, giving more appreciation of Clayton's description that the area was "extremely sandy and heavy traveling."

Despite the rugged trail, the pioneers made 17 miles before camping on the banks of the Sweetwater River about 6:20 p.m. Two Missouri companies were settled within a mile to the west.

The Missourians said one of their men went ahead a few days earlier to scout the route to famed South Pass, a wide valley leading into the Rocky Mountains.

"We are given to understand we have got a long distance to travel without grass or water," Clayton said.

The Mormon campsite offered "plenty of grass on the river banks, but no wood. There are some dry buffalo chips and sagebrush which answer tolerably well for cooking," he said.

Except for the river banks, the countryside was devoid of grass, "perfectly barren except for the wild sage, which abounds. But there is scarcely a blade of grass to be seen," Clayton said.

After the pioneers were settled in camp, Burr Frost, the blacksmith, set up his forge. He set some wagon tires and repaired the wheels of wagons for one of the Missourians.

Other members of the camp ate dinner, tended their stock, bathed in the river and gazed at the mountains in the distance — rugged obstacles they knew they must penetrate in the coming weeks.

"All the mountains that are in sight are covered with snow," Howard Egan said. For the Mormons, most of them from New England, the mountains were more imposing than anything they had seen before.

June 24
THURSDAY

Ice spring discovered 18 inches under prairie

Wagon trains on the Oregon trail continued to leapfrog each other at every chance. Those in front had first choice at the best camping places.

Brigham Young asked the Mormon pioneers to make an early and quiet start this day to get ahead of several Missouri companies camped a short distance away.

"We started at 6:30 a.m. without the sound of the bugle so as not to give notice to the camps ahead,"

Norton Jacob said. "But they got off first," despite the Mormon efforts.

After setting out, Edson Whipple reported that two of his oxen were missing. Howard Egan began a search and soon "discovered two oxen lying down in a ravine near the river."

During the morning march the company found what Jacob called "a great curiosity" — an ice spring buried under the prairie turf. The ice was found when the pioneers dug in a bog where sulpher water boiled out of the ground.

Eight inches under the turf the diggers came upon a pool of strong-smelling water with a nasty alkalai taste.

But about a foot under the water was a layer of ice " as clear as I ever saw and good tasting," William Clayton said. The four-inch thick ice was broken with axes and shovels and passed to members of the company. They enjoyed eating it like a frozen treat.

A supply of potash was discovered nearby which some of the pioneers collected to raise bread with. Also near the ice spring was a supply of salt of such purity that the pioneers were able to use it directly on their food, without refining it first.

Later in the day the Mormon wagon train caught up with one of the Missouri companies ahead of them. They passed the 10 wagons while the emigrants were having a rest stop. But the pioneers made camp early, about 3:30 p.m., at a bend in the Sweetwater River.

The early halt was necessary because the teams were exhausted, hungry and thirsty. The day had been warm, good water was not available and grass had been lacking until the river was reached. Despite the poor conditions and the early halt, the pioneers traveled nearly 18 miles.

They didn't stop to rest the animals for the last 13 miles because there was no water for them to drink.

The campsite was attractive with dense clumps of willows for fuel and feed. The river was about 50 feet wide near the camp and the water was described as "clear and very cool."

Just before dark, John Holman was herding Brigham's best horse toward camp. He jabbed at the animal with his rifle to keep it moving in the right direction. As he did so, the gun caught in his clothing and fired.

The bullet hit the horse in the stomach and the suffering animal died that night after staggering back to camp.

Jacob said the horse was "the best in camp" and cost $150, an enormous sum in those days.

Brigham was much sorrowed over the loss, "but attaches no blame to John, who seems grieved very much," Clayton said. Perhaps Brigham's calm could be explained by the fact that, at first, he thought the accidental shooting was something worse.

Just after the mishap, Holman, 19, came running to Brigham, shouting: "President Young, I have just shot old John." Brigham became quite excited and cried, "John who?"

"Why, old John, your horse," Holman answered.

"Oh," said the president, with a sigh of relief. He thought for an instant that it was John Greene who had been shot.

At sundown in camp that night, Jacob looked toward the Wind River Mountains and wrote in his journal that the snow-capped peaks "present a scene majestic, grand and imposing."

Thomas Bullock, who had been sick all day and unable to arise from his wagon, was given a blessing by Willard Richards and Wilford Woodruff.

Hot days, cold nights and snow in some places

Before the pioneers could get on the road this day, they had to separate their cattle from a herd belonging to a nearby camp of Missouri emigrants.

The animals had gotten mixed up during the night and had to be sorted out by the owners.

The weather was cool as the march began. A wind from the north blew clouds of dust which filled the wagons "so that the brethren were nearly choked."

Just after leaving camp, the pioneers forded the Sweetwater River and made their way through several hills.

William Clayton noticed "a good place to camp" on the banks of the river just a few miles from the previous night's stopping place. It was Clayton's job to notice such things. He was charged with preparing a guide for Mormon companies still to come, advising about possible campsites, watering places and distances between these places.

A short distance from this potential campsite, the pioneers were forced to climb a high sandy ridge blocking their path. It was either that or ford the river two more times. The descent down the other side was "very steep and unpleasant," Clayton said.

Albert Rockwood, one of the wagon train's two division commanders (Stephen Markham was the other), studied the ridge and concluded that "one hour's labor for 100 men" would result in the foot of the ridge being dug down enough to allow wagons to go around it without fording the river.

However, the pioneers didn't have the time to make this kind of major improvement. They pushed on and left the job for some other company.

At 11:30 a.m. the Mormons crossed a small creek and halted for a mid-day rest. The campsite offered excellent grass and plenty of wood. It was surrounded by high hills.

Thomas Bullock, who was feeling better after being sick all the previous day, noted many different kinds of flowers as the wagons moved forward again. He also saw wild strawberries and gooseberries.

As the wagons climbed hills and ridges, the pioneers found snowbanks in shady ravines. Nights were cold "with so much snow around," Clayton said. "It requires considerable clothing to keep comfortable, but in the middle of the day it is equally hot."

Several of the men "amused themselves by snowballing each other," he said. Some of the snow was carried back to camp and Bullock was given a handful, "which I ate — quite a treat for the anniversary of my wedding day."

Albert Carrington explored one of the ridges quite carefully and told the pioneers there was "every appearance of a rich lead mine in the place."

Carrington, 34, was an experienced topographer and surveyor and had once engaged in lead mining in Wisconsin. In the Salt Lake Valley he would aid U.S. government geographical surveys.

One more high ridge confronted the pioneers this day. Wilford Woodruff called it the longest and highest hill the company had climbed since the start of the trek. Fortunately, the descent down the other side was more gradual.

Near the bottom the wagons had to cross a swampy area "quite difficult for the teams to get over without help," Clayton said. The swamp was caused by a number of small streams converging on a creek.

The pioneers made camp near the creek, which was "clear and cold." Some places along the bank had ice several inches thick. This was chopped out and brought to camp.

The ice was used by the pioneers to make their butter cold and hard. Bread was baked and served with the cold butter, "a perfect feast for the wilderness," Bullock said.

"One of the gentile companies is camped about a mile below us, making the third company we have passed lately," Clayton said. "It is the intention to keep ahead of them and have the advantage of good feed and camping grounds."

South Pass, broad gateway to the mountains

The Mormon pioneers reached and crossed the Sweetwater River early this week and entered South Pass — the broad gateway to the Rocky Mountains.

While in the famous pass, they crossed the Continental Divide where rivers begin to flow to the west instead of the east.

On June 28 the pioneers met Jim Bridger, the well-known frontiersman and he spent the night with them. Most of the talk was about the Salt Lake Valley and its possibilities as a home for the Mormons.

The pioneers spent June 30 and July 1 crossing the Green River. Once on the opposite shore they were in what was loosely defined as "California territory."

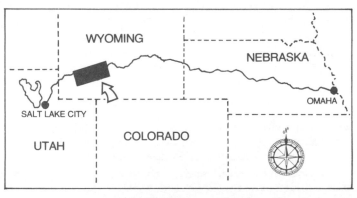

June 26-July 2

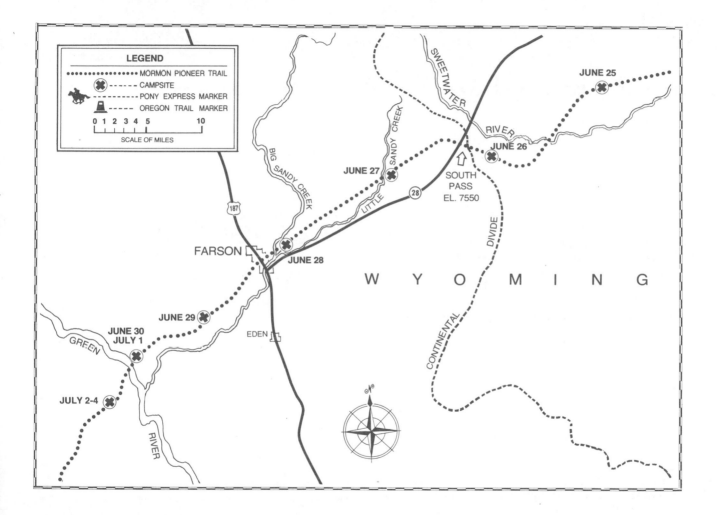

Company moved up broad South Pass plain

As the Mormon pioneers marched into the 25-mile-wide plain that is South Pass, they neared the Continental Divide where waters flow to the west instead of east.

We are evidently at the east foot of the pass,'' William Clayton said as the day's journey began. Sometimes it was hard to tell.

The ascent on the broad plain is so gradual that many travelers crossed the Continental Divide without being aware of it. The pioneers wanted to pinpoint the exact place and sent Orson Pratt and others ahead with a barometer.

South Pass was discovered in 1812, but wasn't used by early trappers until the 1820s. The first wagons were taken over it in 1832. In the two decades from the 1840s to the 1860s, perhaps 300,000 persons used the pass, churning up the turf and wearing broad tracks which can still be seen from the air.

The pioneers' day began bitter cold. "Ice was in the water buckets and milk in one wagon froze solid," Thomas Bullock reported. Banks of snow, six to 10 feet deep, lay in ravines and shady areas.

Several times during the day the pioneers forded streams where the water was described as "clear and cold." Most of the creeks had luxurious grass and

willows growing along the banks. They were considered superb campgrounds.

The wagons climbed a series of rolling hills and the company had "a pleasant view of the surrounding country," Clayton said. Everyone commented on the lack of trees and the snow-covered Wind River Mountains to the north.

At noon the group halted on the main branch of the Sweetwater River, which soon would be left behind. Two stories exist as to how the river got its name.

One tale said early trappers named it "sweet water" compared to the brackish streams lying between there and the Platte River to the east. A second explanation is that French trappers once lost a pack mule loaded with sugar in the river.

During their noon stop the pioneers used a deep snowbank "to cool our milk," Norton Jacob said. Some of the young people in the company cavorted in the drifts and had a snowball fight.

"Soon after we halted, Eric Glines came up," having left the Mormon ferry at the Platte River crossing four days before, Clayton said. Glines had stayed behind to help operate the ferry, despite orders from Brigham Young to accompany the main company. He had little to say about his sudden reappearance.

Glines said he camped one night alone on the trail and the rest of the nights he stayed with Missouri companies.

"He does not give any reason why he followed us," but he evidently decided to repent and obey counsel, rather than continue "obstinate and rebellious," Clayton said.

Glines reported that the level of the Platte River had dropped 18 inches since the pioneers crossed. As a result, the Mormon ferry was moved eight miles downstream.

After a two-hour halt, the wagons moved forward again. The pioneers were unable to find a stream marked on the Fremont maps in their possession. They had veered away from the Sweetwater River and stopped for a time while scouts went ahead to locate water.

Brigham, who led the scouts, came back and ordered the company to change course to the northwest where they encountered the Sweetwater once more and made camp.

Pratt and his party had been sent ahead earlier to find the exact point of the Continental Divide, but they failed to return by dark. Others were sent out to look for them.

The would-be rescuers returned shortly to report that Pratt and his men were staying with some people from Oregon who were traveling east on the trail.

Pratt's group had an enjoyable time reading newspapers from California and Oregon provided by their hosts. Being on the prairie and out of touch with the world, the pioneers often were starved for news.

Based on reports from Pratt, "it is a certainty that we are yet two miles from the dividing ridge of South Pass," which separates the waters of the Atlantic from those of the Pacific, Clayton said.

June 27

Continental Divide was crossed on Sunday

Three years earlier, on June 27, the Mormon Prophet Joseph Smith and his brother Hyrum were killed by a mob at Carthage, Ill. That event was much on the minds of the pioneers this Sunday.

"It was the general feeling to spend the day in fasting and prayer, but the gentile companies being close in our rear and feed scarce, it was considered necessary to keep ahead of them," William Clayton said.

"Our minds have reverted back to the scenes at Carthage jail and it is a gratification that we have so far prospered in our endeavors to get from under the grasp of our enemies," he wrote.

Shortly after getting under way, the pioneer company crossed the Continental Divide, as calculated by Orson Pratt, and reached a place called Pacific Springs where "we have the satisfaction of seeing the current run west instead of east," Clayton said.

Wilford Woodruff drank from a muddy creek and "for the first time in my life tasted water running into the Pacific."

At Pacific Springs the pioneers met a group of 10 Oregonians headed east, carrying mail to the states. The men also had a string of pack mules loaded with furs and skins. Pratt had spent the night with these trappers.

Some of those in the pioneer company had letters which they gave the Oregonians to take back east, a typical informal method of getting mail around the West.

One of the Oregonians, a veteran mountain man named Moses Harris, decided to stay with the Mormons for a short time. He was seeking to hire out his services to emigrants headed for the Oregon-California country where he had trapped and explored for the past 25 years.

"He appears to be a man of intelligence," Clayton said. Harris gave the pioneers a gift of six Oregon newspapers from the month of February.

He also handed over several issues of the California Star, published by Samuel Brannan, a Mormon who took a boat load of church members around the cape of South America from New York to California.

Brannan, who presided over branches of the church in the eastern states, was instructed in 1846 to charter a ship to California for Mormons in the New York area. He was to take along a printing press used for publishing a church paper in New York. A total of 230 Mormons sailed in the ship "Brooklyn" on Feb. 4, 1846, and landed in California July 31 after a long detour to Hawaii.

The emigrants settled at first in a Mexican village called Yerba Buena, where they about equalled the number of Mexican residents. The name of the village was later changed to San Francisco.

Harris, the mountain man, talked at length with the Mormon leaders about the country ahead, especially the Salt Lake Valley, but his reports weren't encouraging.

"He spoke unfavorably of the Salt Lake country for a settlement," Woodruff said.

"From his description," Clayton wrote, "we have little chance to hope for even a moderately good country anywhere in those regions. He speaks of the whole region as being destitute of timber and vegetation, except the wild sage."

The most favorable account by Harris was about "a small region near the Bear River Mountains called the Cache Valley" where trappers hid their robes and furs from Indians. "He said this was a good place to winter cattle," Clayton wrote.

Despite the discouraging reports, "we feel we shall know best by going ourselves," Clayton said. "The reports of travelers are so contradictory it is impossible to know the truth without going to prove it," he added.

After traveling just over 15 miles for the day, the pioneers made camp on the banks of a small stream, which contained only a trickle of water. "But by digging and tramping on the sand, sufficient can be obtained to supply a large company," Clayton said.

An unexpected visit with Jim Bridger

In the afternoon the Mormon pioneers had an unexpected meeting with a famous man they had planned to visit later during their trek to the Salt Lake Valley.

The pioneers encountered Jim Bridger on the trail as he was headed for Fort Laramie and the well-known frontiersman spent several hours describing the area around the Great Salt Lake.

Before meeting with Bridger, the company took leave of Moses Harris, a veteran mountain man and trader who had spent the night with them.

Many in the group traded goods with Harris for the material known as buckskin and also for shirts, pants and jackets made of the same skins. "He sells them high," William Clayton observed.

The buckskin was priced at $1.50 to $2 and pants were $3 to $4, prices which discouraged some of the pioneers. The trader was willing to take rifles, powder, lead, caps or calico in exchange, but "he puts his own price on both sides and it is difficult to obtain even a fair trade," Clayton said.

After leaving Harris, the pioneers trudged across an empty landscape until they reached the Little Sandy, a stream ranging from 20 to 45 feet wide. By 5:45 p.m. all wagons had forded the obstacle and shortly after the march was resumed, the Mormons met the east-bound Bridger.

When told that the pioneers had intended to stop at Fort Bridger to make inquiries about the country, the famed frontiersman asked them to make camp and said he would answer their questions.

Bridger, 43, gave a long account of the country around the Great Salt Lake, but Clayton wasn't too impressed. He wrote it was impossible to get a correct idea of the route ahead or the geography from "the very imperfect and irregular way he gave his descriptions." Bridger apparently had been drinking and this probably affected his talk.

The pioneers first showed Bridger the Fremont maps they had been using and he quickly dismissed them as being of little value.

Wilford Woodruff reported that Bridger said "he was ashamed of the maps of Fremont, for he (Fremont) knows nothing about the country, only the plain traveled road."

Bridger told the pioneers they couldn't follow the Green River because of the rugged mountain country surrounding the river for hundreds of miles.

The visitor wasn't as pessimistic about the Salt Lake region as Harris had been, although he said the great desert "is perfectly barren." He suggested Utah Lake as the best place in the region to settle because there is good timber, plenty of grass and rich land.

Bridger said there were two drawbacks to the region. One was the Indians. He described tham as "a bad people" who would rob or abuse lone travelers or even kill them. He said parties of armed men were in no danger.

The Indlans abound more on the west of the mountains near the Salt Lake, "but we have no need to fear them for we could drive the whole of them (out)in 24 hours," Clayton reported Bridger as saying. "He would not kill them. He would make slaves of them,' Clayton added.

The other problem in the area is the "excessive cold nights" which "he thinks would prevent the growth of corn," although the soil is good, the scribe said.

Bridger praised the country as rich in gold, silver, coal, lead, copper and other metals.

"He thinks Utah Lake is the best country in the vicinity of Salt Lake and the country is still better the farther south we go until reaching the desert about 200 miles south of Utah Lake," Clayton said.

"Such was the information we obtained from Mr. Bridger," he wrote, "but we shall know more about things and have a better understanding when we have seen the country ourselves."

Bridger and two men with him had supper with Brigham Young and spent the night in the Mormon camp.

Twenty-four miles in thirteen and one-half hours

One of the longest days of the trek thus far was recorded this day by the Mormon pioneers, both in miles traveled and the hours until camp was made at night.

They broke camp at 7:40 a.m. and put nearly seven miles behind them in the first three hours. The trail was "a good road through barren land," William Clayton said.

Before leaving in the morning, the pioneers bid goodbye to Jim Bridger, the famous frontiersman who spent the night with them. He had described the Salt Lake Valley and surrounding regions in some detail.

As they parted, Bridger cautioned that it "would not be prudent to bring a large population into the desert basin until we ascertained whether grain would grow,' Wilford Woodruff reported.

As a token of appreciation for the information he provided, the pioneers gave Bridger a free pass for the Mormon ferry back on the Platte River which he would have to cross to reach Fort Laramie.

The pioneer wagons made the first stop of the day on the banks of Big Sandy Creek. A later emigrant guide would warn that from Big Sandy to the Green River in a straight line is 35 miles and "there is not a drop of water."

To avoid this problem the pioneers tried to stay close to the Big Sandy, following it to the southwest, rather than heading straight across open country known as Sublette's Cutoff. Most travelers took the same southern route as the Mormons.

During the afternoon the company traveled over a generally good road, but by 6:15 p.m., a time they normally would have stopped and made camp, they were still in barren country. Brigham Young returned from a scouting expedition and said they must go another six miles to have feed for the cattle.

"He directed the brethren to quicken their pace as we have a long distance yet to a good campground," Thomas Bullock said. The route became worse due to fragments of rock covering the ground, but the weather cooled, "which favored the teams considerably," Clayton said.

Finally at 9:05 p.m. "we found ourselves on the banks of the river again," Clayton said. The camp was formed by moonlight. There was plenty of grass for cattle, but no wood. The pioneers gathered willows for fires.

The company had been on the road for 13 and a half hours. The wagons covered nearly 24 miles, "the greatest day's journey since leaving Winter Quarters," Clayton said.

As they traveled in the afternoon, the pioneers passed a place to become known later as Simpson's Hollow. It was here 10 years later (Oct. 6, 1857, during the Utah War) that Mormon guerrilla leader Lot Smith and 43 of his men would ambush a U.S. Army supply train led by Capt. Simpson and burn all of the wagons. Just the day before, another 52 wagons were destroyed in a similar raid.

As the pioneers made camp, they noted that more men had fallen victim to a mysterious fever which began sweeping through the company three days ago.

"They generally begin with a headache, succeeded by violent fever and some go delirious for a while," Clayton said. Woodruff wrote that John S. Fowler was the latest to become ill. "He complained bitterly at the jar of the wagon and finally was out of his head and wild."

Fowler, 37, recovered, as did the others. After he reached the Salt Lake Valley he found life a little too tough and couldn't see much chance it would improve. He pulled out and went to California where he thought there was more opportunity. His fate is unknown.

Cause of the fever baffled the pioneers. Some blamed it on the alkali picked up en route and used in the baking of bread. "It is considered poisonous," Clayton said.

Others thought the fevers might come from the clouds of alkali dust kicked up by the teams and wagons. Still others blamed the change in climate.

"There has been no case considered dangerous yet, nor any of long duration," Clayton wrote.

In camp that night Bullock had his usual complaint about his inability to get any writing done. "I was sent out to gather dandelions — this instead of writing a journal," he grumbled.

June 30
WEDNESDAY

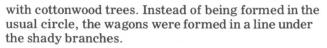

A welcome sight:
the Green River's shady bank

Sickness continued to affect the Mormon pioneer company, but the trek went ahead despite a number being down with "mountain fever."

The ailing were laid in wagons — a jolting ride which didn't do anything to make them feel better. In fact, it may have delayed recovery.

The pioneers left camp at 8:15 a.m. on a hot morning and enjoyed fairly easy traveling, even though the route was sandy and "filled the wagons with dust," William Clayton said.

About three hours later, after covering eight miles, the company reached a welcome resting place — the banks of the Green River. The stream was lined with cottonwood trees. Instead of being formed in the usual circle, the wagons were formed in a line under the shady branches.

The Green River had a greenish color from the slate in the stream bed, but did not have its name because of this. It actually was named after an early trader in the area. At this point the river was about 250 feet wide "and altogether too deep to be forded," Clayton noted.

The only way across was with rafts. The trees along the river were too small to make heavy canoes, so Brigham Young ordered two small rafts built. The work was begun soon after the mid-day meal.

A company of Missourians ahead of the Mormon

wagons had built a raft at the river for their own use, but after crossing "they set their raft adrift, lest it should benefit us," Norton Jacob said.

The campsite on the river was attractive. Clayton saw "many patches of wild apple trees" and "rose bushes abound, bearing pretty roses." Grass for the animals was plentiful, but not as much as had been described by other travelers.

While engaged in building the rafts, the pioneers were pleasantly surprised when Samuel Brannan, a former leader of Mormon branches in the eastern U.S., came riding into camp.

Brannan had taken a boatload of church members from New York to California the previous year and settled them in the area around San Francisco. Knowing that Brigham was en route overland, he had come 800 miles to meet him.

Brannan left San Francisco April 4, 1847, and made his way with two companions through the mountains. At one point he passed the last campground of the ill-fated Donner party. Skulls and bones were scattered in every direction, he said.

The Mormon pioneers rejoiced at the sight of Brannan, although they would reject his pleas to come to California. "We were truly glad to see him," Wilford Woodruff said.

Brannan said church members making the trip by boat from New York suffered 11 deaths en route. Now they were settled in a rich land and were "putting in wheat and preparing for us," Woodruff said.

A report also was given on the Mormon Battalion which had finished history's longest infantry march. They were at "Pueblo de Los Angeles," Brannan said and were in good health, although it had been a hard journey for them.

He brought about 11 issues of the California Star, printed on a press shipped from New York. Brannan stayed with Brigham's pioneer company for much of the rest of the trip, but did not enter the Salt Lake Valley with the party. He eventually was sent back along the trail to meet members of the Mormon Battalion sick detachment traveling just a few days behind Brigham's company.

When it became apparent the Salt Lake settlement would be permanent, Brannan went back to California and parted company with the Mormons when the gold rush erupted. He became famous and wealthy and one of the most important men in the San Francisco area. But his fortune later dwindled away and he died in poverty.

Toward evening a storm blew in from the west. No rain fell in the pioneer camp, but the howling wind was troublesome. It continued to blow the next day and made efforts to cross the Green River very difficult.

Several men went fishing downstream and "caught some nice fish," Clayton said. However, the mosquitoes were so bad that most of the pioneer company could not stand to be out in the open.

Thomas Bullock complained that he had a number of maps to copy and notes to make in his journal, "and yet I was sent out on guard." His constant grievance was that people always gave him other duties and kept him from writing in his journal.

High winds forced halt to river crossing

Work on two rafts was completed early in the day and the pioneers began to ferry their wagons over the Green River. The river was swollen by runoff and the water was 12 to 15 feet deep.

Both rafts were equipped with oars and rudders, but the crossing of the 180-yard wide stream was hampered by strong winds, The pioneers also were short-handed because of a mysterious illness taking its toll in camp.

"We were obliged to desist (ferrying the wagons) because of high winds. Only 14 wagons were gotten over," Thomas Bullock said. Most of the cattle swam over, but with some difficulty.

Those wagons safely on the southwest bank were formed into a separate camp amidst plentiful cottonwood trees.

One of the newly-built rafts "did not work well," according to Howard Egan. The wood quickly became water-logged and too heavy for safety. It was hauled out of the river and cut into pieces. Some of the timber was used in construction of a substitute raft.

About 15 men in the camp were "taken sick with the fever," Wilford Woodruff said. Among them was William Clayton, whose usual detailed journal entries dropped to almost nothing as he suffered "violent aching in my head and limbs."

The raging fever, which made its victims delirious, "is said to be common to emigrants coming from the snowy mountains to the plains and valleys where it is hot," Woodruff noted.

A change in temperature was not really the cause of the sickness, but the fever was never really identified. Modern doctors think it might have been tick fever, but they are not certain.

Bullock was sick in bed, but from what he called "overexertion," rather than fever. He was treated by "drinking tea and chewing ginger root." Willard Richards, who laid claim to some medical training, ordered Bullock to rest in his wagon.

Samuel Brannan, who had joined the pioneers yesterday after a long trip from California, talked continually of the coast area and extolled its virtues. He said "Capt. Sutter was very friendly and wished us to come and settle near him."

This "Capt. Sutter" apparently was John Augustus Sutter, a Swiss emigrant who settled in California and talked his way into a large land grant from the Mexican government, using charm and a phony captain's title.

It was this same Sutter who would one day hire James W. Marshall to build a sawmill on his land. Discharged members of the Mormon Battalion who found work at the mill discovered gold in the river.

That was the beginning of the famous California gold rush in 1849. Swarms of gold seekers poured across Sutter's land, ruined his holdings and finally sent him into poverty.

Brannan was back in California when news of the gold strike broke. He promptly left his church responsibilities and headed for the American River where he established a little one-room store.

He reportedly did a tremendous business, selling anything on credit, except whiskey, for which he demanded payment in gold. He was soon on his way to amassing a fortune. Brannan remained estranged from the church the rest of his life.

While the rest of the nation went wild over the stories of gold, Brigham Young would order the Mormons to stay on their farms and raise food. For the most part, they obeyed, although they could have beaten nearly everyone else to the gold fields.

Homeward-bound members of the Mormon Battalion presented a strange contrast during the gold rush — heading east toward Utah while thousands of gold seekers frantically pushed west to California from all over the nation.

But while Brannan was in the 1847 pioneer camp, all this was a couple of years in the future and Sutter was just a rather well-to-do man known for his hospitality towards Americans wanting to settle in the new land of California.

Despite Brannan's urgings and the less-than-optimistic reports on conditions around the Salt Lake Valley, the Mormon pioneers were not swayed from their goal.

After crossing the Green River with his wagon, Woodruff rejoiced that, "we are now in California." In those days, everything west of the Continental Divide was loosely considered as being in the California-Oregon territory.

Brannan extolled advantages of California

Shrieking winds of the previous day had died down and the Mormon pioneers were able to resume rafting their wagons across the Green River.

One of the rafts had become waterlogged and a replacement was now put into service. Only 14 wagons had crossed yesterday, but before this day was finished, another 47 wagons were on the opposite bank of the river.

William Clayton, one of those stricken by a mysterious fever, got over the river about noon, ''but remained very sick'' and wrote only a few lines in his journal.

Members of the Twelve with the company held a council in a grove of trees. A decision was made to send several men back along the trail to act as guides for other Mormon companies known to have left Winter Quarters.

Brannan met again with the camp leadership and gave more glowing descriptions of California. According to Thomas Bullock, he talked of barley ''with no hull on it,'' oats growing wild, ''clover as high as a horse's belly,'' wild horses scattered all over, geese in abundance and salmon in the rivers.

He praised the weather as pleasant and mild, with plenty of rain seven months a year and a comfortable dry season lasting five months. He tried his best to convince Brigham Young to bring the pioneers all the way to the West Coast.

But the Mormons weren't looking for a paradise which would attract others. They wanted to be left alone to build their own kind of community without interference.

Mormon settlements would one day be founded in California, but only as outposts on the far-flung State of Deseret which the pioneers hoped to establish — an empire covering nearly a third of the present United States.

The major Mormon town in California would be San Bernardino, but even though it became a thriving and prosperous community, it lasted only six years as a Mormon center.

In 1851 Brigham granted the wishes of some church members to colonize an area in southern California (the gold rush was in the north).

On March 22 of that year, 500 persons and 150 wagons assembled at Peteetneet (now Payson) and set forth under the leadership of Amasa Lyman and Charles C. Rich.

After arriving in California they purchased 80,000 to 100,000 acres of an area known as the San Bernardino Ranch, paying $77,000. A town was quickly established and more people came, including non-Mormons. More land was acquired at considerable sacrifice.

By 1856 there were 2,000 Mormons in San Bernardino, but persecution was growing and there was trouble with adventurers, land sharks and politicians in the area.

When Brigham's call came in 1857 to abandon the town and help defend the mountain headquarters in the Utah War, most of the settlers willingly pulled out.

The land which had been acquired at such financial sacrifice and all the buildings and improvements were sold at a loss or simply left behind. The experiment of creating Mormon settlements in California had ended.

Brannan couldn't convice Brigham to accept California as a goal and also had some other people in the 1847 pioneer camp unhappy with him because he refused to part with some books.

Brannan had brought a large box of church books with him, for some reason. They included copies of the Doctrine and Covenants, Orson Pratt's Almanac, and copies of the Book of Mormon. But Brannan "refused to sell one, although he had more than 50 applications," Thomas Bullock said.

On instructions from Brigham, Bullock planted several patches of corn, something he had done at several places along the way to see if it would grow in the wilderness.

Those not engaged in ferrying wagons across the Green River enjoyed the camp, mostly because of the trees.

Being in the shade of trees "was a real treat, I assure you, they being the only ones seen for a hundred miles," said Harriet Young, the wife of Lorenzo Young. Harriet, who had been sickly much of the trip, did not fall victim to the fever which had felled so many of the others in camp.

Through some dry and desolate country

After crossing the Green River and resting their teams for a few days, the pioneers headed south through dry and desolate country. They marched 20 miles before water was found for a campsite.

The camp was just north of what is now the Little America Motel, a major truck and motorist stop on I-80.

Continuing their long marches, the pioneers arrived at Fort Bridger July 7, remaining there two days to repair wagons and do some shopping.

On July 9 they left the fort, embarking on the last 100-mile leg of the long trek. It was here they also left the Oregon trail and once more were alone.

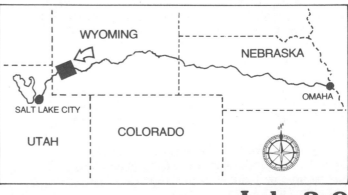

July 3-9

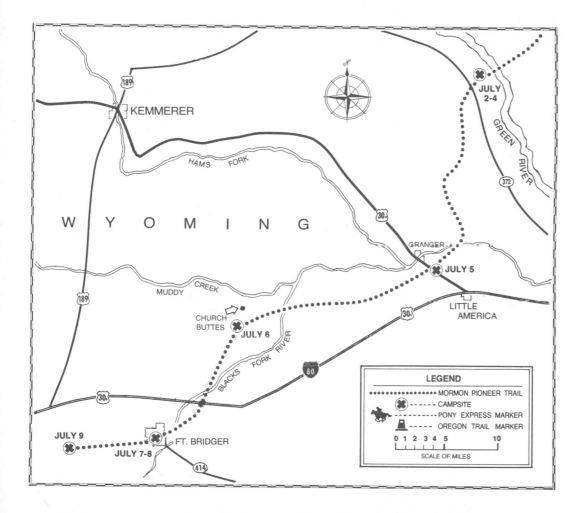

KEMMERER

HAMS FORK

W Y O M I N G

MUDDY CREEK

CHURCH BUTTES

JULY 6

JULY 2-4

GREEN RIVER

GRANGER

JULY 5

LITTLE AMERICA

BLACKS FORK RIVER

JULY 9

JULY 7-8

FT. BRIDGER

LEGEND

.... MORMON PIONEER TRAIL

----- CAMPSITE

----- PONY EXPRESS MARKER

----- OREGON TRAIL MARKER

0 1 2 3 4 5   10

SCALE OF MILES

205

Feed for the cattle, but mosquitoes were bad

The pioneers had been delayed for three days getting across the Green River. Now another Sunday was upon them.

The last wagon was safely carried over just before noon. Because the next day was the Sabbath, Brigham Young ordered the company to move only a short distance to a good camping place.

The teams were hitched up and the wagons moved out at 3:15 p.m., traveling only three miles before stopping where the scouts found plenty of grass for the 300 cattle.

However, the encampment was "in the midst of an army of mosquitoes," William Clayton complained. Swarms of the insects had made life miserable for the pioneers since the approach to the Green River earlier in the week.

Mosquitoes "are more numerous here than I ever saw them anywhere," he said. "Everything is covered with them, making the teams restive." Most of the pioneers stayed in the wagons and tents as much as possible, but this offered only limited relief.

Brigham spoke to the men about the upcoming arrival at Fort Bridger and advised them to use caution in trading at the fort. The pioneers already had learned that prices were high for goods handled by traders in the wilderness.

Willard Richards wrote a letter to Amasa Lyman and C.C. Rich, "which I copied," Thomas Bullock said. Bullock's penmanship was among the best in camp and he often was called to copy the final draft of official papers.

On this occasion he also was asked to transcribe a table of distances between various creeks and campgrounds — a list compiled by Clayton. He wrote out a synopsis of events of the trip between Fort Laramie and the Green River as well.

When combined, this was a large packet of papers and "a troublesome job," Bullock said. But the final product was praised by Heber C. Kimball who said it "could not be better." This comment comforted the scribe.

The apostles in camp (eight of them) met in council, read the papers and wrote their observations in the margins. The information would be sent back with volunteers to a large company of Mormons supposedly already on the trail from Winter Quarters.

The men in the advance party knew that some of their families might be in the group, but they had no way of knowing how things were going.

Five men were chosen to go back, meet the next company on the trail, and act as guides. Named for this task were Phineas Young, George Woodward, Aaron Farr, Eric Glines and Rodney Badger.

"As there are not enough spare horses for each man to ride, Brigham let them have a light wagon to carry their provisions," Howard Egan said. The men would leave the next day to start retracing the trail.

Phineas Young, 48, was a brother to Brigham. This assignment as a guide was the first of three times he escorted companies over the plains and through the mountains.

Woodward, 39, a mason and bricklayer, said the small party traveled nearly 200 miles before meeting the next group of Mormon emigrants. "To my joy, my wife was in the company," he said.

Farr, 28, also met his wife traveling with the next emigrants and accompanied her across the plains. They arrived in the Salt Lake Valley on Sept. 20.

Glines, 24, who had angered Brigham earlier by refusing to follow instructions, did his work as a guide, but after reaching the valley, did not remain. He went on to California — a sign in those days of falling away from the church.

Badger, 24, also was reunited with his wife on the trail and entered the valley Oct. 2. He served as a youthful bishop and county sheriff, but his life was cut short six years later when he drowned while saving a family of emigrants whose wagon capsized in the Weber River.

After making arrangements for the men to leave the pioneer camp the next day, the leaders turned their attention to other problems. Sickness still afflicted many in the camp.

One of the ailing, Norton Jacob, was advised by Kimball to be baptised, so he entered the water with Charles Harper "who baptised me for the restoration of my health." This was an occasional practice in cases of sickness in the early days of the church.

Afterwards, Jacob received a blessing from Kimball and others. He said it "had the desired effect and broke my fever."

July 4

Five returned to serve as future guides

The ranks of the pioneer company were reduced by five men this day, but they also were unexpectedly swelled by the addition of another 12 men.

The five who departed had been assigned to go back along the trail and act as guides for other Mormon emigrant companies expected to be en route.

Brigham Young, Heber C. Kimball and others traveled the three miles back to the Green River to help ferry the five men across.

As they approached, they saw 13 horsemen on the bank, loading their baggage on rafts and preparing to cross the stream. "Who should they be but some of our brethren from the Mormon Battalion," Wilford Woodruff rejoiced.

While the battalion had been making its historic infantry march to California the year before, a detachment of 140 sick men had been dropped at Pueblo, in what later became Colorado, to recuperate.

They had wintered at Pueblo with a company of Mississippi Mormons who mistakenly had gotten out

in front of everybody else in 1846 before they discovered their error.

Knowing the pioneers with Brigham were on the trail, the soldiers began marching west in June. An advance party of 13 was sent ahead to recover some stolen horses.

The scouts caught all but one of the thieves. The one missing renegade escaped with a horse and headed for Fort Bridger with the stolen animal. The battalion party was still pursuing the thief when they learned the whereabouts of the pioneers

The 13 men rode hard to overtake the Mormon pioneers. They said the rest of the detachment was on the trail, about one week's travel to the rear.

"When we met it was truly a hearty greeting and shaking of hands," Woodruff said.

All of the battalion party was rafted over the river, except one, William H. Walker, who was told that his wife probably was included in another pioneer company now en route. Walker turned back and accompanied the five guides on their journey.

After rejoicing at their reunion, the soldiers, now under the leadership of Brigham, returned to the pioneer camp west of the Green River.

Once at the campsite, the members of the battalion lined up in military formation and heard a few formal words of greeting from Brigham, who concluded by asking for a cheer for the returned troops.

A great shout of "Hosannah, hosannah, hosannah, give glory to God and the Lamb," rang through the camp. The men were then dismissed and were quickly surrounded by pioneers eager for news of the past year.

The battalion members who joined the camp were Sgt. Thomas H.S. Williams, who was in charge; Thomas Bingham, John Buchanan, William W. Casto, George S. Clark, Francillo Durfee, Samuel Gould, Allen Hampton, James Oakey, Benjamin Roberts, Andrew W. Shupe and Jesse J. Terrill.

The soldiers handed two letters to Brigham. One was from Amasa Lyman, who had been sent from the pioneer company to Pueblo to help get those people on the trail. The second letter was from Capt. James Brown, commander of the sick detachment.

Addition of the battalion men to the company raised the total of men, women and children in camp to 160. The soldiers reported that a number of those in the sick detachment had died during the previous winter.

No rousing celebration for the reunion was held because it was the Sabbath, but George A. Smith rode to the nearby mountains and gathered a large supply of snow. This was mixed with sugar to make pioneer ice cream.

Many in the camp were still sick with mountain fever, but all appeared to be recovering.

Trouble struck the Robert Crow family again. One of their cows was found dead, "apparently poisoned through eating some kind of weed," William Clayton said. It was the latest in a long series of mishaps afflicting the Crows.

Green finally crossed, and trek resumed

After a delay of several days on both sides of the Green River, the Mormon pioneers once more were moving toward an uncertain future, their goal the desolate Salt Lake Valley.

Although the previous day, July 4, was the nation's birthdate and a major patriotic holiday, especially in the 1800s, it seems to have passed without comment by the pioneers.

They apparently just ignored July 4, not feeling particularly patriotic despite their reverence for the U.S. Constitution and its principles.

The Mormons had been tormented, persecuted, hounded from their homes and many of them killed. State governments had sided with the mobs and federal authorities refused to provide any protection.

Rumors had indicated U.S. Army troops would be used against the Mormons as they prepared to leave Nauvoo — information that helped send them fleeing into Iowa in the dead of winter, with all the suffering and death which resulted.

As far as the pioneers were concerned, the United States was back east. They were in Mexican territory. The Mormons had volunteered troops in the war with Mexico and they would raise the American flag in their new desert homeland. But bitterness against federal authorities was in the hearts of some.

The pioneer company traveled parallel to the Green River for a few miles, then struck west across a barren wasteland. No trees, no grass and no water was available

Fortunately, the rolling prairie provided good travel conditions and allowed the company to make good time. In a few locations the wagons had to be braked to get down "very steep places of descent," William Clayton said.

At one point the company found they could have saved a mile (nearly a half hour's travel), by taking a few minutes to dig down the bank of a hill, "but it was not discovered until most of the wagons had passed," Clayton wrote.

Just before 5 p.m. the pioneers reached Black's Fork, the first water since morning. They had covered 20 miles, "the last 16 and a half without sight of water," he said.

The stream was almost 100 feet wide. The water was not deep, but the current was swift. The thirsty animals drank their fill, but didn't have much to eat. The bottom land around the river had only sparse grass.

Despite the thin supply of grazing, Orson Pratt described the campsite as pleasant and one of the nicer stopping places since Winter Quarters.

In the distance the Bear River Mountains to the southwest were capped with snow. Black clouds poured rain in the mountains, but none of it reached camp, even though a strong wind blew through the area.

Much sickness still afflicted the company. Many men continued to be down with mountain fever. Even Pratt, the scientist in the camp, didn't know the cause of the illness, although he tended to blame it on the "clouds of dust which envelope the whole camp when the wagons are in motion."

The Mormon campsite was near the future location of the hamlet of Granger, Wyo. The town today is not far from the juncture of Union Pacific railroad tracks and U.S. Highway 30 North. The community is just north of Little America, a major motel and truck stop on I-80.

Granger was founded in 1868 as a rails end camp and later became a depot for shipping livestock. Nearby was an Overland Stage station, built in 1850, a stopping place for travelers until the coming of the railroad.

Hardy stagecoach passengers were put up overnight in crude accomodations resembling crowded dormitories. Rough bunks were built in tiers and covered with dirty blankets. The food usually was miserable and flies covered everything. The chief commodity sold at such stations was whiskey.

Granger enjoyed a boom in 1880 when the Union Pacific built a branch line to the northwest. The town became the division point and had a hotel, stores, a saloon and other establishments. But in 1899 the division was moved to Green River.

The final blow was delivered in the mid-1930s when Highway 30 North was moved. The town, once on the main highway, was left a quarter mile to the side.

The 'mountain fever' took its toll, but victims recovered

Illness continued to be a problem in the Mormon pioneer ranks, although most of those striken earlier seemed to be on the way to recovery. More than 15 had been felled so far by the so-called "mountain fever."

"The sick in camp are most universally getting better," Wilford Woodruff noted. One exception was Willard Richards who remained in bed in his wagon.

Many of those who had been sick were like Norton Jacob who said he "rested well and gained strength fast" as the company was halted for the night. Recovery from the fever usually took four or five days although a few cases lasted somewhat longer than that.

Breakfast and morning prayers followed the usual bugle call this day. Teams were hitched and the camp began the day's trek at 7:50 a.m., reaching a stream

called Ham's Fork after traveling nearly four miles.

The water was swift, but only two feet deep and the teams forded the 50-foot stream with no trouble. An abundance of high grass grew on the banks and William Clayton, who was keeping a record of such things, thought it would make a "good place to camp" for some future emigrant company.

A short distance away the pioneers had to cross another stream, this time the larger Black's Fork which was 100 feet wide. However, again the water wasn't deep and the wagons made it over without difficulty.

After reaching the other side of Black's Fork, the pioneers embarked on a long trek over generally barren country. The route was uneven with gullies and ditches "caused by heavy rains washing the land," Clayton reported.

The way was dusty. "Man and beast, harness and wagons, all were covered with dust," Woodruff said. Because of the dry trail, the pioneers did not make their usual two-hour rest stop in the middle of the day. They drove the wagons ahead without pause.

At 4 p.m. the company reached the winding Black's Fork and crossed it once more before establishing camp on the west bank. The pioneers had covered more than 18 miles for the day.

Black's Fork is a tributary of the Green River and was named in 1824 by Gen. William H. Ashley, an early explorer. Ashley led a party of more than 40 men west in 1822 to set up a trading post on the Yellowstone River.

As he traveled, Ashley named many rivers and streams. He changed the name of the Spanish River to the Green River and also named the Sweetwater River.

During their day's journey, the Mormon pioneers passed what is now called Church Butte, a cluster of green and black sandstone some 75 feet high. Early travelers thought it resembled a cathedral. Legend has it that emigrant companies held religious services at Church Butte, another possible source of the name.

The rocks appear today as a green, alien landscape, something lifted from the moon. The famous Lincoln Highway once passed by, following the pioneer trail from Granger to Lyman, Wyo. The highway was closed nearly 40 years ago and now only a decayed road remains to service nearby oil rigs.

The Mormon campsite on the banks of Black's Fork was highly praised by Clayton because of plentiful grass and many wild currants and flowers.

"The prairies are lined with beautiful flowers of various colors, chiefly blue, red and yellow, which have a rich appearance and would serve to adorn and beautify an eastern flower garden," he said.

Also growing around the campsite was "a fine specimin of wild flax . . . considered equal to any cultivated," he added.

Flax is one of man's oldest crops. The silky fibers in the stem could be spun or woven to make fibers ranging from rope to the finest linen. Pioneer settlers often planted flax as a major source of fabric for clothing.

July 7
WEDNESDAY

Fort Bridger was goal this day; pioneers made it

Reaching Fort Bridger was the goal of the Mormon pioneers this day, not because the trading post was important to them, but rather because it marked the beginning of the last leg of thelr long trek.

Beyond the fort lay the Great Salt Lake, slightly more than 100 miles distant — the last part of a journey covering about 1,000 miles from Winter Quarters.

The pioneers broke camp at 7:30 a.m. and after traveling a few miles, forded the twisting Black's Fork for the third time. This was to be a day of crossing many streams, most of them just little brooks.

By noon the company had covered nine miles over a rough trail. Most halted for a midday rest, but a few wagons pushed ahead, hoping to reach Fort Bridger.

The march was resumed in the early afternoon. The path wasn't quite as uneven, but there were occasional places "rendered bad by cobblestones," William Clayton said.

Wilford Woodruff, a fisherman at heart, noted that the company "crossed more than a dozen trout brooks." Some of the men caught some trout,' the first I had seen since I left England," he said.

Finally the wagons entered a beautiful valley dotted with Indian dwelllngs and featuring the wooden trading post known as Fort Bridger. Many Indian ponies grazed in the area.

The pioneers pushed on a half mile beyond the post and established their camp in a vale "where the grass was knee deep and better," Thomas Bullock said.

Everyone in the camp agreed it was "a lovely scene" — peaceful, lush and criss-crossed with small streams created by melting snow. The water ran into Black's Fork.

Clayton said the roadometer showed Fort Bridger was 397 miles from Fort Laramie which the pioneers left June 4.

The final part of the pioneer journey lay just ahead, but athwart the path were rugged mountains far different from what the wagons had crossed earlier. Travel was going to be much slower.

Fort Bridger was not very impressive. It consisted of two double log houses about 40 feet long and joined by a pen for horses. The pen was created by placing 10-foot high poles upright in the ground, "which is all the appearance of a fort in sight," Clayton said.

Howard Egan noted "a full crop of Indian children are playing around the door (of the fort.)"

The structure was built in 1842 by Jim Bridger and opened shop as a trading post the next year by Bridger and his partner, Louis Vasquez. It was the second permanent settlement in what later became Wyoming.

The fort did business in the fur trade with trappers, mountain men and Indians. As emigrants moved along the Oregon trail, the post acquired many new customers.

Location of the fort was a good one, as the Mormon pioneers realized. In 1855 they arranged to buy the post from Vasquez for $8,000. That same year they established Fort Supply six miles to the south where crops were raised for the support of Mormon emigrant companies.

When the Mormons took over Fort Bridger, they immediately made improvements, including a thick cobblestone wall to replace the wooden stockade. Additional log buildings also were erected.

However, they were not long in possession. With the outbreak of the Utah War in 1857, the Mormons burned Fort Bridger and Fort Supply to the ground as the U.S. Army approached. The army spent a difficult winter in the ruins.

Brigham Young and his followers made the final payment on the fort in October, 1858, even though it was occupied by the army and never given back. The fort was rebuilt the next year and served as a military base for 20 years.

Fort Bridger presently is a state park. The only thing left of the 1857 era is a section of stone wall built by the Mormons. All the other buildings date from after the Civil War. The fort is just off I-80, west of Lyman, Wyo.

Many went to Fort Bridger to trade

Having reached Fort Bridger, the Mormon pioneers decided to "stay a day here and set some tires," as well as rest their animals and take the chance to do a little shopping.

The morning was cold. Ice had formed in the water buckets and on nearby streams during the night, but it melted as the sun came up. A brisk wind whipped the wagon covers.

Many in the camp went to the fort to see what they could buy or trade. Howard Egan swapped two rifles in behalf of other men, getting in return "19 buckskins, three elk skins and other articles for making moccasins."

Also visiting the trading post were Brigham Young and Heber C. Kimball. They bought hunting shirts and pants. In addition, Kimball said he acquired "20 good skins."

Prices at Fort Bridger were higher than the pioneers had found at other trading places along the trail — and they thought most of those earlier charges were too expensive. Robes at the fort cost $5 each, shirts $6, pants $6 and dressed skins $3 each.

Several of the pioneers tried bargaining with the French and Indians, but without much success. They weren't able to get high enough offers for their own goods.

At the fort, Sgt. Thomas Williams, one of the Mormon Battalion people, met Tim Goodale, a trapper whose men had stolen Mormon horses and mules at Pueblo. All but one of the animals had been recovered earlier.

Williams cornered Goodale and seized one of his horses, giving him a receipt. He told the trapper he could recover the loss from his own men.

Wilford Woodruff, who had brought a fishing rod and some dry flies back from England, decided to try out the gear for the first time in a stream near the fort.

Many others were fishing in the same stream, using meat and grasshoppers as bait. They said there weren't many fish. Woodruff cast the articial fly into the water and waited expectantly. "It was the first time I had tried it in America, or even saw it tried," he said.

A trout promptly struck the fly and was hauled ashore by the delighted Woodruff. Before he was through he caught 12 fish, most of them weighing about three quarters of a pound..

"The rest of the camp did not catch three pounds all together. This is proof that the artificial fly is best to fish with," he declared.

Woodruff later went to the fort and exchanged his flintlock rifle for four dressed buffalo robes. He valued the gun at $20 and the robes at $5 each — a fair trade.

The rest of the camp was busy with wagon repairs, shoeing horses and generally getting ready for the final difficult days through the Rocky Mountains.

David Grant, 30, a Scotsman and tailor with the company, did his best to keep clothing in good repair. Grant's wife had died at Winter Quarters a few months earlier, leaving him with two small children. Grant crossed the plains again to bring them to the Salt Lake Valley in 1848. He filled a mission to England and was well known as a poet. He died at the early age of 52.

The pioneers met a trapper at Fort Bridger who agreed to carry letters to Winter Quarters as he traveled east. Willard Richards dictated letters to Amasa Lyman and Robert Campbell, giving details of the trek and also news of the Mormon Battalion supplied by Samuel Brannan.

Thomas Bullock copied some documents Brannan had brought with him. These included a description of the Hastings Cutoff from Fort Bridger (which led the Donner party to their doom a year earlier) and also a map of that route.

That evening it was decided to send Sgt. Williams and Brannan back along the trail to meet members of the Mormon Battalion detachment coming from Pueblo.

The 140 men in the detachment hadn't been officially discharged or paid. The pioneer leaders discussed the possibility of sending some men to California to collect the pay for all the others and bring it back to the Salt Lake Valley. The enlistments were due to expire July 16.

From Bridger on Hastings track

A day's rest at Fort Bridger gave the Mormon pioneers a chance to gird for the final push to Salt Lake Valley. Only two weeks were left in their long journey.

The bugler roused the camp, breakfast was eaten, the cattle rounded up and teams hitched to wagons. At 8 a.m. the trek westward was resumed.

As the wagon train left Fort Bridger, the pioneers moved away from the heavily-traveled Oregon trail. Instead, they took the Hastings track, the same path followed by the ill-fated Donner party in 1846. The route, south of what is now I-80, led directly to the Great Salt Lake.

No longer were the Mormons troubled by other emigrant parties. After what happened to the Donner party in seeking a shortcut across the Great Salt Lake desert, other companies were satisfied to stay with the more established route to the north.

The Mormon pioneers were now without a river to act as their guide. All they had were some uncertain maps and written descriptions, plus a dim trail left by the few wagons which had gone that way a year ago.

"Fortunately for us," Erastus Snow said, the earlier travelers left behind a faint track, "though their trail in many places is scarcely discernible."

Reaching a spring from which Three Mile Creek flowed, the pioneers halted to rest and graze their animals. When they resumed travel, the wagons had to climb a long hill over a rough road.

Orson Pratt walked to a high ridge near the top of a bluff, took out his sextant and measured the pioneer position, just like a sea captain.

This was a task he performed every day of the trek, measuring the latitude and longitude and recording it in his journal. He also took barometric readings and the temperature.

It was the kind of a thing only a surveying party would normally do. None of the other emigrant parties going west did anything like it. As long as they had a general idea of their location, that was enough.

However, the pioneers were concerned about making a reliable and detailed map of the whole route. This could serve as a guide for the tens of thousands of Mormon emigrants who would follow in subsequent years.

When Pratt was finished, the wagons descended down the other side of the bluffs, "the steepest and most difficult we have ever met, being almost perpendicular," William Clayton said. The rear wheels were locked and the wagons restrained by ropes during the descent.

After crossing a number of creeks and climbing up and down hills of various difficulties, the pioneers stopped for the day at 3 p.m., pulled into a circle and pitched tents. They had come 13 miles since morning.

The rather early halt was made because of the good grazing for cattle. "There is plenty of tall bunch grass and a good chance for our teams," Clayton explained.

Bunch grass greatly resembled wheat, with a head on top and growing nearly as tall as wheat. The animals browsed eagerly and the growth provided much better feed than the prairie grass which had been their food much of the trip. The bunch grass became much more common as the wagon train rolled westward.

A few cases of mountain fever were reported in camp. Among those stricken were William Carter and Wilford Woodruff, both complaining of intense headaches, pains in the joints, cold chills and hot flashes.

Carter, 25, an Englishman who was a trained glassblower and blacksmith, joined the Mormons in England in his late teens. Like many others he came to America and settled in Nauvoo. His was the first plow to turn soil in the Salt Lake Valley. He served a mission to Canada and later settled in St. George where he worked on the temple for many years. He died in that southern Utah community in 1896.

In the pioneer camp that evening the weather was warm and pleasant. A number of the men gathered near Brigham Young's wagon and serenaded him with hymns.

Brigham's illness stalled company three days

When the pioneers made camp the night of July 10, they had covered 18 miles through rugged country, working hard to improve the trail.

The company almost reached what would one day be the Wyoming-Utah border when Brigham Young was stricken with mountain fever and couldn't travel. This stalled the pioneers for three days.

An advance party was chosen to push ahead in the meantime, but the accompanying map shows only the progress of the main party.

On July 16 the pioneers entered Echo Canyon, a ravine choked with trees and bushes and so narrow the cliffs seemed about to collapse on the wagons.

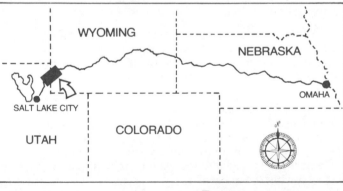

July 10-16

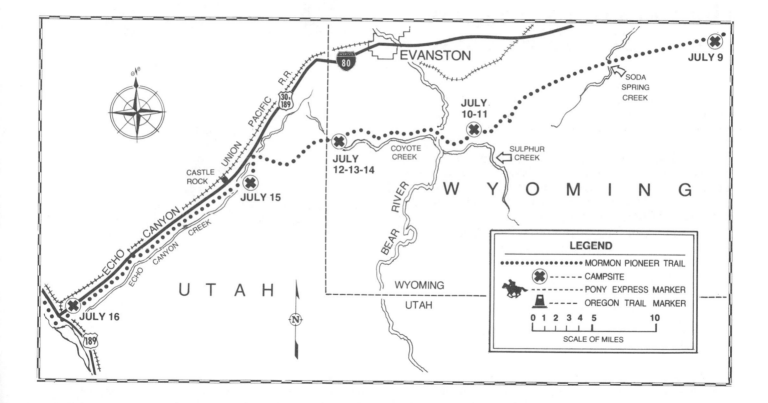

July 10
SATURDAY

The path more rugged as new obstacles arose

In the past, hills and ridges occasionally blocked the pioneer route and made travel difficult, but that was nothing compared to the obstacles the Mormons now began to meet. They were entering real mountain country.

After breaking camp at 8 a.m., the pioneers covered more than three miles, passing through a valley with many cedar trees. They found a spring of copper-tasting water "which had a singular effect on the mouth," William Clayton said.

The water ran over the red sand common to the area and the resulting wet soil "looked like blood at a distance," Clayton noted.

From the spring, the pioneers guided their wagons up a long ridge. Orson Pratt, using a barometer, said the summit was 7,315 feet above sea level.

In order to get down the other side of the ridge, the pioneers had to stop and fix a road for the wagons to use.

"About halfway down there was a place over huge rocks, leaving barely enough room for a wagon, but by labor it was soon made passable," Clayton said.

A little further and the pioneers had to break out shovels again to dig a wider path in a mountain gap. As usual, Brigham Young and Heber C. Kimball were among the most energetic workers, leading the way by example. They "labored hard with a number of others and in about a half hour made a good road," Clayton said.

At 1:45 p.m. the company halted to give the cattle the usual rest for an hour or so. The stopping place was near a body of water that Thomas Bullock called

"Gunpowder Springs" because it bubbled up clear "but tastes like gunpowder and smells like rotten eggs."

After resting for 90 minutes, the pioneers moved out once more and climbed a ridge so steep that the teams and wagons had to make a zig-zag road to the top. The summit was described as "very narrow."

Going down the other side, everybody went on foot and the wagon wheels were locked to keep the loaded wagons from running away down the precipitous slope.

Once safely down, Bullock looked back and said it "seemed like jumping off the roof of a house." He was extremely grateful there were no accidents. "It was long, steep and dangerous.

The pioneer wagons wound around the base of a mountain, seeking the easiest path for the rapidly tiring oxen, mules and horses. They climbed another ridge and finally made camp on the banks of a small stream after coming 18 miles through very rugged country.

"It was a mountainous day's journey," Bullock sighed.

Wilford Woodruff, who had been ill with mountain fever, reported that he was "quite feeble," but said the fever was broken and he was on the way to recovery.

Stories of the Donner party, which met disaster following this same route in 1846 while trying to reach California, had been told by Samuel Brannan and the fate of those people was on Woodruff's mind.

He said the party included people from Clay County and Independence, Mo., who had made threats about what they were going to do to Mormons in California. They set out on their ill-fated journey "with that spirit in their hearts," he wrote in his journal.

The Mormon pioneers explored the nearby hills after making camp and found other campfires belonging to a group with Miles Goodyear, a man they had heard about because he was living near the area they wanted to settle. (Goodyear's cabin was near what is now the city of Ogden.)

Later in the evening, Goodyear visited the pioneers and talked about the region, urging the Mormons to settle near him. He gave a report "more favorable than some we have heard," Clayton said.

Invitations from Goodyear to have the pioneers settle near him were viewed with some suspicion. "We have an idea he is anxious to have us make a road to his place through selfish motives," Clayton wrote.

The pioneer camp was south of the future site of Evanston, Wyo., which was settled in 1868 when the railroad arrived. Soon the town had more than 600 residents, but a few months later a decision was made to transfer the division headquarters to Wasatch, Utah. Twenty-four hours later, Evanston had only two persons left in it.

However, the division headquarters was moved back a few months later and Evanston settled down, becoming a county seat in 1870. At one time it had a large Chinese population.

Pioneers discovered oil, but it helped little

While camped for the Sabbath, some of the Mormon pioneers did a little exploring — and discovered oil.

They used a few buckets of it to lubricate wagon wheels and other equipment, but oil in those days wasn't very important. The discovery was a minor convenience, nothing more.

Whale oil generally was used as a fuel for lamps. Oil from the earth mostly found its way to market as a cure-all medicine. The first oil well and large commercial use was still 12 years in the future in Pennslyvania.

About a mile south of the pioneer camp, John Norton found a spring with a black substance bubbling out of the ground. It "resembles tar and is very oily," William Clayton said

Thomas Bullock called it "a greasy spring" and said when the material was set afire it "burned bright like oil." Wilford Woodruff said some in camp thought it was oil. Norton Jacob had no doubts, calling it a "fountain of petroleum."

Jim Bridger had found a similar oil spring many years earlier and sold oil mixed with flour as axle grease at his trading post. But not until 1912 — 65 years after the Mormon find — was Wyoming to experience its first real oil boom.

The pioneers used the thick liquid to oil their gunstocks and shoes. Some filled buckets with it and used it to lubricate their creaking wagon wheels. The discovery "came very opportunely for we were entirely out of tar (grease) for the wagons," Jacob said.

Brigham Young, Heber C. Kimball and Clayton climbed a mountain that morning to examine the surrounding countryside. As they descended, they found a sulpher spring flowing from the rocks and giving off a strong smell.

A number of people in camp commented on the unusual circumstance of finding a sulpher spring, an oil spring and a spring of clear water, all within a mile of each other.

"It appears as if nature had separated the different productions for the special use of the persecuted saints on their journey," Bullock said.

Miles Goodyear was camped nearby and came to the pioneer wagons, bringing a map he had drawn of the area around the Great Salt Lake.

"He gives a very favorable account of the country

and has a garden planted with all kinds of vegetables," Bullock said. Goodyear wanted the Mormons to settle near him and took some scouts to look at the trail.

Porter Rockwell, Jesse Little and others returned with a negative report, saying the route "leads too far out of our course to be tempted to try it."

Rugged mountains lay ahead of the pioneers. This was very different from the prairie they had crossed. The forbidding peaks around them caused some to have second thoughts.

Bullock was lying sick in his wagon and overheard several men "murmuring about the face of the country."

Clayton said some in camp "are getting discouraged by the look of the country." But he said "thinking minds are not much disappointed" by the terrain.

"We have no doubt of finding a place where the saints can live, which is all we ought to ask or expect," he said.

Two possible paths lay ahead and the pioneers were called together after dark to decide which to take. It was voted to take the right hand, or northern road, despite the private feelings of the apostles that the other would be better.

"But such matters are left to the choice of the entire camp so that none may have room to murmur at the Twelve hereafter," Clayton explained.

With the uncertain feelings in camp about the mountainous country ahead, the pioneers bolstered their spirits that night with a rousing singing meeting.

Company reached bank of Bear River

Ever since leaving Winter Quarters, one of the most active men in the entire company was Brigham Young, working as a scout and pathfinder and generally setting the pace. Now illness was to strike him down.

The Mormon pioneers broke camp at 7:15 a.m. on a cool, cloudy day. They climbed a steep hill and covered about two miles to reach the banks of the Bear River near what is now the Utah border.

The river was "a very rapid stream," about 100 feet wide, two feet deep and the bottom was covered with large, round stones, William Clayton reported.

Because the river was shallow, the wagons moved ahead, fording the clear water which "came up to our axles," Thomas Bullock said.

Along the banks of the stream were willows, good grass, many wild strawberries "and the soil looks pretty good," Clayton observed. Wilford Woodruff was not impressed with the "long looked-for Bear River," saying it "wasn't very interesting" at the place where the pioneers crossed.

Perhaps it wasn't interesting because he was on the lookout for fishing holes. Ever since his success with fly fishing near Fort Bridger, Woodruff kept his fishing gear close at hand and continually tried his luck at catching trout.

Mostly he fished from horseback and occasionally would find a quiet eddy where "fish would jump at the hook as though a bushel of trout were in the hole."

Just before noon the pioneers halted in Coyote Creek Canyon, flanked by ridges of high, rough rocks and just east of a rock formation known as The Needles.

"There are scarce any wagon tracks to be seen. Only a few wagons of the Hastings company having come this route. The balance (the Donner party) went the other road and many of them perished in the snow, it being late in the season. Much of their time was lost quarreling over who would improve the road," Clayton wrote.

Disquieting news now swept through camp. Brigham, their stalwart leader, was ill with the same fever that had afflicted so many of the pioneer company recently.

After a two-hour halt the company moved on. But Brigham was too sick to travel, even as a passenger in a wagon — a rough ride for a well person. Eight wagons, including those in Heber C. Kimball's group, stayed behind in the camp as several friends took care of the ailing president.

This was the beginning of a division the next few days that would see three groupings in the pioneer company — an advance guard, the main body, and a few wagons as a kind of rear guard with Brigham and some of the other sick.

The pioneers, after leaving Brigham and his party behind, crossed creeks, climbed hills, made their way around the base of other hills and marched through a number of small, but rich bottom lands.

"We passed through some fertile valleys where that eyesore — wild sage (sagebrush) has disappeared," Norton Jacob observed with satisfaction.

The wagons covered a total of 16 and a half miles for the day before camping near a very small creek. During the afternoon's march they crossed what would one day be the Utah-Wyoming state border.

Near the campsite a cave was found by R. Jackson Redden. It was four to six feet high and 30 feet deep. The pioneers believed it was a place used by trappers or others to store property. They called it Cache Cave and also Redden's Cave, after the man who found it.

Plenty of grass was available near the campsite, but it was parched. "This country evidently lacks rain," Clayton said in something of an understatement.

The pioneers waited for Brigham's wagons to catch up, but they failed to arrive by nightfall.

Others were sick in the company. Among the worst was Albert P. Rockwood. Thomas Bullock also was still ailing. His wagon was being driven by Horace Thornton, 25, who would cross the plains a second time to bring his family. Thornton later would help colonize parts of southern Utah. He died in Manti at the ripe old age of 92.

Brigham Young was ailing, and his absence delayed the company

The Mormon pioneer company was delayed by the absence of Brigham Young, left the previous day with a small group about seven miles to the rear because he was too sick to travel.

Anxious for their ailing leader, Wilford Woodruff, John Brown and Joseph Mathews rode back early in the morning to Brigham's camp "to learn the state of his health," Norton Jacob said.

The delay in travel was a worry to many in the company who already were afraid they would reach their destination too late in the year to plant crops. The growing season already was far along.

Shortly before noon, Woodruff and his party returned, accompanied by Heber C. Kimball and Howard Egan. Kimball was second in command of the pioneer company and had instructions for the camp.

A meeting was called, "but suddenly dispersed by a thundershower," William Clayton said.

After the rain ceased, the meeting was resumed. Kimball proposed that an advance guard be formed under the leadership of Orson Pratt to "try and find a pass over the mountains," Clayton reported.

Kimball asked that "some 20 wagons go ahead to explore the road through the mountains separating the pioneers from the valley of the Great Salt Lake."

As they traveled, the advance guard also was assigned "to make a road" and smooth the way for subsequent wagons, Woodruff noted.

Kimball said that Brigham was "a little better this morning, but last evening was insensible and raving." Albert Rockwood also was sick at the rear camp and was "quite deranged" from the fever.

The advance party assembled by Pratt included 23 wagons and 43 men. Those in the group were Stephen Markham, Porter Rockwell, Jackson Redden, Nathaniel Fairbanks, James Egbert, John Freeman, Marcus Thorpe, Robert Crow, Benjamin Crow, John Crow, Walter Crow, George Therlkill, James Chesney, Lewis Myers, John Brown, Shadrach Roundy, Hans Christian Hansen, Levi Jackman, Lyman Curtis, David Powell, Oscar Crosby and Hark Lay.

Also with the forward company were Joseph Mathews, William Carter, Gilbroid Summe, Green Flake, John Gleason, Charles Burke, Norman Taylor, Alexander Chesley, Seth Taft, Horace Thornton, Stephen Kelsey, David Grant, James Stewart, Robert Thomas, Charles Barnum, George Wardle, John Eldgredge, Elijah Newman, Francis Boggs and Levi Kendall.

This advance guard pushed off in the early afternoon. To these men would belong the honor of being the first to enter the Salt Lake Valley, several days before the official arrival of Brigham and the last few men in the pioneer company.

After the Pratt company moved out, Kimball and Egan returned to Brigham's rear guard, accompanied by George A. Smith. Those left in the main camp turned their attention to a variety of other activities.

Many visited nearby Cache Cave and commented on the more than 50 bird nests attached to the roof. Some of the men carved their names in the side of the cave and noted the place was "swarming with bugs."

Thomas Bullock used the time to catch up on his journal. Others dug a well closer to camp, "but the water has a sulphurous taste," he said.

Hunters went out and bagged 12 antelope and brought the meat back to camp. Willard Richards and Woodruff did a little exploring, looking for springs of fresh water.

As they walked, "we talked over old times" in connection with their missions in England, Woodruff said.

The weather was hot and sultry and "mosquitoes are very troublesome," Clayton noted.

Because of the illness and absence of Brigham and other leaders in the rear guard, plus the departure of many with Pratt's company, the atmosphere in camp was subdued.

When darkness fell, "the camp was very still, more than since we left Fort Laramie," Bullock observed.

Pioneers now split into three companies

The Mormon pioneer company was now broken into three separate groups because of the illness of Brigham Young — an advance guard under Orson Pratt, the main body, and a rear guard tending the ailing president.

For the second straight day the main group of pioneers did not travel, waiting for their sick leader to recover and rejoin them from his camp some seven miles to the rear.

Wilford Woodruff and Barnabas Adams rode back to Brigham's small camp of eight wagons to see how he was getting along. They found him "convalescent" and looking forward to joining the other pioneers the next day.

Albert Rockwood, who had been stricken with the mountain fever about the same time as Brigham, was "much the sickest man in camp," Woodruff reported.

The apostle and some others joined in a special prayer for the suffering Rockwood. Afterwards they were "convinced we should find him better in the morning."

Adams, 34, who accompanied Woodruff on the visit to Brigham's encampment, was a quiet, soft-spoken Canadian. He crossed the plains again with his family in 1848 and settled near Little Cottonwood Canyon. At age 56 he injured himself internally while lifting the bed of a wagon and died a few days later on June 2, 1869.

In addition to those ill in the rear guard, the fever also continued to cut into the ranks of the main camp. "Several more were taken sick yesterday and today," Norton Jacob wrote in his journal.

William Clayton said the fever was "very severe on the first attack, generally rendering its victims delirious for some hours, then leaving them in a weakly condition."

He said a dose of pills or medicine was good to break the fever. The patient then needs some kind of stimulant to "brace his nerves and guard against another attack," Clayton noted. He suggested diluted spirits as a treatment.

In the main camp the usual guard duty, caring for stock, cooking and washing went on. Many men went hunting and five antelope were killed and divided amongst the pioneers.

Thomas Bullock went to nearby Cache Cave and sat in its cool shade all day. The weather was hot and sultry and many of those not hunting sought relief from the heat in the darkened cavern.

The cave contained many bird nests and the swallows were very busy "attending to the wants of their young," Bullock said. In addition to bird watching, he caught up on entries in his oft-neglected journal.

That night the bugle was blown as the signal to retire, but many of the men continued to sit up and talk "as usual," Bullock said. But a sudden rain shower sent them running to their wagons "and reminded them of the fifth law of the camp (getting to bed at the sound of the bugle)."

Meanwhile, the 23 wagons under the command of Pratt had pushed forward during the day. Their task was to find the best route to the Great Salt Lake and also improve the road for wagons through the mountains.

Much of the time would be spent with shovels filling in ravines, digging up tree stumps and otherwise making the rugged trail more passable.

Pratt's party followed a mountain stream into what is now known as Echo Canyon. The leader described his group as being "shut up in a narrow valley, 10 to 20 rods wide, while on each side the hills rise very abruptly 800 to 1,200 feet."

For most of the way since leaving the main camp "we have been walled in by vertical and overhanging precipices of red stone," he said. The rocks have been carved into "many curious shapes, probably by the rain."

In modern times Echo Canyon has been cut and filled for highways and the feeling of being crowded on both sides no longer is as dramatic as it was for the pioneers.

Pratt said the way was "quite rough" for the wagons which had to cross and re-cross the stream in the bottom of the canyon a number of times. Despite the difficulties, he described the geography "interesting and exceedingly picturesque."

July 15

An ailing Brigham was returned to the main camp

Early in the morning Wilford Woodruff hitched a horse to his carriage in the main Mormon pioneer camp and drove back along the trail to where the ailing Brigham Young was staying with a group of eight wagons.

Brigham and Albert Rockwood had been the two sickest men in the company and were left behind because travel was too agonizing for them.

"I found them much better in health," Woodruff said. They thought they could travel so he fixed a bed for both of them in his carriage because "it was the coziest vehicle in camp."

Going carefully, he drove once more along the trail and reached the main camp about noon, much to the relief of those waiting there. The pioneers felt lost without the dynamic presence of Brigham.

"The president is much better," William Clayton rejoiced. Rockwood, who had been stricken about the same time, also appeared to be recovering. "They appeared very cheerful and quite comfortable," Norton Jacob said.

While waiting for Woodruff to bring back their leader, Jacob explored along the creek with John

232

Pack, seeking a possible camping place. They soon found a nice place with "a fine spring, wood and grass."

Later he climbed to the top of a mountain ridge in company with George A. Smith and Albert Carrington. They reported much scrub oak and with a spyglass "saw large quantities of pine."

After the arrival of Brigham, the camp was ordered to hitch up teams, thus ending a stop of more than two days. While the pioneers were getting ready, a thundershower broke upon them. Clayton described it as "very refreshing."

Travel this day was very limited — only a two-hour march covering four and one-half miles. The short trek was dampened by two more rain showers. Camp was established beside a spring of "good, clear, cold water," Clayton said.

The campsite was at the foot of some high red bluffs about a mile from what would one day be the Castle Rock station of the Union Pacific railroad. Thomas Bullock said he was able to gather "seven varieties of flowers within 20 yards of my wagon."

Meanwhile, the advance company under the leadership of Orson Pratt had crossed the Weber River near the future site of Henefer and made camp. They looked for the faded tracks of the Donner party a year earlier. New grass had nearly obliterated all traces.

"We traveled about six miles," Pratt said, noting that the canyon into which the Weber River flowed was impassable for wagons. He and John Brown rode ahead on horseback, trying to find the Donner party trail.

Clusters of willows were all around, "making very close thickets for bears," he said. He sighted many large tracks and saw large holes caused by their digging for roots and concluded that bears "must be very numerous." But none were actually seen.

Among those in Pratt's advance company were John Sunderlin Eldredge; a black man, Green Flake, and a man with one of the most unusual names in camp, Gilbroid Summe.

Eldredge, 26, later served a three-year mission in Australia. On the way home his ship was wrecked on a coral reef and five passengers drowned. Twenty-nine other Mormons were with Eldredge. They spent weeks on an uninhabited island until rescued. He became a farmer in Wasatch County and died of a heart attack at age 52 while plowing a field.

Flake, 22, was born a slave on a North Carolina plantation. His owners joined the church and he later became a member himself. He crossed the plains in the advance pioneer company while his white master came along later. He eventually gained his freedom and lived in Salt Lake City until late in life, remaining a devoted Mormon. He died in Idaho Falls in 1903 at age 78.

Summe, 44, became an Indian fighter and was a tireless colonizer. He was among those who founded San Bernardino, Calif., and later helped establish a number of settlements in southern Utah. He died in 1867 at age 65.

Travel was rough on wagons as party got to Echo Canyon

Travel was extremely difficult as the main body of Mormon pioneers pushed into the massive mountain range surrounding the Salt Lake Valley.

The company entered "a narrow ravine" (Echo Canyon) and attempts to travel along the bottom proved to be a struggle. Occasionally teams had to be doubled to get over obstacles.

A wagon owned by Harvey Pierce was damaged trying to cross the creek. It had to be unloaded and repaired. Solomon Chamberlain's wagon broke a front axle and couldn't continue. In camp that night another wagon was unloaded and sent back for him.

Chamberlain was still sick with mountain fever.

The company penetrated further into the canyon. As they did, "the mountains seem to increase in height and come so near together as to barely leave room for a crooked road," William Clayton said.

Porter Rockwell, who had been with the advance company under Orson Pratt, came back to report that they had found the trail used by the Donner wagons last year and expected to reach the top of the mountains that day. The advance party was more than 20 miles in front.

When the main company resumed the march after a midday halt, the path at the bottom of the canyon became even narrower "until it seemed strange that a road could ever have been made through," Clayton said.

The canyon was rich with currant and elderberries. Many flowers blossomed and the area was thick with willows, bushes and birch trees. Thomas Bullock said in some places the pioneers "could not see two wagons ahead."

The variety of plants, vines, berries, flowers and wild wheat in the mountains convinced the Mormons that the weather couldn't be too bad and frosts were not likely to kill off crops as Jim Bridger had warned.

By nightfall the company had made 16 and a quarter miles through the rugged canyon and "we are yet enclosed by high mountains on every side," Clayton said. The campsite was the first reasonable stopping place since noon because of the narrow canyon.

Grass was plentiful most of the way. At the camp it grew to six feet high. Along the banks of the creek it was eight to 10 feet, the pioneers noted.

Brigham was worn out by the day's rough going and seemed to suffer a relapse. Wilford Woodruff again had provided his soft-riding carriage for the sick president and Albert Rockwood, but the canyon "was a bad road for the sick to travel."

The leader was still sick that night and Woodruff went fishing, catching a trout to feed Brigham for dinner.

As the company made its way through the narrow defile, Clayton commented on the echoes which were to give the canyon its name.

"The rattling of wagons resembles carpenters hammering at boards inside the highest rocks. A rifle shot resembles a sharp crack of thunder and echoes back and forth for some time," he said.

"The lowing of cattle and the braying of mules seems to be answered beyond the mountains." The bugle was blown and "music, especially brass instruments, have a very pleasing effect," he noted.

Because of the echoes, the high rocks on both sides, and the narrow ravine, Clayton thought it was "at once romantic and more interesting" than anything he had seen before.

Norton Jacob said several small rain showers had fallen and the canyon "looks more cheering than the arid desert we have been passing through."

After the pioneers formed camp, Clayton climbed the mountain slope on the south, having to go on "hands and feet" part of the way. Once at the top, he could see the fork of the Weber River a mile away.

"But in every other direction, nothing but ranges of mountains, much higher than the one I was on. It was wild and melancholy," he said.

Meanwhile, the advance party with Pratt also found the going rough. He sent a dozen of his men ahead with shovels to make the road passable, "which required considerable labor."

A thundershower provided "nearly enough rain to lay the dust, which is more than usually falls," he said.

Ahead lay 36 miles of rugged mountains

Following the route of the ill-fated Donner party the year before, the Mormon pioneers exited Echo Canyon and moved to near what is now Henefer.

Ahead lay 36 miles of rugged mountains that taxed the strength of the pioneers and their teams. Orson Pratt's advance guard was some distance in front of the main body, trying to improve the trail.

Pratt and Erastus Snow were the first to enter the Salt Lake Valley on July 21 and a larger group followed July 22.

Brigham Young had fallen sick again and was bringing up the rear with eight wagons. He was among the last to enter the valley, but his arrival July 24 made it official.

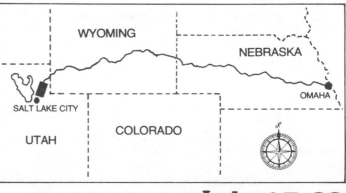

July 17-23

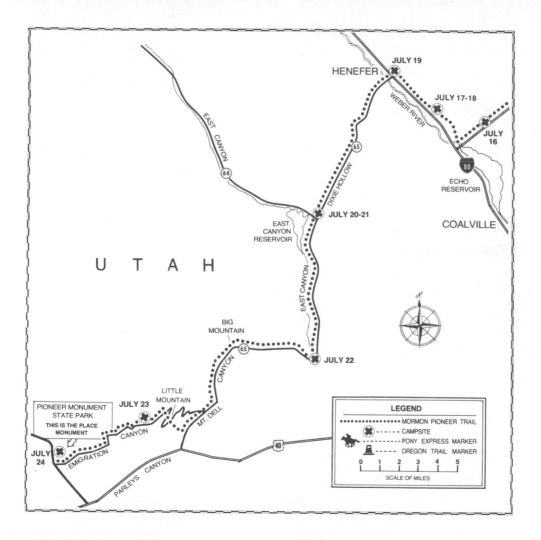

JULY 19

HENEFER

JULY 17-18

WEBER RIVER

JULY 16

EAST CANYON

66

65

DIXIE HOLLOW

80

ECHO RESERVOIR

EAST CANYON RESERVOIR

JULY 20-21

COALVILLE

U T A H

EAST CANYON

BIG MOUNTAIN

65

JULY 22

CANYON

LITTLE MOUNTAIN

PIONEER MONUMENT STATE PARK

THIS IS THE PLACE MONUMENT

JULY 23

MT. DELL

CANYON

40

JULY 24

EMIGRATION

PARLEYS CANYON

LEGEND

●●●●● MORMON PIONEER TRAIL

⊗ -------- CAMPSITE

🏇 -------- PONY EXPRESS MARKER

🪧 -------- OREGON TRAIL MARKER

0 1 2 3 4 5

SCALE OF MILES

237

July 17
SATURDAY

Livestock responded to answering echoes

Progress by the Mormon pioneer company was very limited this day. A late start was made and the wagons covered less than three miles before halting. Brigham Young once more was too sick to continue.

When the pioneers arose in the morning, nine of their horses were missing. Blacksmiths set up a forge and repaired the broken axle of Solomon Chamberlain's wagon which had snapped the day before in the rugged canyon travel.

Brigham had spent a very sick night and was reported by Wilford Woodruff as "poorly this morning."

All the cattle and mules in camp "seem very uneasy and continue lowing and braying all the morning," William Clayton noted. 'I suppose it is in consequence of the echoes, they (the cattle) no doubt thinking they are answered by others over the mountains.'

About 9:40 a.m. most of the company assembled and moved out "while some took the repaired axletree to Chamberlain's wagon where it had been left in the canyon and others went to look for the lost horses," Norton Jacob said.

The wagons reached what the pioneers called the Red Fork of the Weber River after only a mile's travel. They moved along the banks for a short distance and camped near what later became the site of Henefer, Utah.

"The reason for our stopping so soon was in

consequence of President Young being suddenly taken quite ill and he could not endure any further travel today," Howard Egan explained.

In the meantime, the missing horses were found about 10 miles away and finally brought back to camp.

From the new campsite Clayton said he could see ahead to the mountain pass (Main Canyon) which the pioneers would take because they were unable to follow the Weber River any further. That route was impassable due to rocks and a narrow passageway which seemed to block wagon travel.

The day was hot and the mosquitoes plentiful. A few of the men went fishing in the river and "caught some fine trout," Clayton said. Among them was Woodruff, still happily using his artificial flies.

In the afternoon several men "went into the mountaintops to pray for the president and those that are sick," Clayton said. The prayer group included Heber C. Kimball, Willard Richards, Ezra T. Benson, George A. Smith, John Pack, Howard Egan, Thomas Bullock, Erastus Snow, Lorenzo Young and Albert Carrington.

When they finished their prayers, they reverted to little boys and "rolled many large rocks from the top of the mountain, to witness the velocity of their descent." Some of the rocks smashed into pieces.

Later that evening, Kimball, Smith and Egan went ahead to explore the canyon, but did not return until after 10 p.m., "which caused some uneasiness in camp," Bullock said.

John Dixon also had been out exploring and found an unusual thistle which Clayton said he had "never seen before, nor ever read about".

Dixon, 28, an emigrant from England, would serve with the first Mormon missionaries to the Hawaiian Islands in 1850. Three years later he was hauling wood in the Wasatch Mountains when a band of Indians opened fire, killing him.

Clayton mused in his journal that this was his 33rd birthday and said his mind was "on my family" back in Winter Quarters, living in unknown circumstances.

Meanwhile, the advance guard under Orson Pratt also was halted for the day. The party was camped on flat ground near the bank of East Canyon Creek, a site later to disappear under water from the East Canyon Reservoir.

The way had been so difficult that Pratt went back to the rear on foot "to see if there was a more practicable route . . . than the one we had come." But he was soon satisfied that "we had taken the best and only practicable route."

He ordered the entire company to "labor on the road over which we had passed yesterday" while he rode ahead. He found things just as bad up front with the trail "almost impassible and requiring much labor." A stream had to be crossed and re-crossed 13 times and the banks were choked with willows.

Pratt climbed a mountain for a better look and was confronted with a discouraging view.

"The country exhibited a broken succession of hills piled on hills and mountains on mountains in every direction," he observed.

July 18
SUNDAY

A special day of prayer and fasting on the Sabbath

The pioneers realized they were near the end of their long journey, but they were worried about the repeated delays caused by the sickness of Brigham Young.

Despite this concern, the company followed its usual custom of remaining camped for the Sabbath. It was decided to make this a special day of prayer and fasting, of preaching and of humility.

The day began with the pioneers awakening to "a severe white frost," Norton Jacob said. But the vegetation in the mountains "is of such a hardy nature that the frost does not seem to injure it."

Heber C. Kimball called the company together soon after the camp was up and about. He reported that Brigham was "a very sick man" with mountain fever.

He asked the men in camp to meet together for prayer instead of scattering about the countryside as they often did on a Sunday, some hunting, some fishing and some climbing the surrounding mountains.

The pioneers were urged to "humble ourselves before the Lord that we may obtain power with him to turn away sickness and disease from our midst," Jacob said.

It was decided to assemble at 10 a.m. in a small grove of shrubbery created for such a meeting. The tops of a number of trees had been cut off and planted opposite the wagons to make a green bowery.

The bugle was blown to call the camp together, but for some reason, "John Norton manifested a spirit of contention and instead of attending the meeting, he went to bed," Jacob wrote in his journal.

All the others met as planned and heard Kimball propose that most of the wagons travel the next day toward the valley. The pioneers should "proceed immediately to put all our seeds in the ground," he said.

William Clayton said Kimball urged them to find a good place and plant potatoes and other crops that might thrive late in the season "as we have little time to spare."

It was proposed that eight or 10 wagons remain behind with Brigham and some of the other sick members of the company "until the president should regain his health sufficient to travel," Jacob said. The suggestion was voted on by the camp and received unanimous approval.

A number of people expressed their feelings and then the meeting was adjourned until 2 p.m. when the group reassembled for preaching by Kimball and other leaders.

"The bishops broke bread and the sacrament was administered. Good feelings seem to prevail," Clayton said. Howard Egan said the preaching "done my soul good."

Kimball said the Lord had heard and answered the camp's earlier prayers, explaining that when Brigham was washed and anointed, "he fell into a deep sleep and awakened much refreshed."

Later in the day, Kimball, Ezra T. Benson, Howard Egan and Wilford Woodruff rode over the ridge they called Pratt's Pass (Hogsback Summit) for a look at the forbidding mountain country still ahead.

Afterwards several of the party had prayers together in behalf of the sick. Woodruff described the experience as "a good time." He said the small group "conversed much concerning the kingdom of God."

Meanwhile, the advance guard under Orson Pratt also remained in place for the Sabbath after expending considerable effort the day before in attempts to improve the trail for the wagons to follow.

The little community of Henefer would be founded in 1859 near the campsite of the main body of pioneers. The town was begun by James and William Henefer, who started out as blacksmiths to aid travelers, but later turned to farming.

More settlers joined them. A townsite was surveyed in 1861 and named Henefer. A fort was built in 1866 as a protection against Indians and the Union Pacific railroad line was constructed within a quarter mile of town in 1869.

Pioneers were tracing the trail of Donner party

As the Mormon pioneers struggled into the rugged mountains east of the Salt Lake Valley, they were following in the exact footsteps of the ill-fated Donner party which met a tragic end the year before.

From Fort Bridger in 1846, a group of 87 men, women and children under the leadership of George and Jacob Donner and James Reed, made a fateful decision.

Following the advice of a promoter, Lansford W. Hastings, they chose a "shortcut" through the mountains, around the Great Salt Lake and across the desert wasteland to California, a route Hastings said would save more than 200 miles. But he failed to mention the rugged mountains or the lack of grass and water west of Salt Lake Valley.

The Donner-Reed party made its way through Echo Canyon to what is now Henefer. There they found a note from Hastings, who was about a week ahead, scouting for other emigrant groups. The note said Weber Canyon was impassable, but he could show them a better way.

(The earlier emigrant parties, ignoring Hastings' advice, made it through the narrow canyon and rough water, although with great difficulty.)

The Donner-Reed group delayed near Henefer for six precious days while Hastings was chased all the way to Black Rock on the south shore of the Great Salt Lake and brought back. He pointed out a "shortcut" over Big Mountain, the summit of the Wasatch Range, and left again.

However, that route was neither shorter nor safer. It turned out to be a nightmare of struggling up and down mountain slopes. Discipline broke down and travel was delayed by arguments over who should be doing the work. It took 16 vital days to move 36 miles through the mountains.

The final day was a back-breaking, animal-killing climb over what later was known as Donner Hill, a terrible ordeal that could have been avoided — as the Mormon pioneers did — by cutting a road near the mouth of Emigration Canyon with about four hours work.

All the effort left the Donner-Reed party exhausted, way behind schedule, short of supplies and still facing the terrible desert. Eventually, unusually early winter storms caught them in the Sierra Nevada mountains. Nearly half of them died in an ordeal of cold, starvation and cannibalism.

As the Mormon pioneers left the future site of Henefer, they would have a difficult time, but they would cover the 36 miles through the mountains in four days instead of the Donner-Reed party's 16. And once in the valley they were home.

Brigham Young was still recovering from mountain fever and remained behind in a rear guard group of wagons which would move more slowly while the main body pushed ahead.

The wagons in the main company set out over a road "very rough on account of loose rocks and cobblestones," William Clayton said.

Entering Main Canyon, they climbed the ridge known as Hogsback Summit and zig-zagged down the other side, a task dangerous for the wagons. The wheels of George A. Smith's wagon collapsed inward while going downhill. It was one of a number of small accidents during the day.

The view from the top of Hogsback was disheartening, with high mountains in all directions. Wilford Woodruff called the terrain "the worst road we have had on the journey."

As they moved down the other side of the summit, into what later became known as Dixie Hollow, the pioneers spent considerable time improving the road. From Dixie Hollow they slowly made their way into East Canyon where they spent the night in a thick patch of willows. The site is now covered by East Canyon Reservoir.

The rear guard with Brigham moved more slowly and was some miles behind. The president "stood the morning's ride quite well," Woodruff said, but noted that by evening he was "quite weary."

Meanwhile, an advance party under the leadership of Orson Pratt was out in front of everyone. Pratt and John Brown climbed Big Mountain on foot and caught a glimpse of the valley through an opening in the canyons.

A light blue sky "seemed to be sinking into a plain of gold," Pratt wrote. Two small patches of level ground were visible from the vantage point.

Most of the rest of the advance guard remained busy improving the trail, and the main body of pioneers drew closer during the day.

Some of the most difficult travel of trek

Although they were close to the Salt Lake Valley, the Mormon pioneers had some of the most difficult and slowest travel of the entire trek as they struggled through the towering Wasatch Mountains.

They still were moving, like beads on a string, in three separate groups — an advance party under Orson Pratt, the main body, and a rear guard of a few wagons with the ailing Brigham Young.

Pratt's party continued to move slowly, both because of the rugged terrain and the need to improve the trail for those following. This advance group climbed Big Mountain, about nine miles in front of the main body of pioneers.

The major company was late getting started this day, being "delayed until 11 a.m. with wagon repairs," Thomas Bullock noted. A number of wagons had been damaged in the previous day's travel.

Some time was spent making a coal pit so the blacksmith, Burr Frost, could repair the wheels of George A. Smith's wagon. The wheels had collapsed on a steep hill.

The pioneer camp was in East Canyon where most of the trail has since been submerged by the East Canyon Reservoir.

While waiting to get started, the pioneers greeted

one of the men from Pratt's group who rode into camp looking for stray cattle. "He said the road is very rough from here," William Clayton wrote.

As the main company moved out, three wagons were left behind. Henry G. Sherwood, Benjamin Franklin Dewey and James Case all had come down sick with mountain fever and were unable to travel. But it was already late in the year for crops and the pioneers couldn't delay any longer.

While the wagons struggled through the canyon, Clayton went ahead on foot nearly four miles "and picked many gooseberries, nearly ripe. They are very plentiful on this bottom."

Movement was slow as the pioneers labored to improve the road, which was still filled with obstacles despite the preliminary work by Pratt's group.

"The road over which we have traveled is through an uneven gap between high mountains and is exceedingly rough and crooked," Clayton said. Dense willow groves choked the canyon and made it hard to find any stopping place.

In the latter part of the day the willows proved a real obstacle, the growth reaching over 20 feet and tangled with other bushes, poplar and birch trees.

"Although there has been a road cut through (by Pratt's group and the Donner party the previous year), it is scarcely possible to travel without tearing the wagon covers," Clayton said. In addition, the wagons had been forced to cross and recross the creek 11 times during the day.

Clayton said the route was the most crooked he ever saw. Even where the willows had been cut, the stubs still made it "very severe on the wagons." Bullock agreed it was "a crooked and rough day's journey."

Norton Jacob gave Pratt's advance party credit for doing much. The Donner party the year before also had worked on the trail. But despite this and the improvements made by the main body of pioneers "there is room for more labor."

Clayton said there were many springs in the canyon, but he was doubtful about the quality of the water. The canyon also had some swampy areas which the pioneers tried to improve by laying down layers of willows.

"We have got along today without much damage, which is somewhat favorable, for the road is awful," he said. He described the canyon as "truly a wild looking place."

The main body of pioneers managed more than seven miles for the day and camped not far from Big Mountain.

Meanwhile, the rear guard with Brigham broke camp at 5:30 a.m. so as to "travel in the cool of the morning," Howard Egan said. The small party made good progress and the health of Brigham "continues to improve."

While scouting ahead for a campsite, Heber C. Kimball came upon the three wagons left behind with the sick men from the main company. The rear guard pushed forward late in the day and joined these wagons, having covered more than 12 miles for the day.

Two scouts are first to enter the valley

All the months of weary trudging across the plains were rewarded this day when the first Mormon pioneers — two scouts ahead of the advance party — set foot in Salt Lake Valley.

Erastus Snow, carrying a letter dictated by Willard Richards, had left the main body of pioneers and rode ahead to find the advance guard under Orson Pratt.

Once he reached Pratt and delivered the letter (mostly instructions about entering the valley and planting crops as soon as possible) the two men went ahead to scout the way.

They made their way four and a half miles down Emigration Creek, which Pratt called Last Creek, to near the mouth of what is now Emigration Canyon.

To avoid the rugged canyon mouth, the Donner party of the year before had struggled up "a steep and dangerous hill (Donner Hill)," Pratt noted.

He and Snow climbed the same hill and from the summit "a broad valley stretched out before us."

The sight, after having been shut up in the high mountains for many days, was overwhelming. "We could not refrain from a shout of joy which almost involuntarily escaped from our lips the moment this grand and lovely scenery was in our view," Pratt said.

"We immediately descended into the lower parts of the valley and although we had but one horse between us, traversed a circuit of about 12 miles before we left the valley and returned to camp," he said.

The rest of the advance party (43 men and 23 wagons) had remained in Emigration Canyon, slowly moving forward and trying to improve the route as best they could.

The main body of pioneers further to the rear had spent the night in East Canyon and started at 6:30 a.m. on what was to be one of the last and most difficult days of the trek. The march began near the base of Big Mountain and the wagons soon began to be pulled up the slope.

"Much time was necessarily spent cutting down tree stumps, heaving out rocks and leveling the road. It is an exceedingly rough place," William Clayton said.

The ascent gradually grew steeper, the worst part being near the top, but at last all the wagons reached the summit where the pioneers found the ruins of considerable timber which had been destroyed by fire.

From this ridge the pioneers could see glimpses "of an extensive valley to the west, but on every other side are high mountains, many of them white with snow," Clayton said. "It seems as though a few hours travel might bring us out of the mountains."

The wagons plunged straight down the other side of Big Mountain, the pioneers first locking the rear wheels of their wagons to keep them from running away.

"We found the road down exceedingly steep and rendered dangerous by the many stumps of trees left standing in the road (by earlier clearing work). The brethren cut many of them, which delayed us much," Clayton said.

About a mile downslope the pioneers found a temporary bridge built by Pratt's group. Small trees were piled on top of one another to fill a deep ravine. It was steep on both sides of the ravine and Joseph Rooker's wagon overturned while trying to cross the bridge.

However, the mishap didn't cause much damage and the pioneers continued the slow descent, now less abrupt. Four and a half miles from the summit of Big Mountain they found a good camping place with a spring of cold water and plenty of grass for the cattle.

The teams had been in harness for about 10 hours without eating "and the feeling of many was to stay here," Clayton said. But others, anxious now that the end was near, wanted to push ahead. So the trek continued.

Soon the company began to ascend another high ridge (Little Mountain), but the uphill pull was too much for many of the tired animals "and some of the teams began to fail," Clayton said. However, all finally made it to the top.

The descent down the other side wasn't quite as steep as down Big Mountain, although the wagon wheels had to be locked again. The pioneers halted on the banks of Emigration Creek, having covered 14 miles in 13 hours. The grass was poor for the tired cattle.

Stephen Markham of the advance company came back and said Pratt's party was camped only a half mile ahead. He helped the weary pioneers assemble their camp for the night.

Meanwhile, the rear guard with Brigham Young had not moved that day because of the sick with them. They remained camped in East Canyon many miles behind the others.

Almost all but Brigham saw valley

All of the Mormon pioneers entered the Salt Lake Valley this day — except Brigham Young and his small group bringing up the rear of the exodus.

Orson Pratt, who briefly explored the valley with Erastus Snow the day before, rode back to the main body of pioneers in Emigration Canyon to find out what to do next.

He talked with Willard Richards, George A. Smith and others and agreed to choose places in the valley where the Mormons could plant their first crops.

Taking Smith, Porter Rockwell, J.C. Little, John Brown, Joseph Mathews and John Pack with him, Pratt "rode into the valley to explore." Members of a 42-man advance party were left to clear the mouth of the canyon of thick timber and underbrush. This job would save a back-breaking climb over Donner Hill.

Pratt and his companions rode toward the Great Salt Lake for about five miles, then swung north, checking out the land for farming possibilities. The early part of the ride found the soil "of excellent quality," but as the men came closer to the lake, it "began to assume a more sterile appearance."

After a 15-mile ride the party turned back to the mountains on the east and found the wagons of the advance guard camped five miles into the valley, their clearing of Emigration Canyon completed.

In the meantime, the main body of pioneers continued to travel in the canyon, taking considerable time to improve the trail and grade the mountain slopes.

While most of the men were thus engaged, William Clayton climbed to the top of a hill and was "much cheered by a handsome view of the Great Salt Lake".

Sitting down to look at the scenery, he described "an extensive, beautiful, level-looking valley from here to the lake." Judging from "numerous green patches (the valley) must be fertile and rich."

The area appeared well supplied with small streams. There was little timber in sight anywhere in the vast valley, "but we have not expected to find a timbered country," Clayton said.

The lack of trees was "about the only objection which could be raised, in my estimation, to this being one of the most beautiful valleys and pleasant places for a home for the saints which could be found," he said.

"There is no prospect for building log houses without spending a vast amount of time and labor, but we can make Spanish brick (adobe) and dry them in the sun," he said.

"If the land be as rich as it appears, I have no fears but that the saints can live here and do well," Clayton declared.

The scribe said he would rather live at peace in this wild-looking country amongst the saints than "dwell amongst the gentiles with all their wealth and good things of the earth" and be "eternally mobbed, harrassed, hunted, our best men murdered and every good man's life continually in danger."

Clayton's major concern was for his family and he dreaded the long journey back across the plains to collect them and expose them to the dangers of a similar trek.

"I could almost envy those who have got safely through, having their families with them (the Robert Crow group), yet they will doubtless have a hard time of it this winter," he said.

The main company of pioneers finished cutting their road and about 4 p.m. "turned around a hill and came in view of the Great Salt Lake in the distance," Thomas Bullock said.

"A very extensive valley burst upon our view, dotted in three or four places with some timber." He could not help shouting, "Hurrah, hurrah, hurrah, here's my home at last."

Like Clayton he noted the general absence of trees as a drawback, "but there is an ocean of stone in the mountains to build stone houses and walls for fencing."

Only one thing was lacking — fuel. "If we can find a bed of coal, we can do well and be hidden up in the mountains to the Lord," Bullock said.

The wagons in the main party made a "very rapid descent" down the foothills and camped beside a small stream, not far from the wagons of Pratt's advance party.

Pioneers assembled, offered a prayer of thanks

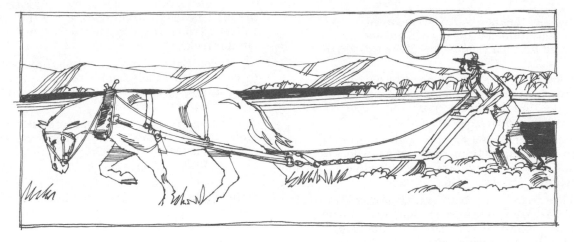

Two riders were dispatched back into the mountains to tell Brigham Young's small party that all the other Mormon pioneers were safely in the Salt Lake Valley,

The men carrying the good news were John Pack and Joseph Mathews. Their information spurred the rear guard, still about 15 miles from the valley, to move more quickly.

In the valley below, the main company of pioneers had joined Orson Pratt's advance group in a single camp near a stream they named City Creek.

At 9:30 a.m. the pioneers assembled and offered "a prayer of thanks to the Almighty for the preservation of the camp, their prosperity in the journey and their safe arrival in this place," Thomas Bullock said.

The prayers were led by Pratt and Willard Richards. They "consecrated and dedicated the land to the Lord," and immediately set about plowing the earth near what later became Main Street and just north of the present Salt Lake City and County Building property.

The first furrows were turned about noon by William Carter, George W. Brown and Shadrach Roundy. The soil was reported as fertile, although baked rather hard by the sun. Several plows were broken as the work progressed.

Crops to be planted in the newly-turned ground were potatoes, corn, beans and buckwheat — those things the pioneers thought would have the best chance of maturing despite the extremely late date in the growing season.

The pioneers were urged to plant the seeds they had brought across the plains "without question as to who would eat the fruit of them," Bullock said. First priority was to get a crop and never mind who owned what share.

Assignments were made in all directions. Charles A. Harper, Charles Shumway and Elijah Newman were named as a committee to see that drags and plows were available to those turning the ground.

Stephen Markham was given the responsibility for having fresh teams available for the plowing every few hours.

Other men were put to work building a dam across City Creek for irrigation and digging ditches to bring the water to the land marked off for plowing and planting. All those with special duties were empowered to call on the rest of the company for equipment and labor as needed.

About 2 p.m. water from City Creek was diverted into the farm land — the first step in the irrigation system which would one day bring renown to the pioneers for its extensive and efficient use.

After the water had soaked the ground a bit, plowing was resumed and proceeded much easier.

At 4 p.m. some men began preparing a stretch of ground for a turnip patch. Others worked on construction of a coal pit under the direction of Almon Williams. This same Williams went back to Winter Quarters in 1848, but apparently never returned to Utah.

Meanwhile, Brigham's small group of wagons continued to make their way through the mountains.

Starting at 6:45 a.m., they left East Canyon and climbed Big Mountain. The descent down the other side was difficult and the company later halted for a two-hour rest in a grove of birch trees.

Resuming the march in the afternoon, the small party struggled to the top of Little Mountain. Pack and Mathews, who earlier brought news of the other pioneers, left Brigham's group at this point and rode their horses back to the valley, making faster time than the ox-drawn wagons.

At 5 p.m. the company called a halt on the banks of what was known as Last Creek (Emigration Creek). It was as far as the still-recuperating members of the group could go that day.

Entry into the Salt Lake Valley would have to wait until July 24.

Brigham arrived, the trek was officially over

Brigham Young and the last handful of Mormon pioneer wagons reached the foothills overlooking Salt Lake Valley after being delayed by sickness for many days.

Traveling six miles through Emigration Canyon "we came in full view of the great valley or basin," Wilford Woodruff said.

"A land of promise, held in reserve by the hand of God for a resting place of the saints," he thought, and declared this moment "an important day in the history of my life and the history of the church."

All those in Brigham's small party "gazed with wonder and admiration upon the vast, rich, fertile valley, abounding with fresh water springs," Woodruff said.

"Our hearts were surely made glad. We contemplate that in not many years the house of God would stand in the tops of the mountains," he said

Brigham hadn't yet regained his strength after a severe case of mountain fever, but "expressed his full satisfaction in the appearance of the valley as a resting place for the saints and said he was amply repaid for the journey," Woodruff wrote later.

Nothing was mentioned in Woodruff's journal at the time about Brigham having said, "This is the place." That famous statement was first described 33 years later by Woodruff during a speech celebrating the church's 50th anniversary.

In recalling the 1847 event, he said Brigham had seen the valley in an earlier vision. Looking over the expanse below, the president saw the future glory of the valley and said: "It is enough. This is the right place, drive on."

At last, the 111-day trek had ended safely. The

long trek was over — this time. Many in that first company of pioneers would trudge across the plains several more times.

Most of the 157 men, women and children in the advance party had entered the valley July 22-23. Now Brigham's arrival made it official and stamped the date in history.

After looking at the scenery for a time, the group descended into the valley to be greeted by the pioneers already at work there.

They had been busy plowing, planting and digging ditches to irrigate the land because no time could be wasted. The planting season already was extremely late.

"By noon five acres of a potato patch had been plowed and planting commenced," Thomas Bullock said. The soil was hard and several plows were broken, but the work continued unabated. Some corn also was planted.

The plowing took place near the present location of the Salt Lake City-County Building. City Creek was dammed a ways to the north to create a pool of water for irrigation.

Shortly after noon the last of the ditches was completed and the water turned loose on the potato patch. The system seemed to "answer very well" for the lack of rain, Bullock observed.

At 2 p.m. Brigham and company arrived. "All rejoiced to see them, especially as they are better in health." Bullock said.

Most of the pioneers seemed pleased with their new home, William Clayton said, "but some complain because there is no timber." A few, including the women in the party, said the valley was too barren to sustain life and thought it would be better to push on to California, despite the hardships.

However, most agreed that the soil was rich "and there are good prospects for sustaining and fattening livestock with little trouble," Clayton said.

"The only objection is a lack . . . of rain," he said, but added that God would send moisture "in season if the saints are faithful" and cited a thundershower which wet the ground briefly the day before.

"We can easily irrigate the land at all events," he added, "for the springs are numerous and the water appears good."

Howard Egan, noting the irrigation already begun, said the valley was "admirably adapted" for such a system because of the "many streams descending from the mountains." The water from these "can easily be turned to any portion of the land at pleasure and little labor."

After looking around, Egan said: "This is the most safe and secure place the saints could possibly locate themselves in." He said a lack of timber probably was the main reason others hadn't settled the area. "But I think we can find sufficient timber up the creeks and also coal in the mountains."

"The saints have reason to rejoice and thank the Lord for this goodly land unpopulated by gentiles," he said.

Epilogue

One hundred and fifty years have elapsed since the first Mormon pioneers settled in Salt Lake Valley, but the impact of their trek continues today.

A modern skyline rising above a tree-lined Salt Lake City is only one part of their legacy. For the pioneers did not simply found a thriving city — they established an empire.

Before the linking of the transcontinental railroad in 1869, nearly 70,000 Mormon emigrants crossed the plains by wagon and handcart. An estimated 6,000 died along the way, almost all buried in unmarked graves.

After the railroad was available they still came, but such immigrants no longer were given the lofty title of "pioneer." Sometimes the late-comers were referred to as "Pullman pioneers" because they arrived by rail.

Soon after the first Mormons reached the valley they fanned out in all directions in the greatest program of organized colonization the world has ever seen — founding more than 350 communities from Canada to Mexico (and even across those borders) and from Nebraska to California within 30 years.

Side by side with this far-flung expansion they forged a religious empire, creating a theocracy that met not only their spiritual, but also their civil needs. In the early years they often simply ignored the usual government system and handled their affairs through the church organization.

This, and the practice of polygamy, infuriated the non-Mormons among them and helped fuel a conflict that would last more than half a century and include, among other things, a bloodless "war" with the U.S. Army.

The hoped-for isolation they sought in a desert empire was only partially achieved. The land soon became U.S. territory as a result of the war with Mexico. Mining, commercial ventures, the California gold rush and the railroad, all brought so-called gentiles into the midst of the Mormons.

The peace the pioneers wanted thus eluded them, but their empire was far enough removed that they were in the majority and not subject to the mob violence that had driven them from their earlier homes.

After reaching their goal on July 24, 1847, the first Mormon pioneers did not give a sigh of relief and settle down to build their private lives. They were more like troops in a religious army, dispatched here and there by the orders of Brigham Young.

In the first week they explored the valley, sent expeditions south to Utah Lake and north to Cache Valley, met with local Indians, chose a site for a temple, investigated the nearby canyons, made crude roads into the mountains for timber, plowed and planted 53 acres of vegetables and other crops, and started building a boat.

They surveyed the city, assigned farming plots according to family size and laid down a number of rules, a chief one being that no land could be privately owned. It wasn't to be bought or sold — just used.

Five days after their arrival the ranks were

swelled by another 200 persons when the Mormon sick detachment, which had wintered at Pueblo, Colo., marched into the valley accompanied by some Mississippi Mormons who also spent the winter at Pueblo. These additions raised the total number of pioneers in the valley to about 350.

Bricks were made, timber cut, and work was started on a fort where Pioneer Park is now located. Corrals were built for cattle.

A baby, Elizabeth Steele, was born Aug. 9, the first Mormon infant in the valley. Two days later, George Therlkill, age 3, wandered away from camp, fell into City Creek and was drowned, an accident that brought gloom to all the new settlers.

Only three weeks after the pioneers entered the valley, many of them turned around and started the long, weary journey back across the plains to Winter Quarters, Neb.

A total of 71 men with 33 wagons under the command of Tunis Rappleye and Shadrach Roundy were sent on the return trip to collect their families and guide others across the plains. They made a quick trip, reaching Winter Quarters in only 67 days.

Rappleye, Roundy and company left Salt Lake Valley Aug. 16 and were followed Aug. 26 by a larger group of 108 men led by Brigham Young and Heber C. Kimball, which made it to Winter Quarters in 68 days.

Samuel Brannan, John Brown and others also left the valley for California with instructions for the Mormon Battalion members there, as well as the New York Mormons who had sailed to the west coast with Brannan earlier.

Departure of all these groups left less than 180 persons in the valley to tend the crops, finish building the fort and get along as best they could until more help arrived.

But their numbers soon were increased by arrival of the "Big Company" — a large group of pioneers who had left Winter Quarters in June and were thus on the trail before the advance pioneers with Brigham reached the valley in July. The various divisions of the Big Company began arriving in the valley in September. By early October more than 1,500 persons and 556 wagons had reached the goal.

Brigham Young and the others who went back to Winter Quarters in 1847, returned in 1848 with companies totalling 2,000 Mormons and 4,000 animals of many kinds.

Many of the pioneers in the original company would be on the move much of their lives — an experience common to thousands of the early Mormons. A dozen of the historic first party died violent deaths in accidents or at the hands of Indians. For years, they and others suffered hardship, poverty and hunger. Just as they would get reasonably comfortable, they would be called to move again.

The example of George Wardle was typical. A musician and wheelwright and a native of England who had emigrated to Nauvoo in 1842, he was among those chosen for the historic first trek.

After crossing the plains, he went back for his family and brought them to Salt Lake Valley. When he arrived the second time he was asked to start a dancing school, organize a choir and put together a brass band, in addition to working as a wheelwright and blacksmith.

Later he was called to settle in Provo, but had barely finished his house when he was asked to move to Midway, Wasatch County, where he promptly built another home. Then he was moved again to Glenwood, Sevier County, where he prospered for a time.

Because the town of Midway had problems, he was called back there. A few years later he was asked to settle in Vernal, where he died at age 81.

To Brigham Young, the test of a man's faith was his willingness to uproot himself and his family time and again and start life anew where he was needed.

The early years of Utah contain thousands of individual stories of hardship, sacrifice, heroic work and devotion to church assignments at incredible cost.

When the area became a U.S. territory, it dashed the hopes of the pioneers to create a "State of Deseret" stretching across what is now several western states. Federal officials appointed to administer the territory often were political hacks of little ability and frequently hostile to everything Mormon.

Friction grew, culminating in the Utah War of 1857 when U.S. troops were sent to quell a non-existent "rebellion." The conflict ended by negotiation and resulted in soldiers being stationed at what is now Fort Douglas.

Life was never the same for Mormons after that. Their troubles with the gentiles escalated over the years, mostly about polygamy, but also regarding struggles over political and economic control of the territory.

Finally, with many of their leaders jailed or in hiding, church property confiscated and church members deprived of the right to vote or hold office, the Manifesto of 1890 was issued renouncing the practice of polygamy.

Eventually, church property was returned and in 1896 Utah was admitted as a state, finally getting rid of what Mormons had considered "carpetbag" government by appointment.

In the 20th century most of the old conflicts faded away and Mormons rose to prominence in political, business and cultural life all over the nation.

But their strict living habits, their placing of their religion as the pivot and center of their lives, and devotion of their time and resources to the church, have kept the Mormons somewhat apart as a "peculiar people."

The gathering to Zion which the trek of the pioneers represented finally ended. The flow began to move in other directions as Mormons flourished elsewhere, supported by a rapidly expanding missionary effort.

Although Utah is still the headquarters of the church and holds a special place in the hearts of Mormons, the church has become a world-wide institution and its members number in the millions.

But the story of the pioneers remains vibrant and alive — the heritage of all Mormons, including tens of thousands who have never set foot in the United States.

Index